HISTORY OF
MUSIC

THE TEACH YOURSELF

HISTORY OF
MUSIC

By
ALLEN PERCIVAL

with drawings
by
RACHEL PERCIVAL

THE ENGLISH UNIVERSITIES PRESS LTD
ST. PAUL'S HOUSE WARWICK LANE
LONDON, E.C.4

First printed 1961
Second impression 1967

SBN 340 05616 9

*Made and Printed in Great Britain for the English Universities Press, Ltd., London
by C. Tinling & Co. Ltd., Liverpool, London and Prescot.*

CONTENTS

CONTENTS

PREFACE

No one can pretend to write about music unless he can analyze sounds into melody, harmony and rhythm by ear. But how is he able to describe his analysis without using many technical terms and, above all, how is he to describe what any piece sounds like without being subjective? A historian who specializes in Renaissance music may write about the 'excitement' of a motet for two choirs, brass bands and orchestra by Gabrieli, and the contemporary critic about an 'exciting' performance of Walton's *Belshazzar's Feast* for the same resources. The word 'excitement' tells us nothing about the actual sounds of the music; but if your knowledge of musical history is musical, you will know before you hear either of these pieces what sort of sound to expect and within the limits of a particular period's style the word 'excitement' takes on more meaning. The first chapters of each section in this book attempt to help the reader who knows enough to pick out notes on a piano (and can remember a tune when he hears it again) to distinguish between different periods in musical history by ear.

The chapters on the sounds must use some technical terms, but most of these would explain themselves if only they were in English; so, literal translations are given as the terms occur. If you are more interested in music as social or economic history—who paid who for what and why?—or if you are fascinated by the detective work of the musicologist (how do we know what troubadour songs sounded like and is the evidence material or hearsay?) the chapters headed 'The Sources' can be read continuously.

No book of this kind would have been possible without the work of men like Parry, Stanford, Colles, and Scholes in the first part of this century and up to 1939, to mention English scholars alone. They wrote for a wide public and when the large one-volume histories of German musicologists (among them Lang, Einstein and Sachs) became available in English during the 1940s, English students were ready to tackle them, despite their length and, sometimes, difficulty. Gramophone record histories began in the 1930s with Scholes's *Columbia History of Music through Ear and Eye* in England and Sachs's *Two Thousand Years of Music* and *Anthologie sonore* on the Continent; since the Second World War, the only comprehensive collection has been *The History of Music in Sound* (associated with the *New Oxford History of Music*), but catalogues now include almost every kind of music known to us. Record enthusiasts will know, beside those of the huge recording companies, the specialized labels of Archive, Argo, Cantata and Oiseau-Lyre. Since 1945, too, collections of printed music designed deliberately to show the development of musical history have appeared (mostly in America), led by Apel and Davidson's *Historical Anthology of Music*.

To these general histories must be added the particular histories which have become set reading for serious students: Sachs on the music of the Ancient World, Reese on the Middle Ages and the Renaissance, Dent on opera, Apel on musical notation, Fellowes on Elizabethan music and so forth. The Master Musician series, published by Dent, includes some of the most reliable studies in short biographies and Hutchinson's University Library series on Music deals clearly and in some cases brilliantly with various sides of history. A fair bibliography would take pages and there is no room in this book. Any good public library should have its Grove's *Dictionary of Music and Musicians* (1954 edition) and a glance at the entry 'Histories' or at the bibliographies after each major composer's entry would give most of us reading matter on musical history for the remainder of our lives.

History never stands still, nor does it divide neatly into compartments. In this book, the sections overlap each other deliberately by some 50 years to point this. Every quarter, every month, almost every week (on the radio), new theories or discoveries throw more light upon musical history and papers like the *Musical Times*, *Music and Letters*, and *Opera* (among many others) require our attention. At no other time in musical history has so much information, opinion and argument been printed or aired. If this book teaches you to seek more information so that you may form opinions and argue from knowledge, it will have found its proper use.

ALLEN PERCIVAL

CHAPTER ONE

MAGICIANS

MUSIC and magic are inseparable among primitive tribes. In war or peace, at work or at play, music has great power for them. No important event in life—birth, puberty, betrothal, marriage or death—can pass by without a celebration in music. Music can deliver them from evil spirits, bring good weather for farming, or bring disaster to an enemy. So the best dancers, singers and players are the tribes' witch-doctors—but every primitive man tries to be his own magician as well. Even where no magic is needed, music helps as a woman rocks her baby to sleep, fishermen haul in their nets, or a farmer plants his crops. Singing and dancing help them to work; instruments help them to play, and to pray.

Many primitive instruments have been brought back to Europe and we learn a good deal from examining them. Percussion instruments are used more than any others. Drums are made by stretching skin over cooking pots or over the ends of a piece of hollow tree-trunk and are in all sorts of shapes and sizes; very common is the hour-glass drum made by binding two pots base to base; they are almost all without pitch, though some will sound different notes if you beat the two ends. Drumsticks are usually the spoons from the cooking pot. Various rattling instruments and 'dancing sticks'—clappers of wood—are common to most tribes. Bone-whistles and reed-flutes are still used in Africa, and a hunting-bow with one end stuck in the mouth is plucked like a 'Jew's Harp' by the oldest known surviving tribe, the bushmen of the Kalahari Desert in Bechuanaland. Some of the flutes have three holes in them, which gives them a range of four notes; others have no holes but are plugged at different places and bound together like panpipes to provide a wider range.

The number of primitive tribes today is negligible and we still know too little about their music. Until a few years ago historians had to rely on the musical knowledge and memory of explorers if they wanted to imagine what tribal songs and dances actually sounded like, but now tape recordings from Africa, the South Seas, the Far East, Northern Europe and South America give us more reliable evidence. From these tapes, a pattern of five notes (= pentatonic) emerges as a common factor in the make-up of primitive songs. Example 1 shows these five notes as the pattern looks from middle 'C'. Very few primitive songs use all these notes: some use only one (*a* in example 1, from Africa) in a rhythmic monotone which suddenly leaps to a higher octave; and many children sing as they play games, to two- or three-note tunes (*b* and *c* in example 1, from several parts of the world). More advanced folk tunes use all five notes in more than one octave, and other notes can be heard as the singer slides through the gaps in the pattern (marked with a wavy line in *d* of example 1, from the Hebrides). The gaps are filled by notes which vary according to their place in the melody—between 'E' and 'G' might be 'F sharp' or 'F natural' or a slither through both—but the pentatonic notes are always the same, and this pattern seems to be as old as any in the world.

Folk song collectors find it increasingly hard to track down singers who are keeping old songs alive in civilized countries; when these are found, no one can be sure how much the tunes have altered with each new generation of singers. Children's songs like those in example 1 are much the same in places as far apart as Mongolia, Finland, Germany and England, but tunes based on the four-note patterns suggested by instruments vary in different parts of the world. The ethnologist analyses them to guess at common origins. Here are four basic divisions of the instrumental four-note pattern into which a great many folk

Example 1

tunes can be analysed, with two transpositions to show how the pitch may change to an overlapping or adjacent fourth.

The first two patterns are common to most Western races and we call them 'Major' and 'Minor'; the third was particularly adopted by pre-Christian Greece; the fourth is most common in Arab music.

(a) transposed,   (b) transposed,
    adjacently   overlapping (note 'A')

Example 2

Collectors can also prove the existence of models (like the children's chants) on which tunes are built in different countries. In example 3 are three folk tunes. The basic patterns on which the tunes work are shown by the square brackets and you will

Notes marked * vary, according to the tetrachord in use

Example 3

be able to follow them if you look back at example 2. Though the patterns are different you will hear—if you play them one after the other—that they are on the same tune model. As this is already a much-travelled tune model, most of the examples in this book are also built upon it.

The rhythm of folk tunes yields only one sure conclusion: if you are singing for a dance, you must make the beat clear; but if no one has to dance to your song, you may sing it in free rhythm, just as the mood takes you.

All dance steps are counted in two or threes, and the ethnologists find that the nearer you get to Eastern countries the more freely these units are combined. In Austria, most dances are in threes (e.g. Waltz), and in England we count either '2' or '3' or multiples; but in Greece and the Balkan countries they frequently count '2+3' or '3+2+2' making totals of 5, 7, 8, 9, 11 and so on. No matter what you count, the speed of counting is usually constant in these countries, but in Spain and Arab countries they often count '2' slowly, then a quicker '3' taking

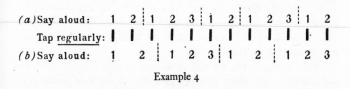

Example 4

up the same time-length. (Example 4 shows the difference.) Further East still folk dances are usually not very complicated. (although professional musicians in India and China use the numbers '2', '3' and '5' in a spider's web of rhythms). All this points to the Near East as the home of complicated rhythm.

Folk singers sometimes use their voices in ways which seem strange to a foreigner; those who sing through the mouth will think those who sing down the nose sound quaint—and vice versa. The further west you go, the more open the throat; the further east, the tighter the throat gets and all the countries in the

Near East prefer nasal singing. Three features are common to most folk songs:

1. Rubato, robbing one note of some of its value, but paying it back by holding the next note a fraction longer.

2. Portamento, sliding from one note to the next.

3. Parlando, speaking quickly on one note; these are often tongue-twisters.

Four features equally well-known, but confined to certain places, are:

1. Cadenza, suddenly improvising at great length on one syllable; particularly Southern Spain and the Near East.

2. Vocalise, wordless singing found in many mountainous countries from the Alps to the Scottish Highlands; may be 'crooning' or a series of rhythmical syllables which make nonsense but are good to dance to.

3. Yodelling, jumping deliberately from the normal voice to the high falsetto and back in vocalise, with cadenzas; mostly heard in Swiss villages, but a very formal type, in regular rhythm and often in elementary harmony is sung in Austria.

4. Yelping, shown in the African tune of example 1; the sharp 'hi!' which ends some Cossack songs is heard in other parts of the world where horse or cattle are bred, down to the 'yippi-i-o' in cowboy hill-billies.

Many instruments are still primitive in folk music: collectors regularly record small drums (nakers), clappers of wood (castanets) or brass (cymbals), spoons, the Jew's harp and various pipes, either open (flute) or blown through reeds (oboe). Some plucked strings are very ancient as is the most popular of all stringed instruments: some form of fiddle, played with a bow. The names of folk instruments—handed down by word of mouth—have come in for close analysis and it begins to look as if many derive from Indo-Germanic roots by way of Greece, Rome and Spain to the West, through Indian dialects to Chinese in the East.

Most musical instruments are made of fragile or perishable materials and the songs and dances of early or primitive societies

were never written down. So musicians fare badly in the museums
of prehistoric art. All we can see are a few fossilized bone-
whistles, a wooden horn (called a 'Lur') from Stavanger in
Norway, reproductions of a painting in a French cave which may
show a hunter using his bow as a Jew's harp—and a frieze of
ornate signs in a Spanish cave which one writer claims as
musical symbols. These exhibits can be made to fit in with the
deductions of anthropologists, but that is all.

Even though we do not know what their music sounded like,
we know something about the part music played in men's lives
from about 3000 B.C. onwards. During the last hundred years,
the remains of vast civilizations have been found on expeditions
which have taken archaeologists to Persia (now Iran), Mesopo-
tamia (Iraq), Arabia, Egypt, Palestine (Israel and Jordan), Asia
Minor (Turkey), Syria and Greece. Down to 400 B.C., Persia and
Arabia were the only unconquered countries; Egypt and Palestine were constant enemies until the Persians swallowed all
(sixth century B.C.); Asia Minor and Syria gradually became the
meeting-place of East and West. By 400 B.C., Greek civilization—
much of which came from Asia Minor—was ready to influence
East and West in the Hellenistic period of history.

Persia and Arabia

The ruins of three great capital cities have given up many
secrets: Susa, the capital of Sumeria; Babylon; and Nineveh, the
chief Assyrian monument. From these tribes, it seems, all the
higher civilizations got their musical instruments and, perhaps,
their musical ideas. Primitive drums, tambourines (round or
square drums with jingles) and rattles have been dug up varying
in date from c. 3000 to 600 B.C. Pictures in bas-relief at Susa
made as early as 2600 B.C. show musicians at the temple gate
playing flute, oboe, horn and bow-string instruments. Some
actual harps have been found at Babylon, where two-stringed
harps with upright or horizontal strings, lutes, lyres, curved
horns and straight trumpets of brass were used from c. 2000 B.C.
onwards.

Nineveh fell to the Chaldeans (612 B.C.)—a far from bar-
barous tribe, as the excavations at Ur proved thirty years ago—
and Nebuchadnezzar's alliance with the great Persian Empire
finally connected the Semitic-Arab peoples with the Asians. All
these tribes have left their words behind them, though the
various scripts have been deciphered only during the last hundred
years. The writers were not historians and they tell us nothing of

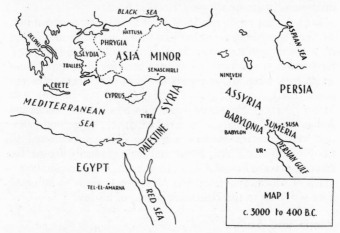

MAP 1
c. 3000 to 400 B.C.

where the music came from or what it sounded like, but these
words, written by a Sumerian in 2400 B.C., say what it meant
to them:

> 'Music fills the temple courts with joy,
> chases the city's gloom away,
> calms the passions,
> and stops weeping.'

Egypt and Palestine

The earliest attempts at musical history were made by the
writers of the Old Testament; but first a word or two about
their more powerful enemies, the Egyptians. The beautifully-
drawn pictures which were revealed by excavations at Tel el

Amarna and—on pottery—at many other places on the banks of
the Nile give us a tantalizing glimpse of the work of their
professional musicians. As in Babylon, they sing and play
at feasts, but there are also Egyptians using pipes as magic
wands at harvest-time and wine-pressing—and some even appear
to be taking music classes. In the earliest pictures, workers dance
and sing in the fields; later paintings, dating from c. 1600 B.C.—
after the invasion by the Hittites and Hebrews—show singing-
girls performing and many Semitic instruments being played.
Of the many classes of Egyptian instruments now in museums
all, including the famous trumpets of Tutankhamen, were
known earlier in Babylon. Egyptian writing tells us a little of the
part that music played in the temples but many technical terms
for music appear to derive from Hebrew and it seems that the
Egyptians were not specially skilled in music until they had
known their first defeat at Semitic hands.

In the writings of the Old Testament it becomes clear that
the Hebrews were highly skilled and that they had acquired their
skill from regions further East. Why else should the first
reference to music indicate a place so precisely? The Book of
Genesis says that Jubal was 'the father of all that play the
lyre and harp'; he and Tubal, the brass founder, were descended
from Cain; and Cain had been banished 'eastwards'.

The Book of Psalms shows that the Hebrews were famous for
their music. The Psalms were written c. 1000 B.C. in the reign
of the musician King David, himself a fine player of stringed
instruments. They were certainly not written for amateurs like
the singing-girls who had so attracted the Egyptians—for we
know from the First Book of Chronicles how carefully the music
of the Temple was to be organized. The Temple was to have
seventeen singers, three 'cymbal' players, eight 'psalterers' and
six 'harps'; the chief Levite was to be 'songmaster, because he
was wise'; seven priests were to blow the trumpets. The names
of instruments in the Authorized Version of the Bible are
often translated very loosely and no one should quote them as
evidence in a history of musical instruments; here they are

quoted only to show how highly detailed Temple music was by 1000 B.C. Five hundred years later, a writer tells us that it took five years' apprenticeship to join the chorus.

The words of the Psalms show, it is believed, that choruses, responses and antiphonal singing (that is, by a choir divided into two sides) were intended, but perhaps the most important scraps of information are contained in the preambles to each psalm and in words like 'Hallelujah' or 'Selah'. 'Hallelujah', 'Amen', and 'Hosannah' were evidently congregational shouts or even songs (possibly on the simpler tune models such as example 1*b*). 'Selah' meant 'pause here' or perhaps 'interlude' when instruments were to play. Phrases at the head of some of the Psalms are translated in the Authorized Version as 'to the chief musician X upon . . .' followed by a word which seems to be the title of the tune-model to be used. None of these tune-models are known to us, but evidently there were strict rules on how the words were to be fitted to them and only those instructed by the chief Levite knew the secret. The word 'Maschil' at the head of a psalm means that it was a teaching piece. It is even possible that some superscriptions should be translated 'on the principal note X' instead of 'to the chief musician X', which would make the directions even more precise.

The Old Testament as a whole reveals the ground of music from its primitive track to the steps of Heaven: in the early Books, music is associated with harvest, work like well-digging, revels and saying 'good-bye'; by the Book of Samuel, music itself has become divine—'it is *good* to sing praises unto the Lord'.

Asia Minor, Syria and Greece

Bas-reliefs found in two eastern cities of Asia Minor—Hattusa and Senaschirli—show that the Hittites of *c.* 1500 B.C. were as musical as the Persians, for the lyre, flute, oboe, trumpet and usual percussion instruments appear many times, joined by the long-necked guitar. The Canaanites in Syria (called Phoenicians) living round Tyre and the Greek peoples settling on the western coasts of Asia Minor were the communities who leads us to 'the glory that was Greece'. The three most powerful tribes were remembered in the names which Greek writers in the fifth century B.C. gave to the first three patterns in example 2: 'Lydian', 'Phrygian' and 'Dorian'. Plato and Aristotle maintain that the Dorians were the greatest of Greek wanderers and that theirs was the tune-pattern by which Greek music became known. The first writer to describe the system by which composers worked in Classical Greece gives us the names of all these patterns, together with two others—'Aeolian' and 'Ionian'—named after wandering Greek tribes. Writing in 400 B.C., he tells us that his predecessors thought of patterns in two sets of four, called 'harmoniai' (= tunings). This is the first detailed description of the various ways in which an early civilization chose the component parts for building tunes from basic four-note patterns (= tetrachords). Whether the names given to the harmoniai really signify which patterns were commonly used by the different tribes in Greece is doubtful: each tuning set its own mood (or 'mode') and every mode had its own moral value, uplifting, tranquillizing, or lascivious; perhaps their names simply reflect the moral character of the different tribes, as Plato and his contemporaries saw them.

Plato and Aristotle faithfully record the part music played in their society. An educated man needed to know about music as a sign of wisdom and as a social asset; young people danced and sang to the gods (specially Dionysus) on any excuse; and professional poet-singers were a source of wonder to the non-practising musicians. Classical Greek music was divided into five categories:

1. Hymns
2. Dirges
3. Songs of victory
4. Songs of revelry
5. 'Songs' for instruments

Each had its own style of melody, harmony and rhythm and it would have been quite wrong to have composed or played a dirge in the same mode as an ordinary hymn. The power of these modes was so great that slaves were sent into the theatres to be educated and indoctrinated by musicians.

All early poems were sung or chanted—that is the meaning of the word—and poet-singers are famous in Greek history. They were all enchanters: Terpander, Sappho, Polymnestes before 500 B.C.; then the tragedians with their choral poetry— Aeschylus, Herodotus and Pindar. In the fourth century B.C. there came a new outlook in Greece. Timotheus with his lyre (or cithara: see drawing at the head of this chapter) kept the old magic alive with a lighter touch, and new playwrights like Euripides would have none of tradition. Aristoxenus explained how the magic worked in far greater detail than his predecessors like Pythagoras. Music was becoming an art to listen to for its own sake. It need no longer be thought of only in terms of ethics and religion; it had its personal appeal, as 'music'.

The emotional and ethical powers of tunes-with-words made the Greeks call them 'music' (= belonging to the Muses). The Muses were personifications of the seven kinds of spoken word (epic, loving, lyrical, tragic, comic, eloquent and historic), of dancing, and of astronomy. Why astronomy? To the ancients, music was a bridge between heaven and earth, between gods and men. The sound of music was the sound of heavenly voices and these could be heard in the stars, the wind and the sea, and in materials like the wood from which instruments were made. Myths and legends from Greece and China (as well as the Old Testament) provide music with a divine origin and give instruments direct connections with the earth and heaven. According to Homer, the Greek gods Apollo and Orpheus (who lived *east* of Greece) first breathed music; and music was magic— 'Orpheus with his lute made trees'. The Chinese sage, Confucius, repeated that the first Divine Emperor's minister was sent to a mountain in the far *West* to cut bamboo to make pipes, and that it was

these pipes that made music magical. The Bible has Jubal;
and the Magi were wise men 'from the East'.

East of Greece, west of China and east of Palestine; the
myths and legends agree with each other remarkably on the
birthplace of music—and of its magic. More often than not,
myths and legends turn out to be history in disguise.

CHAPTER TWO

ENTERTAINERS

The declining civilization: 400 B.C. – A.D. 250

The turn of the century around 400 B.C. marks a violent
change in the sounds of western music, not as important in its
musical as in its social effect. The new professionals in Greece—
Timotheus and Philoxenus outstanding—were making music
purely to entertain an audience. The idea that music had
moral undertones meant nothing to them; they were free to
sing and play as they liked and the public was free to hear
and idolize them. In sounds, this meant that the singers began
to use ear-catching tricks (exaggerated portamento amongst
them) and, in experimenting with new ideas, made up rhythms
and melodies which broke all the old rules of the modes.

This new music started a musical revolution which kept
faith with its leaders afterwards because it did not know how
to succeed them. One hundred and fifty years after Timotheus
died, professional musicians were still singing his songs and no
one wrote new ones; everyone was nostalgic for the old music—
the few fragments of Greek music which have survived are
almost all in the old tradition though they were all written after
250 B.C.—and highbrow professional entertainment was,
musically speaking, a living museum piece. (Something of the
kind occurred in England in the eighteenth-century worship of
Handel long after his death.)

Star performers were actors and virtuosi, not creators;
their patrons and fans wanted well-staged entertainment not
new songs. The music hall of late Greek and Roman days (the

pantomime and the amphitheatre), as you might imagine from the heading of this chapter, was a pretty low affair of belly dancers, acrobats, bawdy sketches and songs. A few of the first-rate singers who could sing the music well were, however, treated like heroes and gods in much the same way as present-day prima donnas. It may be that through their pupils something of their art survived the Dark Ages, but we have not enough evidence of their songs to compare and it seems unlikely we shall ever know. The remaining professionals were available to play the pipes or cithara and sing 'for all occasions'; some were good value, others just 'made a joyful noise'. But the profession was sufficiently organized to have its own trade unions.

No music of the home-made entertainment which we would now call folk song and dance has reached us for certain from these early days. We know that Greek children were taught to sing and even took part in inter-city festivals, that eminent Roman citizens did at one time take part in dignified panto-mimes, and that some Roman Emperors were talented singers and cithara-players (e.g. Nero), but we have no record of what they sang and played.

The Dark Ages: 250 – 1000

The first of the barbarians attacked Western Europe from the north about A.D. 250 and not a note of music has survived to show us what was sung and played outside church for the next 700 years, except a few trumpet calls which may be remnants of the highly-ordered system of signals that the Romans used.

It is impossible to doubt that people did sing and dance on all the usual occasions but we can only guess what it sounded like. Five assumptions are fairly safe:

1. Bands of musicians still travelled about with acrobats, jugglers and mummers to earn a living, but they had lost much of their old skill.

2. Folk songs of the ordinary people must have become a confusion of the old Eastern and the new Northern types; neither style can be assessed by listening to any modern folk music, which is all much more recent.

3. Scholarship began again after Charlemagne became the first *Christian* Emperor of the new order (800). The songs which are our direct heritage (that is, in regular accents rather than in which each word or phrase has its own lengths) must have been written after this.

4. The intelligent amateur musicians of the old governing families were absorbed by the Church or became advisers serving the new masters. Some barons of the new order must have become interested in their music.

5. Islam preserved something of Arab, Persian, Syrian, Egyptian, Greek and Gothic music as the Muslim world spread westwards from about 650 to the fifteenth century. European musicians undoubtedly had some contact with the creators of the lavish *Arabian Nights*, since the Caliph Haroun-al-Raschid and the Emperor Charlemagne maintained ambassadors at one another's courts.

The Early Middle Ages: 1000 – 1300

The five assumptions just listed are made, of course, in the light of what we know about the early Middle Ages; for the first three, we can find material evidence in the actual music which survives from the later period.

The decline in the ballad singer's musical standard is shown in the monologues with very little tune which are called Chansons de Geste. Literally, these were songs about great deeds in which words and mime were all-important. The music only added the magic touch of enchantment and the 'jester' repeated the same musical snippet over and over again until the end, when he changed his tune to emphasize the last few words. These tunes were traditional and the only written evidence seems to be in a quotation from an old jester which appears in a pastoral play about 1285. This is quite revealing, for the jester sings his tune on one of the earliest tune-models (see example 1), like this:

Example 5

Evidently the medieval jester was, musically, a primitive; and probably the tunes which people sang and played for their dancing had also gone 'back to nature'. The words, however, of the jester's songs were in the new language of the conquerors, the Franks, and—even if the tunes were old—songs were at least being written again. The Roman mime and even the Greek actor survived in these minstrels, who described the great virtues of the Holy Roman Emperor Charlemagne or of the saints of the Christian Church in place of the rulers and gods of the earlier days.

Another pin-point of light shines on the Dark Ages in the Latin poetry written down by travelling scholars, called Goliards, (after an imaginary Bishop 'Golias' who was fond of wine, women and song). The disreputable picture of these students which we often read is perhaps exaggerated. They travelled from place to place seeking out new masters and, like any bunch of students, they were often poor, sometimes thoughtless and usually high-spirited. But this need not mean that they were no better than beggars or that they were vulgar renegades. Their songs, like those in any student song book, were a mixture of silly nonsense, doubtful puns, sharp satire, open-hearted sentiment and moral uplift; the tunes were often converted hymn tunes or in that style. As the words of Goliard songs are in Latin verse, we could use the rhythmic modes (see page 40) to transcribe them—if we had the tunes. Only one Goliard

melody has come to light, written down in a kind of tonic sol-fa (see page 57), to tantalize us with its lilting freshness: the twelfth-century 'O Roma nobilis' which was also sung to a disreputable love-poem 'O admirabile' 200 years earlier. The meeting of these two types of musician—professional jester and amateur goliard—produced the troubadour and his minstrels and provides the last two assumptions of what music went on in the Dark Ages.

The new masters of Europe spoke kinds of French, Spanish and German. As their sons grew up and studied, like the goliards they began to write songs—but in their own languages, first mixed up with Latin then entirely in native dialects. Their songs had different metres and rhyme-schemes which were gradually copied in the music. The forms into which the songs can be analysed are so numerous that there is room here only for a summary of general characteristics.

These educated gentlemen were usually of high birth and their chivalrous love-poems matched their nobility. For their music they relied at first on their jesters, so the melodies were short, constantly repeated, and usually around the first tune-model in example 1. Some can be analysed in one or other of the Gregorian church modes (see page 33), but it is easier to think of them as extensions of the pentatonic pattern, which result in our major scale and—more important—in new tune-models based on three-note patterns (triads). The example-tune would not be out of place in a troubadour's song book if it were written like this, starting with one of these major three-note patterns:

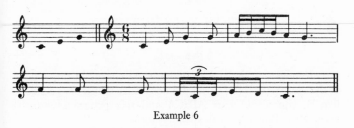

Example 6

The decoration and the extension of the range depended on the skill of the singer; so did the rhyme-scheme, both in words and music. Two types of solo song emerged from the old chansons de geste:

1. Lay (French 'Lai', German 'Leich'), which had several contrasting verses, each having a new musical idea but each ending in the same way as a kind of rhyme in music; more

rhapsodical than the chansons de geste, sounding something like church Sequences; used for telling Bible stories or crusader's tales.

2. Ballad (French 'Canzo', German 'Bar'), which had one tune repeated for each verse except the last; the last verse, like the last line of a chanson de geste, had a 'summing-up' tune (AAB).

Songs with choruses, well known in all folk music, also had two main branches:

1. Virelai, a lay with a chorus before and after (ABA); sounds specially modern to us because the chorus had a half-close cadence:

Example 6A

2. Rondeau, a virelai with a shortened chorus in the middle of the verse (ABaB'A); if you did not realize that B' was actually like B, you would hear ABaCA and this pattern eventually became the Rondo (Italian spelling) form.

The choruses sometimes had one word only (e.g. 'Eya', 'Eya') or a string of nonsense; if the chorus section of a virelai or rondeau had a lot of words which meant something, the poet was probably merely using the form but sang the whole thing himself.

One last class of vocal music remains to link the sounds of entertainers with those of priests and scholars in the Middle Ages. In it are the songs in troubadour forms which were sung by people walking on pilgrimage or in penitential processions, at special church plays, or for open-air dancing. Pilgrim songs were found, naturally, in those countries which had the most hallowed shrines: Italy (Rome) and North-West Spain (Compostela). In Italy, they were 'Laude Spirituali' and in Spain 'Cantigas'. Laude for processions were normally virelais in form, but some were so ornate that they sound like church chant at its most ecstatic. Cantigas also mostly used the virelai form, with one extra feature which we have already met as a Spanish folk idiom: the change of time from '2' to '3' which keeps the same overall length of time in each bar (see example 4). Here is the opening of the example tune as it might be in a cantiga:

Example 7

Some cantigas were very passionately ornamented and must have been sung at various stopping-places on the route. Even nowadays, in Spanish religious processions at Easter, such a solo song may come from any penitent in the watching crowd as the procession passes by.

Dancing songs called 'Carols' go back certainly as far as the pagan dances of the Greeks. The origin of the word may be from the Greek *choros*, through *choraules* (meaning dances accompanied on the aulos, see page 307), that is 'outdoor dances'; or it may be from *Kyrieleison*—giving the Dutch carol word 'Leisen' and the English 'Kyriol' or 'Carol'. The medieval carol is always in virelai form. The refrain is called 'Burden', the verse 'Stanza'. The words were probably composed by go-ahead clerics who saw in this form a much better place for a sermon than the pulpit, particularly as they could use the crowd's native tongue (rather than Latin) and dramatize theology. The music is very likely to preserve many old virelai tunes, for carols remained popular well into the sixteenth century. Perhaps the two most famous early carols are 'Orientis partibus' (called, in England, the Song of the Ass), and the Annunciation Carol 'Angelus ad Virginem' (which originated in Ireland).

Carols were songs to dance to, but some dance music was played on instruments alone. Instrumental dances used the form of the lay and there were three different kinds:

1. Ductia, a processional dance probably with loud instruments.

2. Estampie, more often accompanied on stringed instruments.

3. Rota, which is as yet only a name to us, mentioned often in medieval literature.

Very few of these tunes have survived and the whole repertory of instrumental dance music of the early Middle Ages would only fill five or six pages of this book. They were played on reed pipes, recorders, drums, viols and—above all—the fiddle (which may have come through Islam, as one of its names—'rebec'—suggests). The troubadour opened his performance with something on the string hurdy-gurdy, another dance instrument (which the French call 'vielle', but which is best described by its Latin name *rota* since you made the strings sound by turning a wheel). At a royal or military procession you would have heard brass instruments as well. If you add various bells *and* the bagpipes to this list, you can imagine how entertaining the sounds of the early Middle Ages could have been.

CHAPTER THREE

PRIESTS AND SCHOLARS

Plainchant: Psalms

In the early Christian Church, the songs of the East remained. The psalms of the Jewish synagogue were the basis of church music but the sound of chanting gradually developed its own style in the West. The simplest form of psalm chant, in all Christian rites, had an opening phrase (intonation); a reciting-note (tuba = trumpet, perhaps because, like most early trumpets, it had only a single note); and various kinds of phrase-endings (cadence = falling). At first, each psalm had an 'Amen' or short verse (like 'Glory be to the Father . . .') at the end for the congregation to sing, but, with the foundation of the monasteries in the fourth century many changes were made.

In monastic houses, which had no congregations, the psalms were sung antiphonally as in the old Jewish service (page 18), while, in churches open to the public, congregations were given increasing numbers of hymns to sing and the psalms were left to the choir. Latin replaced Greek as the singing language in the west. The intonation soon became so long that it needed a separate name, 'antiphon'. Here lies confusion, for 'antiphon' in this sense means simply something which went before the psalm, and not necessarily that it was sung by two sides of a choir, that is, 'in antiphony'. Many tunes were taken from the Jewish chant, but they developed regional variations so that there were soon at least fifteen collections of Christian chant in use (sixth century) as well as the original uses in Syria and Byzantium (Asia Minor). Of these, the most important were those used in

31

Rome, Milan (Ambrosian), Spain (Mozarabic) and France (Gallican). It is now very difficult to sort out the different dialects of this musical language; it was not much easier for the great Pope Gregory, after whom Gregorian chant is named. He seems to have classified the chants, according to the patterns (modes) they used, towards the end of the sixth century. Example 8 shows the development of a plainchant psalm.

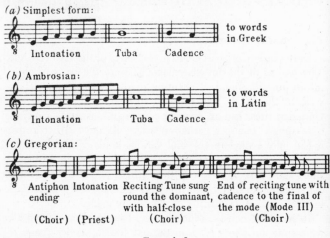

(a) Simplest form:

Intonation　　Tuba　　Cadence

to words in Greek

(b) Ambrosian:

Intonation　　Tuba　Cadence

to words in Latin

(c) Gregorian:

Antiphon　Intonation　Reciting Tune sung　End of reciting tune with
ending　　　　　　　round the dominant,　cadence to the final of
　　　　　　　　　　with half-close　　the mode (Mode III)
(Choir)　(Priest)　　(Choir)　　　　　(Choir)

Example 8

Plainchant: Modes

Gregorian modes were thought of in sets of eight, not—as with the Greeks—sets of four, and each mode was built on a definite pitch. The reciting-note fixed for psalms (tuba) was called the 'dominant' (= master note) and the note on which the psalm ended (final) was the lowest, on which the whole mode was built. All the modes used only intervals of tones or semi-tones—steps which came naturally to western voices—and they can be played on the white notes of the piano. The four modes which St. Ambrose had distinguished between were classed as 'authentic'; to each of these Gregory added a second, called 'plagal' which started a perfect fourth below its 'sister' mode but kept the authentic final. Here are the eight Gregorian modes:

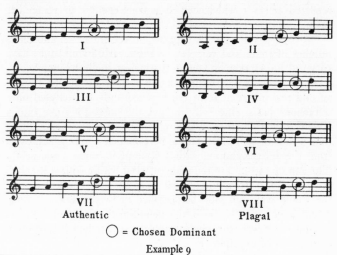

○ = Chosen Dominant

Example 9

A warning about the names of Gregorian modes: in the fifteenth century, a theorist re-classified them and added others, giving them all Greek names ('Ionian', 'Dorian', 'Phrygian', 'Aeolian' and so on) but, despite their similarity, Gregorian modes have no direct connection with the ancient Greek tetrachords—and in Gregory's day no Greek names were used at all.

Plainchant: Hymns

To begin with, all Christian hymns had words paraphrased directly from the Scriptures. After a while, the Eastern Church allowed increasing numbers of religious poems put together by its bishops and monks and eventually the Western Church began to collect its own body of original hymns, written at first to Eastern tunes, then to new melodies. The hymn composers of the early Christian church were interested in tunes only as far as they fitted their words easily and could be remembered. Most words had one note to each syllable, except for a few like 'Alleluia' which developed a tune of their own, and tunes often had repeated phrases which helped a congregation to remember them.

No congregation can be expected to remember an enormous number of tunes and very few of these early hymn tunes have survived, but you can find one or two in most modern hymn books. They can usually be classified in one of the eight modes, though an odd few inherited from the East can only be analysed on a tetrachord basis, since—if you put the notes they use into a scale (Latin *scala*, as in 'escalator')—they have an interval other than a tone or semitone. This is part of such a tune which came from the Jewish church, with a scale of its notes underneath. The gap of 1½ tones in the scale (marked with a square bracket) is an interval which could not belong to any Gregorian mode and the whole scale can only be classified in two tetrachords (nos. 2 and 4 of example 2). If the penultimate note had been 'C natural' however, the mode would have matched a Gregorian class (no 1 of example 8).

Example 10

Plainchant: Spiritual songs

Composers could concentrate on the musical side of their art in the spiritual songs which stemmed from the shouts of praise in the old Jewish church, the 'Hallelu' (= 'praise ye'). The Christian 'Alleluias' soon became showpieces for the choir and a soloist as the final syllable was extended into an entire piece of music. It was, St. Augustine said, 'praising without words' and came

near to entertainment rather than worship. Between the eighth
and tenth centuries, the moral guardians of the church (deans)
and the musical guardians (precentors—chief singers) fell to
guarding against each other, as deans and choirmasters may
still do today. By 800, the poet-composer had hardly any work
to do in the church: Gregorian chant was universally accepted
for the psalms; hymns were more or less traditional and new ones
unpopular; all, thought the poet-composer, was stagnation. So he
added to the Alleluia a piece of music in its own right with
words specially composed, called a Sequence (= following
piece). Similar interpolations at other parts of the service were
called 'Trope' and 'Prose'.

The words of the Sequence, Trope and Prose were not always
—as the third name shows—poetry; the tunes had several
repetitive sections, each of which took a different turn at the end,
as the name 'Trope' (= turning) implies. They were most useful
at great festivals like Easter or Christmas, when they covered long
processions. Some were so long that they were dramatized
and eventually became the mystery-plays. Such a Christmas
sequence, where the Magi sang as they followed a 'star' which
moved on pulleys down the roof of the aisle, was immensely
popular; the Easter sequence, 'Whom do you seek in the
Sepulchre?' was probably the most widely known of all.

So far, so good; but when precentors began to have the choir
singing to cover every movement the priest made during the
service—even when the lesson readers approached him to ask
his blessing—the deans took a firm line. Music was becoming too
obtrusive and detracted from the spirit of the service.

Plainsong: The Mass

The order of the Church's greatest service was finally established by 1000. The 'Ordinary', or unchanging parts of the
Mass, were:

1. Kyrie Eleison	Lord, have mercy	Greek, ex Pagan.
2. Christe Eleison	Christ, have mercy	Gregorian addition

3. Gloria in excelsis	Glory to God in the highest	Latinized from the Greek *c.* 600.
4. Credo	I believe in God	Added *c.* 1000.
5. Sanctus	Holy, Holy, Holy	Jewish.
6. Agnus Dei	Lamb of God	Added in the eighth century.

It may be that the congregation knew some settings of all these well enough to join in, though in many countries they would find the language hard to sing. The Creed, as the most personal part of the Mass, always had a simple tune so that every man could sing his own statement of faith; if the setting of other portions of the Mass was complicated, congregations probably waited until the end and joined in the 'Amen' much as they do today.

Other parts of the service changed daily or seasonally and certain words and tunes were proper to certain days. The 'Proper' of the Mass for a normal day—not a feast or a fast—was, and is:

1. Introit	Introduction to the service	Choir.
2. Graduale	Introduction to a reading	Choir, Soloist, and Choir again.
3. Offertorium	While gifts were being offered	Choir
4. Communio	Sung during the congregation's communion	Choir

There were also two lessons proper to each Mass, chanted on a single note with the ending falling or rising one tone.

Added to these sections were several acclamations, 'Deo Gratias', 'Amen' and 'Alleluia', perhaps extended by a precentor; and other choral items or long solo songs (Tracts = drawn-out) whenever there was a break in the continuity of the priest's part. Time must have been very short to rehearse all these and it is no wonder that accurate musical notation became absolutely necessary—especially as composers were now attracting still more attention to their music by experiments in part-singing with many solo voices (= polyphony).

Polyphony: Improvised

Adding a second part to a plainsong would today be called 'harmonizing' but the tenth and eleventh centuries called it 'organizing'. The word 'organ' meant 'an instrument'—something that worked—and the popular church instrument was the pipe organ with a compass of ten or twelve notes. Small pipe organs were later carried in processions (see illustration on page 44) but, in 950, they were much too big and some had more than one set of pipes. The second set of pipes was possibly tuned to the plagal mode a fourth below and sometimes two players played together at the same instrument. When singers copied the sounds of such an organ duet—part-singing in fourths—they said they were 'organizing' and called the whole process 'Organum'.

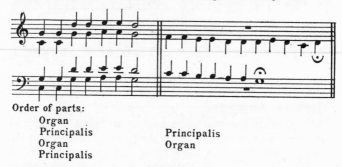

Order of parts:
    Organ
    Principalis   Principalis
    Organ   Organ
    Principalis

Example 11

Organum first moved in parallel lines of fourths with the lower part ending on the final of the mode ('G' in example 11). No one can stop a musician from decorating a simple tune, given the chance, and soon the first voice (principalis) began to improvise an ornamental ending while the organ-voice held on to the final (so being called 'Tenor' = 'holder'). Simple two-part organum could easily be made into four by doubling each part at the octave, so long as the parts remained parallel; decorated organum was safer in two parts only.

One huge organ in England was that of Winchester, which needed seventy men to blow it. Two men played it together but how many notes they played we do not know. Englishmen, however, had their own way of improvising harmony. In the thirteenth century, they often sang in thirds (gymel = twin-like) and even invented an ingenious way of improvising in three parts, called 'English Descant'. This had parallel lines of thirds and sixths with an organum-like beginning and end. Here is the example tune, first at the bottom then (as occasionally happened) at the top, in English descant. When the tune was at the top, the lower parts were said to be in 'fa-burden' suggesting that the technique was used in choruses (see page 29).

Example 12

Polyphony: Composed

So far, organizing was something to be learnt by ear and each singer was in effect his own composer. When particularly gifted choirmen began to experiment by singing tunes that moved in the opposite direction to the organ-voice throughout, part-singing became an art of written composition. The organ-voice was no longer added to the principalis with the first voice having his fling in the cadence; the organ-voice held on to the notes of the tune while the principalis sang another tune which was quite deliberately composed against the plainsong, in what is called 'counterpoint'. In the hands of precentors, this kind of harmonization was often used to accompany a procession or to conduct the preacher to the pulpit and became known as 'conductus'. At such a place in the service, the composer was not obliged to use plainsong and he could write both parts himself. It was 'free' composition, but sounds like this would only have been heard in big churches—and then only on the highest festival days:

Example 13

As early as 1200, organa had three parts and even, rarely, four; but these were the work of the most gifted. A modest choirmaster could put together a simple conductus type of organum for his choir fairly easily with a few rules about intervals in mind. If the tune he thought of did not fit exactly with the plainsong he could always hold up the organ-voice for a note or two until it could move on to a correct interval. These slow tenors were obviously suited to the organ rather than a second singer and the organist probably took over the whole of the plainsong, leaving the singer with the freshly-composed countermelody. Two parts written in this way were never thought of as 'high' and 'low' but as equals, so that the singer often crossed the organ tenor like this:

Example 14

Performers must have found these pieces difficult to remember: the organist could easily lose track of the singer's second part

(duplum) and fail to move off his long note at the right place;
and the duplum was in such free rhythm on one syllable only that
he might easily forget a flourish here or a roulade there. Composers found two remedies. The first was to give the duplum a
regular rhythm so that the tenor could count a pulse. Some
plainsong had been sung always in free rhythm—e.g. the psalms
—but other plainsong was rhythmical—e.g. for processions—
composed of long notes (two beats) and short ones (one beat).
Medieval theorists and teachers of music and poetry codified the
possible arrangements of long and short notes or syllables just as
Gregory had classified tones and semitones in certain arrangements. There were six rhythmic modes; since a singer or
speaker needs breathing space, the end of each phrase is a rest.
Here they are, in modern transcription:

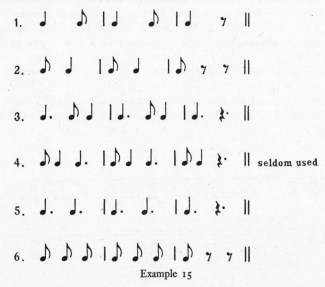

Example 15

When the duplum in two-part organa sang as rhythmically as
this, the tenor sometimes held his note in the old style for

several bars, but occasionally he might move more quickly and
in even time—say at the beginning of each bar. A section like
this might appear at any point in the piece and was called
'puncta' (= 'point') or 'clausula' (= 'little close').

Example 16

In three-part organa, by the early thirteenth century, the
duplum and the third part (triplum) fitted together easily as they
were in the rhythmic modes; the tenor alternated between even
movement and long-held droning. By now, the top two parts
were equal and the tenor was usually below, but it could still
cross the others at any time if the composer wanted it to.

The poet side of the composer provided the second aid to
remembering quick-moving added parts in polyphony. In
clausulae, composers often wrote separate texts for the duplum
and triplum to sing. As new texts had lengthened the alleluias
in plainsong to make them into sequences, so extra texts added to
counterpoint above the plainsong tenor's words gave their name
to a new type of polyphonic composition: the 'motet' (= 'little
word').

Polyphony: Motet, 1250 – 1300

Early motets thus evolved from the clausula. Before long,
composers even missed out the plainsong tenor altogether and
used their own duplum from a clausula as a basis for two new
added parts, so that all three were really 'counterpoints' and
there was no trace of the original plainsong. Sometimes he might

write his motet words in a different language for each part; on the other hand, he might connect all three parts melodically. All these variations worked very well rhythmically, for the modes all fitted together. The harmonic results were sometimes, to our ears, crude. In the first half of the thirteenth century, the harmony at any point where the tenor moved or on any strong beat

Example 17

was usually made up of fourth and fifth in old organum fashion. One of the first contributions which England made to the development of European music was made through the adoption by Norman and Burgundian composers of some of the sounds of

English descant in their motets during the second half of the century.

A thirteenth-century motet in three parts, with an organ playing the tenor and soloists singing the duplum and triplum in different languages is a strange mixture to listen to, but it has a freshness which must have matched the entertainers' music outside church—particularly as it seems from paintings and miniatures that no one minded if you played other instruments in church as well. Ex. 17 is the opening of the example tune as it might have been used for a motet during this early period of polyphony—called, in comparison with what was to follow, the 'Ars Antiqua'. Some of the instrumentalists who might have taken part in the same service are shown in the heading to Chapter IV.

CHAPTER FOUR

THE SOURCES:

400 B.C.—A.D. 1300

THE evidence of musical history in these years is largely hearsay in the writings of theorists and commentators, or from dumb witnesses such as paintings and musical instruments. Only after musical notation became fairly accurate (and as we learn to decipher the different scripts) can material evidence be assembled for judgment.

Material evidence: 400 B.C. – A.D. 1100

Two stone carvings, six papyri with fragments of melodies on them, and four tunes in ancient textbooks are all the Greek music that we have. The first stone, uncovered at Delphi in 1893, has two hymns on it; the second, part of a tomb found near Tralles in Asia Minor, records a drinking song as an epitaph to a man called Seikilos—both pieces, the sacred and profane, are now over 2,000 years old. The papyri date from the fourth century B.C. to the third century A.D. but no piece on them is complete and they remain a frustrating collection of notes for songs in plays, incidental music for an unspecified instrument and half a line of a lyrical song. There are tunes in Greek textbooks but often—like most of the examples in this book—they were only built to demonstrate a teaching point and can hardly be taken to represent truly what music was being performed when the book was written. So the number of authentic complete pieces of ancient Greek music stays at two.

The republic of Rome has left us no memorial in music script of any kind and the earliest surviving manuscripts of Christian chant were copied in the eighth century. The earliest complete collection of Ambrosian chants for the daily services throughout the year dates from the twelfth century; and part of it (for winter) is in the British Museum.

Charlemagne (crowned Holy Roman Emperor in 800), forbade the use of the Gallican rite and no complete service has survived his edict; but practically all the yearly service music in Mozarabic chant is preserved in Spanish manuscripts from the eighth century onwards, coming from Toledo and Leon cathedrals.

The main language made up of these earlier dialects—Gregorian—is first apparent in copies of Antiphoners (containing all the choir's music) from different parts of Europe, made during and after the eighth century. The Gregorian manuscripts which have come down to us in the cathedrals of Southern France such as Toulouse and the enormous red brick building of Albi give us a 'flashback' of the earlier dialects. Despite the ban on the Gallican rite and the swallowing-up of the Mozarabic, some of the earlier tunes were too good to lose and hymns survive to throw up two names from the gloom of the Dark Ages: Fortunatus of the Gallican rite, whose 'Salve festa dies' ('Hail, thou Festival Day!') is known to many a choirboy as the long processional hymn for Easter, Ascensiontide and Whitsunday; and Mozarabic settings of one of the earliest Christian poets, Prudentius, including 'O sola magnarum urbium' which we now know as 'Bethlehem, of noblest cities'.

Geographically, the only cultured Western country untouched by barbaric invasion until late in the Dark Ages was Ireland. Irish Christianity provided a strong link, if not the only tie, with classical literature and music. Converted by St. Patrick, a Roman, in the fifth century, the Celtic monks were scholars and missionaries: through men like Columba, Aidan and Cuthbert, Latin poetry and grammar were carried to Scotland; from Iona and Lindisfarne as far south as Sussex; and finally, in the seventh century, back to Europe and particularly to the Irish monastery of St. Gall near Lake Geneva in Switzerland.

In the archives of the monastery at St. Gall are the earliest written version of the Easter Sepulchre drama and a large number of beautifully-copied pages preserving sequences and tropes. Two monks of the monastery about 900 must have been among the greatest poet-composers: Notker (nicknamed 'Balbulus' = The Stammerer) for sequences and Tuotilo for tropes.

MAP 2
400 B.C. to A.D. 1300

ST ANDREWS
LINDISFARNE
DUBLIN
YORK
WORCESTER
HEREFORD
READING
SALISBURY
WINCHESTER
CANTERBURY
PARIS
CHARTRES
REICHENAU
BENEDICTBEUERN
POITIERS
ST GALL
LIMOGES
CLUNY
PADUA
COMPOSTELA
LEON
NAVARRO
ALBI
TOULOUSE
MONTPELLIER
MILAN
LUCCA
PISA
FLORENCE
AREZZO
ROME
TOLEDO

Meanwhile, Roman Christianity had taken firm root in England, based on St. Augustine's see of Canterbury, but also with many Benedictine monasteries. In one of the latter, at Winchester (capital of Wessex), the Easter Sepulchre drama appears again in a Troper dating from about 980. In the same Troper is the earliest extant polyphony as used in performance apart from teaching: no less than 164 two-part organa. It lies in Corpus Christi College, Cambridge, but its notation cannot yet be deciphered and it will need minds such as have defeated the 'Linear B' Minoan script, together with new finds for comparison, if it is ever to be re-heard. Indeed, our only examples of organum written before 1100 which can be performed are one leaf from a book in Chartres Cathedral, and a short piece in a library at Lucca.

Material evidence: 1100 – 1300

By 1100, plainsong notation looked much as it does today and this makes the modern transcriber's task easier, for at least he can reproduce the pitch of a melody accurately. There are, however, no defined rhythmic symbols until the six rhythmic modes were adapted in the mid-1100s; yet, by 1300, you could tell the length of a note by its shape just as we do today. These tremendous strides were taken by the only people who could write, who had time to think out ways of passing on traditional tunes, who were singing together daily and so discovering how to compose polyphony—the monks and their choirmasters in the monasteries and cathedrals.

The foundation of Benedict's order in the fifth century, the numerous Irish monks of the Dark Ages, and the Benedictine offshoots of Cluny (910) and the Cistercians (1098) made the map of Europe between 1100 and 1300 look like a honeycomb of monastic cells. In England alone, Benedictine houses and cathedrals were to be seen from Durham to Dorset, Worcester to Wells and Bridlington to Bury St. Edmunds; Cistercian abbeys stood at Robertsbridge, Tintern and Thame; and in the far north, the heirs to the first of St. Augustine's converts outside Canterbury lived and worked at St. Andrew's. If we add to these cells the pilgrim cities of Compostela and Rome and the new universities—among them Oxford and Cambridge, Paris, Toulouse and Montpellier, Bologna, Pisa and Padua—we have a wide choice of places to search for polyphonic music. Six hundred years, however, is a long time for manuscripts to survive. Then as now, successive choirmasters must have destroyed out-of-date music rather than clutter up the library, and at a time when parchment was so scarce and expensive, music was often cut up to stiffen the binding of new pieces.

The most interesting discoveries of twelfth-century music

have been made in the Cathedral Library of Compostela. The Compostela volume, called the Calixtine Manuscript (*c.* 1137), provides a telescopic view of one corner of church music: it contains pilgrim song tunes, plainsong sequences and tropes for the feast of the patron saint St. James, and twenty-one pieces of two-part organa (some conductus and some slow-moving tenors). One remarkable two-part pilgrim song, 'Congaudeant catholici' even has a third part which was added later and points the way to the thirteenth century. Twenty-two tropers from St. Martial (at Limoges) and the surrounding district are now housed in libraries—mostly at Paris, but one in the British Museum—and they, too, contain fine examples of early organa.

One last piece of early composed organum is worth mentioning, partly because it was found in the fly-leaves of a later manuscript and we are lucky to have it at all, partly because it shows that the English were by no means behind the field in harmony. It is a three-part version of a tune on a favourite model of the Middle Ages (see pages 25 and 27), called 'Verbum Patris humanatur' ('The Word of the Lord is made flesh'), now in Cambridge University Library.

A manuscript now in Wolfenbüttel, Germany, forms a bridge to the thirteenth century which spans Europe geographically as well as musically. The book was written about 1250 in St. Andrew's, Scotland, and its eleven sections range from two-part tropes and alleluias in twelfth-century organum to three- and four-part organa with clausulae for instruments in them. The clausulae are written separately and may first have been played without their parent organa—perhaps to cover a priest's actions when he had no words to sing—or even outside church as dance tunes for a religious procession.

A series of manuscripts still in Paris came from St. Victor half a mile from Nôtre-Dame cathedral, and were being written about the same time as the Augustinian monks of St. Andrew's were copying their collection. In the Nôtre-Dame school, the new rhythmic modes were strictly applied to two upper parts above a slow-moving tenor (as in example 17). Later clausula were probably provided by a new choirmaster as alternatives to the earlier pieces, and many of them have added texts in the upper parts, making them the earliest motets. The motets were sometimes in Latin, sometimes in French and occasionally in the Anglo-French of the Norman (or Angevin) noble; probably the Latin was used when they were performed in church, the modern language when they were sung outside—such double uses of the same music were well-known. Copies of organa, conductus and motets written by composers attached to Nôtre-Dame have been found in England, Scotland, Spain and Italy, to prove how international the style of Pérotin—the greatest composer of the 'school'—and his companions became in the thirteenth century. Their music is the finest of this early period of polyphony, the 'Ars Antiqua'.

It was as common to use the same polyphonic music with alternative words inside or outside church in 1300, as it had been for the goliard to use the same Gregorian chant for his devout or vulgar poetry. Troubadour tunes and even earlier forebears were often heard in church motets, sometimes only a phrase, occasionally intact in the duplum (as in a famous collection of motets in the style of Pérotin at Montpellier University). From such motets many troubadour tunes (particularly rondeaux) have been reconstructed.

Latin song tunes (except for 'O Admirabile': see page 26) are lost to us, though the poetry remains to record the names of many who kept civilization alive during the Dark Ages: Ausonius, Prudentius, Boethius and Fortunatus of Roman stock; St. Columba and his numberless Irish namesakes called 'Colman'; Alcuin, the Yorkshireman who taught Charlemagne to value literacy; Strabo, Abbot of Reichenau, writing across the lake from his friend and master Grimold, Abbot of St. Gall; and the 'Archpoet', spokesman for the anonymous wandering scholars. The rhythm and metre of their poetry, as with Greek play songs and the Hebrew psalms, suggests musical forms—but no more. The two most famous collections of Goliard verse are *The Cambridge Songs*, an eleventh-century scholar's song-

book copied by an Englishman, and the *Carmina Burana*
(thirteenth century), also copied carefully from various original
love-songs, drinking songs and serious songs which a scholar
had collected on his journeys. Some he learned at the Universities, some he heard from Minnesinger (= Love-singers, the
German troubadours), and some he made up himself. Both
collections were preserved in monasteries (Canterbury and
Benedictbeuern).

The only manuscript approaching a chanson de geste (except
the tiny extract mentioned on page 25) now available to us is a
thirteenth-century story with music about *Aucassin and Nicolette*
—a touching tale of derring-do involving a fair young couple in
love, which was guaranteed to cure any man's grief and fill him
with joy, said the preface, 'such is its sweetness'. This last
is the 'tag' line which rounds off each verse of repeated music
with a fresh strain.

The melodies for troubadour and trouvère poetry were not
written down in any numbers until the professional hands of the
thirteenth and fourteenth centuries began their skilful and
elaborate chansonniers (= song books) for wealthy patrons. There
is no knowing what the later masters did to the old tunes when
they wrote them down, but we rely mostly on these chansonniers
for the large collection of minstrel melodies which are now
available in modern editions. Names of minstrels sometimes
come into their songs—e.g. Marcabru—and among those we
know something about are the noble troubadour William of
Aquitaine, Count of Poitiers, the royal trouvère Thibaut, King
of Navarre, the strolling minstrel jester Colin Muset, and the
travelling minnesinger Walther van der Vogelweide. The
evidence of the tunes proves that troubadours did not suddenly
begin to write a new kind of music: they first adapted popular
tunes, whether these were hymns or dance tunes; then they
asked trained musicians to supply them; finally, they became
skilled enough to write their own. The small last group were
strongest in Germany where, first as minnesinger in citizen gilds
and then as the Gilds of Mastersingers, the poet-composers of

unaccompanied melody practised until the sixteenth century. The Gild actually lived on in name until 1839 and was given an apparently everlasting memorial by Wagner in his opera *The Mastersingers of Nuremberg* (1868).

The last material evidence to be called for this period proves that troubadour songs were taken up by the most zealously religious parts of Europe in the late thirteenth and fourteenth centuries. In Spain, the *Cantigas de Santa Maria* were collected by Alfonso the Wise, King of Leon and Castile and another large volume has come from Las Huelgas. They can both be bought in modern transcriptions and some of them have been recorded: in them are many changes of time like that in example 7, most are in virelai form, and all describe some miracle of the Blessed Virgin. The biggest collection of Laude Spirituali comes from Cortona, near Florence, and they coincide in date with the formation of the earliest brotherhoods of friars, dedicated to the work of God outside church. St. Francis of Assisi is known to have written at least one of these hymns in the first years of the thirteenth century. We now sing it as 'All creatures of our God and King' and it opens yet again with the celebrated tune-model of the Middle Ages:

Example 18

Hearsay evidence: 400 B.C. – A.D. 900

The laws of musical history must allow much hearsay evidence whenever it can be made to fit known fact, and tend to accept it when it comes from a known expert witness. So we tend to believe much of what Aristoxenus (a trained professional musician) wrote, yet mistrust a man like Boethius (whose musicianship was only scholar's knowledge to go with astronomy, mathematics and astrology). The few Greek scholars—Pythagoras among them—who wrote about the sounds of music (as opposed to the place of music in society) set out to analyse it as a science, not as an art. Their analyses had no more to do with what the man in the street heard, than their astronomy had to do with what he saw in the sky.

Aristoxenus, however, belonged to the age of revolution in Greek thinking and worked, as his teacher Aristotle recommended, 'by ear to understanding': that is, by practical experiment and observation. But his analysis of music was never intended for practical use and nothing which he wrote can be said to have affected future composers. To the musical historian, he confirms that all Greek music was built on tetrachords and that the intervals of the fourth and fifth were perfectly in tune to a musical ear. Beyond that, as he pointed out himself, any amount of description of the component parts of Phrygian or Dorian music will not help us to know *why* one piece sounded 'Phrygian' or another 'Dorian'.

Greek philosophy and science to do with music travels down to us along the North African coast through the commentary on Aristoxenus by Ptolemy of Alexandria (second century A.D.), the translations of Aristotle and Plato into Arabic (with the additional experiments of Moslem theorists), and the re-translation of the Arabic into Latin by the Spanish priest-scholars of the Middle Ages. To the medieval mind, Boethius was the only philosopher who, as a Roman, seemed to provide a direct link with the ancient civilization. Just as Galen was the only man who knew about medicine, Boethius invented or developed everything in music. Boethius—eminent as the translator of Aristotle, trusted councillor of a barbarian conqueror (Theodoric), and an unforgettable poet in his *Consolation of Philosophy* —seems to us to have added nothing practical to the history of music. In his writings he used, for the first time, an alphabetical system to identify pitches, but no one after him used it (though for centuries the way of using alphabetical letters as we know it was said to be 'Boethian'); his descriptions of Greek modes were, in the light of what we now know, very confused; and though he provided food for thought resulting in page after page of medieval theory, Boethius can now almost drop out of musical history books.

Descriptions of the use of music in Roman days and Arabian nights abound in the Latin and Moslem chroniclers. What you see is easier to describe than what you hear, and the valuable parts of these chronicles are those that say what instruments looked like and when they were used. Roman and Moslem writers refer to funeral processions, marriages, feasts and rituals—all the primitive times for music—but they also refer to concerts given by singers with stringed and wind instruments. These concerts gave the professional composer his chance both as singer and player: the Roman mime-jester and the Arab court minstrel are often portrayed, with singing girls and dancers. Plutarch, Suetonius, Pliny and Petronius head the list of Roman writers who record these concerts; the war historians, Pollux and Procopius, tell us how charge and retreat were sounded by cavalry and infantry trumpeters, while bugles played the routine calls of the watches. As for Islam, the Great Books of Songs—twenty volumes on the history of Arabian music which took half the tenth century to compile—describe types of music which were current in Europe only in the following 300 years; but, alas, there is no Arabic musical notation before the thirteenth century.

The earliest Christian writers on music began by ridiculing and condemning Greek music as pagan, mocking the mythical inventors of music in favour of the Biblical interpretation of the original 'Word' as the voice of God. Practically, this meant that they disapproved of the lyre and cithara but liked the voice. Such men as Clement of Alexandria wrote that the music of King David was 'the true music', and that the coming of Christ brought the Word again—a 'new song'. St. Basil of Caesarea, whose liturgy is still used in the Eastern church, preached constantly on the virtues of singing psalms to the 'psaltery' (or dulcimer)—a soft, stringed instrument played with the fingers—rather than to the 'brassy' accompaniment of the cithara and lyre. St. John Chrysostom, whose prayer still closes every

Anglican Morning and Evening Service, repeatedly commended psalmody, since there was no need for the cithara with its 'artificial' plectrum. The influence of Jewish singing and hallelus was still strongest in the Near Eastern countries, and the greatest of all the great Christian scholars in the Byzantine church, St. Jerome, exhorted all Christians to *sing* their praises, particularly in the psalms which contained the word 'Alleluia'—however bad their voices were. The deeply emotional Hebrew style of singing in the Eastern church passed into the West through Milan, where St. Ambrose used Eastern forms of chant in antiphony, and also introduced hymn singing for all.

St. Augustine, a pupil of St. Ambrose, first sounds a note of caution about over-adorned psalm-chant in the Western church during the fifth century, although he is inclined to allow it for the weaker members of the congregation who 'by the delight taken in the ears [may] be roused up into some feeling of devotion'. For himself, he is afraid and ashamed that he may be moved more by a beautiful singer than by his song, and prays for guidance. Here is the first open statement of a problem which has continually cropped up in church musical history: should we only have the austerest musical settings (or none at all) so that the words are shown as all-important, or should we use the power of music to increase a congregation's devotion? Augustine may have left this question unanswered but he gives us a fair-minded account of church music in his day.

The performance of Mass in the time of St. Gregory the Great is described in great detail by the anonymous authors of the Roman Ordines (official guides to the Papal Mass), the first of which was written in the eighth century, more than 100 years after Gregory had died. The true scope of Gregory's influence has many times been questioned: to medieval biographers, Gregory 'founded' Church music, just as Boethius had 'invented' notation. Yet the standardization of the Mass and of the various types of plainsong dates inescapably from his Papacy, and there seems no reason to doubt that he was personally in charge of the editing.

The ultimate authorities for us to consult about post-Gregorian liturgy and its plainsong are the handbooks to the various Uses (= forms of service) current in the Middle Ages at York, Hereford and Salisbury (in England), the Vatican, and many continental cathedrals. Their prologues often claim to say what Gregory had ordered and the directions for performing the music help us to reconstruct what the service looked like, if not precisely how it sounded. Their musical information apart, these books are also interesting in their record of how cathedral music was administered. Many Latin words used in small parish churches today show their medieval ancestry: the choir still has a 'Decani' and 'Cantoris' side, and the 'Vicar', 'Rector' or 'Canon' takes the service. All these titles explain themselves if you read the Uses. The Decanus (= Dean) was in charge of the conduct of all the priests living under the Canons (= rules) of the cathedral; the Cantor was in charge of a canon's musical training, in some cases from being a choirboy onwards. Each dignitary sat immediately behind the choir screen on opposite sides of the aisle which divided the choir into two antiphonal sides, our 'Decani' and 'Cantoris'. In some places (e.g. Southwell Minster) the choirmaster is still called 'Rector Chori' (= 'Guider of the Choir') and our parish Rector is still the 'guider of his flock'. If a canon provided a substitute, this relief singer was called, in Latin, 'Vicarius'. So we get our clerical titles, many of them connected, as was the entire medieval service, with music.

Hearsay evidence: 900 – 1300

The way to write early polyphony, from organum to motet, is analysed by a remarkable series of abbots and monks living in the monasteries of England, Flanders, Switzerland and Italy. Improvised organum is first mentioned by Hucbald of Flanders in the tenth century, who says that organizing was generally common in his day. Similar vague references to organum and gymel are made by English writers between 1100 and 1300: John Cotton, Gerald of Wales and Walter Odington. Organizing was popular everywhere. You were as likely to hear singing in

thirds in Welsh taverns of the Middle Ages, if we can believe
Gerald, as you would be in some 'Nelly-Dean' areas today;
according to Cotton, you might also have heard parallel fourths
or fifths and even parts improvised in contrary motion.

Rules for composing organa are first found in *Enchiridion
Musices* (= Manual of Music) written, possibly by the Abbot
of Cluny himself, St. Odo, about 935. Almost 100 years later,
Guido of Arezzo in his *Micrologus* gives practically the same
rules. Textbooks were to help a performer to know something
about how his music was contructed so that he could read it and
interpret it better; we teach elementary harmony to all intending
professional musicians today for the same reason. To this end,
the rules reduce music to a set of patterns which can be put
together again to make a well-known shape. Composition of this
kind will not make a man a professional composer, but if he
has the gift of composition to begin with, a traditional background will help him to keep in touch with his public. Writers
who believed this—Odo, Guido, Franco of Cologne and Hermann
the Cripple of Reichenau—followed Notker and Tuotilo of St.
Gall as teachers who, in helping their own generation to understand, help us today in two vital directions: they tell us how to
read their musical notation; and they teach us how their instruments were tuned, in great acoustical detail.

Acoustics, the theory of sounds, is outside the scope of this
book; but the reading of notation is essential to any musical
historian, in this book or in an immensely learned thesis.
The musical staff grew up during the tenth century. Notes first
followed an imaginary horizontal line so that the reader could
begin to see how they went up and down; next, the line was
actually drawn in red; and finally, a set of parallel lines each
an interval of a third apart—like our five lines—became normal.
The copyist used only as many lines as he needed for his tune,
not wasting parchment on lines which would have no note on
them.

Guido of Arezzo was probably the greatest teacher of the
century. He had invented a series of syllables to help his pupils

to distinguish between degrees of modal scales, which were revived in much the same system a hundred-odd years ago in England. Guido called his system 'solmization' and used the syllables 'Ut, re, mi, fa, sol, la'; Curwen, in the 1840s, called it 'Tonic Sol-fa', replacing 'ut' by 'doh', rhyming 'doh' with its major-scale dominant 'soh' (for 'sol') and adding a seventh syllable 'te' (which rhymed with the syllable leading to the other semitone in the scale, 'me'). The place of the semitone was just as difficult to remember in the modal system as it is in our scales, so Guido always coloured the places where semitones occurred (before 'F' and before 'C' in all modal music), whether on a line or in a space, red and yellow. When his pupil could read without the coloured guides to the semitones, he was reminded only by the letters 'F' and 'C' written at the appropriate place at the beginning of each set of lines, just as we are today. Our bass and alto clef signs are only ornately-printed versions of the letters 'F' and 'C'.

Guido tells us how his contemporaries learned to read pitch; Franco of Cologne tells us how his pupils learned to read rhythms. In his *Ars cantus mensurabilis* (= The Art of Measured Song), written about 1260, he explains the rhythmic modes and describes three main symbols for notes. The Long was worth three or two of the next shorter value, the Breve, according to its position; in a slightly different shape, the Long doubled its length, becoming 'Duplex' (very useful for slow-tenor organum). The third symbol was for the shortest note then in use, the Semibreve (= 'half-short'). Apart from these three, Franconian notation had several kinds of grace notes, rests and composite shapes for whole patterns of notes ('ligatures'). The reading of music had already become a long and complicated business, but thanks to Guido and Franco we can at least now read much of the material evidence of music in the early Middle Ages which has come our way.

It is difficult to know much about the men who provided the considerable material evidence of two- and three-part pieces in the twelfth and thirteenth centuries. As far as the

Nôtre-Dame 'school' is concerned, the only writer to tell us anything about it is an anonymous student in Paris, probably an Englishman, who took lecture notes on the construction of three-part music and added a few comments. The same writer also writes of a flourishing 'school' around Worcester Cathedral (where only a few fragments of material evidence have been found). The names of the two eminent precentors of Notre-Dame, Léonin and Pérotin, come from this source, but the masters of Worcester remain unknown. Three English composers are named in an index of the polyphony which used to belong to Reading Abbey, but we have none of their music.

Before 1300, no scholar thought popular music was worth writing about. The idea of music being beautiful in itself and not connected either with theology or science was as alien to the early Western scholars as the idea of music being an entertainment was to the Classical Greek philosophers. The new spirit among scholars which we call 'humanist' was as revolutionary as Greek ideas in the fourth century B.C. and was the beginning of the Renaissance. Had two writers not looked at the world around them at the turn of the century and commented even on popular songs, we should know even less than we do about minstrel music. Happily, these two—Johannes de Grocheo in Paris and Dante Alighieri in Florence—tell us not only the forms of troubadour song in detail but also something of their place in people's hearts. Grocheo is prosaic but kindly, suggesting that chansons de geste should be sung to old people or hard-working peasants after the day's work, so that their own hardship may not seem so great beside the sufferings of the jester's hero. Dante is the poet, devoting two verses in his *Paradise* to describing the beauty of a single song by the trouvère Bernard de Ventadour.

In Florence, Dante spent the year 1300 turning himself into a scholar-poet; in Assisi, Giotto was painting warm human beings in memory of the liberator of religion, St. Francis; the Bible, Missals, Psalters and Books of Hours shone out of the hands of illuminators in monasteries the length and breadth of Europe; the cathedrals of Northern Europe stood then as many still do, monuments to their Gothic architects and sculptors. Master craftsmen in all the crafts had become artists, and looked towards the Renaissance.

CHAPTER FIVE

MASTER CRAFTSMEN

MODERN ears find the music of the Renaissance easier to listen to than the music of earlier times, for experiments in rhythm and melody produced sounds which are still, in different ways, used to-day. This is not to say that Renaissance music sounds 'modern' but it is true that modern popular music draws remarkable parallels.

During these three hundred years (roughly 1300 to 1600), the weaving of more and more strands of melody into logical patterns made music sound ever richer. Two-part music became less fashionable (except for experiments in canon or to make short periods of contrast) and first three-part (1250–1450), then four (1450–1550), then five became usual.

Range of Voices

Motets in the old style, based on a borrowed plainsong or clausula tune which slowly unravelled in the tenor, were en-livened by more ornamented upper parts and these began to stand out. The second part (duplum) came to be used to keep the bottom or hem of the pattern in good shape. As you can see for yourself, a tune will not always make a firm basis for two other parts, and so the composer tacked another part round it, some-times above, sometimes below, which acted as a buffer (or what they called 'counter') whenever the tenor took an awkward turning. We still use the Renaissance term 'counter-tenor' (which replaced 'duplum') to describe a high male voice. The third part (triplum) was then the top; again, we still call the top part of vocal music the 'treble'.

In four parts, the texture of the music became thicker by adding two parts to counter the tenor, one above (contra alto) and one below (contra bassus), giving us our remaining terms: contralto (or, more usually, alto) and contrabass (as the bass is called in string music) or plain 'bass'. By then the tenor was well disguised in the whole, and as the top part lost some of its decoration, all parts gradually reached equal importance.

Isorhythm

The rhythmic modes of the thirteenth century, which did not allow division by two but only by three, restricted impatient composers, and from about 1280 onwards motets began to make some use of duple time. In place of the strict modes, the new rhythmic structure was that of isorhythm (= same-rhythm). In explanation it sounds mechanical, just as any other analysis of musical structure will—whether modern, like the twelve-note system, or established like sonata-form—but it was a stimulus both to the composer and to the intelligent listener. Basically, it involves two different ways of repetition: you either repeat the *rhythm* of a section exactly but put new pitch to it, or you repeat the *pitch* of a section exactly but change its rhythm if you wish. The first kind of section was a 'talea', the second a 'color'; both kinds of repetition were used in the same piece but the color (in the slow tenor) was a longer section.

The craftsman took as his tenor a snatch of plainsong, clausula tune, or—why should the Devil have all the best tunes?—a popular song. In example 19, the tenor is 'God save the Queen' (first three notes). Because this does not make a very satisfactory bass, a counter is added which will; this bass is freely added and does not have to repeat in the second color as the tenor must. The top two parts repeat their two-bar rhythm (talea) three times; the triplum is the most ornate and harks back to the triple division of the rhythmic modes, as well as being based on the example tune; the duplum is in the 'new' duple time.

This detail shows clearly one way in which composers of the fourteenth and fifteenth centuries achieved that unity which all

Example 19

artists—painters, poets, sculptors, architects or composers—
sought at the time. The arabesques of a painting, the lyrical
ecstasy of a poem, the tracery of a building, the delicacy of
the upper tune in a piece of music—all these attract the eye
or ear first, but beneath each is the craftsman's foundation,
strong yet supple.

A piece of this kind could have been sung throughout by
voices, when only the top voice would sing all the words of the
piece and the others would probably vocalize; but usually the
lower parts, because of their long notes, could only be played
on instruments, most often the organ. The first complete
setting of the Ordinary of the Mass in the fourteenth century
uses isorhythm for all its sections.

Melody

In the fifteenth century, the cross-play of rhythms was
all-important. Being wise after the event as all historians are,
we can suggest why. An isorhythmic motet was rhythmically so
complicated that the congregation heard only a general sound and
the appeal—like that of all strange music—was primarily
emotional. Only the accustomed and very intelligent listener
could follow the complications in the mind's ear. If they tried
to understand music at all, most people listened to the top tune.

A melody which never repeats itself, like the talea of an
isorhythmic motet, may sound sublime for a short time, but the
memory does not retain rhythms easily and the attention will
wander quite soon if phrases are only connected by their rhythm.
In the fourteenth century, composers tried to keep the attention
by delaying the melody rhythmically or by dividing it between
two voices so that the note is repeated with an extra rhythmic
'kick' which would stick in the memory. Both devices were
called 'hocket' (= 'hiccup').

By 1450, however, congregations had become used to listening
to the tune of motets with deliberate concentration. They no
longer wanted it broken up in hocket style: 'musical appreciation' was fashionable. The teachers of musical appreciation today

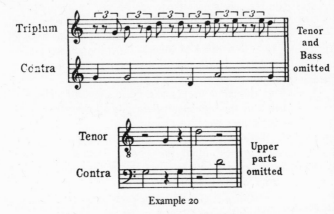

Example 20

usually start by suggesting that a pupil listens for the tune:
once the ear has become used to concentrating on one part,
memory begins; once you can remember easily the beginning, at
least, of a tune, you can begin to follow that opening through
different voices in the piece. Imitation of the same tune by
different voices occupied the inventors of polyphony from about
1250 to 1600. Strict rules ('canons' in Latin form: see below)
were continually made about imitation, only to be broken by the
more sensitive composers in the interests of musical beauty.

Canons

The workable laws or canons of the fifteenth and sixteenth
centuries were very intricate. Here, using familiar phrases,
are just a few of the ways in which the contemporaries of Raphael
and Michelangelo made a tune imitate itself.

The last, glorious tune in Example 21 is included in many
hymn books today in its original form as a straight forward
canon (that is, one which is like a round) under the name of its
composer, Thomas Tallis.

The next problem for composers to solve was to find out
how many tunes, played together, could be followed by the ear

Example 21   (continued overleaf)

(a) In augmentation

(b) In diminution

(c) In inversion (lower part moves by the same steps as the tune, but in the opposite direction).

(d) In retrogression (lower part is the tune backwards).

(e) Mirror Canon (upper part is the tune in retrogression as it appears upside down).

Example 21 continued

and the memory. If you sing a straight canon like 'Three Blind Mice' you can hear the melodies intertwining continuously and this adds to the pleasure, but what happens when you are only a listener? You hear the entries of the different voices and recognize them but once they are all singing, the music becomes a blurred mass of parts and you will find it more and more difficult to separate the lines so that you can 'follow' the music.

The sixteenth-century composer had no false illusions about his listeners' ability to analyse by ear. The more obscure canons of example 21 were retained as materials only in a few compositions which were meant to delight the eye of someone examining the manuscript, and no one expected his most complicated ingenuities to be recognized and applauded solely by ear. Whatever complicated construction had gone on under the surface, the composer was concerned that the listener should find the surface beautiful; but just as the architect left some of his basic materials in full view so that the visitor can see the order of his designs as well as their overall beauty, the composer usually made his tune-openings memorable enough for his listener to follow the order if he wished. The whole building was the harmony: points of imitation can be very expressive and add to the keen listener's enjoyment, but it is the harmony of several parts which goes to the heart.

Cadences

Punctuation marks in music, called cadences, also acquired new laws in the Renaissance. Modal Gregorian cadences were in order as long as the voice returned to the final at the end of

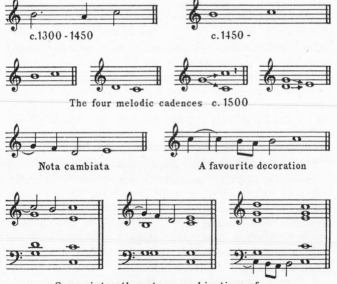

c.1300 - 1450

c.1450 -

The four melodic cadences c. 1500

Nota cambiata

A favourite decoration

Some sixteenth century combinations of
the four melodic cadences

Example 22

a chant, either falling on to it or—occasionally—rising to it. In polyphony, trebles began to return to the final always from below, by hopping (*c.* 1300–1450) or by step (*c.* 1450 onwards). By 1600, four such ordered cadences governed everyone; to them could be added the decorated 'nota cambiata' (= 'changed note') or—to make the harmony richer—two repeated dominants ('G' in the second treble of the last cadence in example 22).

All these cadences were 'perfect'; if a phrase ended on the first half of these cadences, unresolved, the cadence was 'imperfect'.

Harmony and discord

Organum harmony had been thought perfect in chords made up of fourths and fifths; Renaissance harmony had only two concords, both involving thirds. Counting inclusively above the bass, these can be expressed in figures: 5/3 and 6/3. Discords were seconds and sevenths (still dissonant to many modern ears) and the fourth if it clashed with the bass. No discord was forbidden —in fact, dissonance was encouraged—provided that it was smoothed out ('resolved') within the beat, but composers usually preferred also to prepare the listener for the discord by letting the dissonant note start as a concord in the previous beat.

Church Music: The Construction of the Mass

The devices of rhythm, counterpoint and harmony were moulded into music in motets, but it was only in the Mass that the music became a huge structure comparable with the Gothic cathedrals. The plainsong of the various sections served as a firm foundation ('cantus firmus') on which to build a polyphonic structure in most early settings, but between 1400 and 1600 there were four possible schemes (and an able composer eventually knew how to work to them all):

1. Cantus firmus Mass, of two main types, used throughout the period. Type A: the tenor of each section was a Gregorian chant appropriate to that section (that is, a plainsong Kyrie chant served for the polyphonic Kyrie); two upper voices sang an

elaborate version of the same chant; some passages were in two-part canon; and the Gloria was still troped (see page 35). Type B: a chant taken from a plainsong antiphon or a secular song served for the whole mass, using successive phrases for successive numbers or making one phrase do for all the sections by using the devices learnt in experiments on canons and isorhythm; usually four parts; cantus firmus in the tenor was in danger of being lost in the middle, so it was the last to enter and was doubled on the organ.

2. Alternating Mass, of four types, succeeding each other chronologically. Type A: until *c.* 1420, in which plainsong for the choir alternated with passages in polyphony for soloists. Type B: between *c.* 1420 and *c.* 1500, a wholly polyphonic setting in which the choir still sang only the plainsong while instruments played the other two parts, alternating with more difficult passages for three unaccompanied soloists. Type C: fifteenth century onwards (into the early eighteenth century) the so-called 'Organ Mass', in which unison choir and organ divide sections or verses alternately. Type D: late sixteenth century, in polychoral music, where two choirs alternated, one singing simpler polyphony in block chords, the other more complicated sections of counterpoint.

3. Parody Mass, of three types, all in use during the sixteenth century. Type A: in which the composer took a three-part secular song and used all three parts (or as many as he wished) in turn, either as a cantus firmus—usually in the bass, not tenor—or as points for imitation. Type B: in which the composer took one part of a secular song and let each voice sing it in turn; the other voices sang various borrowed bits of the other two parts of the song against it. Type C: in which the composer took all three parts of a sacred or secular piece—his own or someone else's—and made a long Mass out of a short motet or chanson by elaborating and interchanging the tunes of the original with his own added fourth part.

4. Fantasy Mass, the height of unaccompanied polyphony in the sixteenth century, in which the composer derived every-

thing in the Mass from a chosen model, but never let the model itself appear; the model might be a plainsong melody, a scale, a few sol-fa syllables or even one of his own ideas; the fantasy relied for its shape on a reminder of the intonation here or a snippet of scale there, particularly at climaxes.

The Mass and motets in the sixteenth century had four or five voices—occasionally eight, ten or even (once) forty—which began in strict imitation one after the other until everyone had entered; then came the first cadence. Words were repeated where the length of a part made it necessary or where emphasis was needed. In the cadence, one voice always started the next section, so no join was audible between the phrases; this section then grew to its cadence and so on. The descant cadence (see example 22) required a rising semitone and some of the cadences ended upon a final in a new mode, so that to make the semitone an accidental might be necessary; such 'modulation' began to relate certain modes to each other and led to the diatonic key system (see page 105).

Tunes moved smoothly, mostly stepping from note to note in fragments of scales, or up and down 5/3 and 6/3 chords; if a voice jumped outside the notes of one of these chords it always returned immediately within the distance. Yet, despite this apparent cramping, many tunes of lasting beauty were written. The lessons that composers had learned from working with isorhythm left an inheritance of intricate cross-rhythms which have a feeling of accent even if you cannot beat time to a piece in convenient divisions of three or four.

The Fantasy type of Mass marked the end of the Renaissance attitude to listening: variations on unknown themes are hardly easy to follow logically; they speak to the heart, and by-pass the mind.

Laude

Masses and motets were for trained choirs. Ordinary folk sang praises to God in processions outside church, rarely in the services, as they had done in the Middle Ages. Carols and virelais were still the main types of laude and cantigas, but with the spread of English descanting they were harmonized more often, and a few composers began to write simple harmonizations especially for congregational singing which contributed a good deal to the most popular style of secular song in the late fifteenth century, the frottola.

Popular song: 1250 – 1450

In any age, people expect to hear popular songs at parties and dances. Renaissance men and women were no exception, and their favourite topic was love. Family parties varied, of course, according to the social scale and so did the kinds of dances. A wealthy father—king, prince, duke, baron, merchant or banker— could afford to hire professional musicians to entertain his family and their guests. The more money he had, the better the performance! These singers were often also in the church choir and the songs they sang at parties were no less than motets in disguise (hence the alternative words in many early motets). Motets changed with the style of church counterpoint and led in part to the sixteenth-century madrigal, but they were rather too dignified to provide a satisfactory after-dinner entertainment. Dance songs became more popular, sung by a group of singers or by one singer with a small dance band, or simply by a singing guitarist (or lutenist); the troubadour and his minstrels gave way to the 'pop' singer, his vocal group and an instrumental ensemble. The new entertainers took over some troubadour forms and added some of their own. They had four main types:

1. Virelai, a medieval favourite, which was kept alive by up-to-date arrangements of the old tunes until the middle of the fifteenth century; shortened virelais after that were called 'Bergerettes'.

2. Rondeau and Ballade, also medieval forms, which remained fashionable because of the opportunities for clever rhyme in the words; some were very complicated and used as church pieces; some had instrumental refrains; most had the tune at the

top, but in arrangements for vocal groups it might be in the middle.

3. Ballata, the Italian version of the French ballade, which had a more flowery tune and very simple instrumental accompaniment; used for laude as well as dance songs.

4. Caccia (= Hunting Song, French *chace*), which first described hunting scenes in duets full of quick-fire imitation or canon over a slow-moving bass; later novelties imitated the sounds of a market, a military parade, the return of a fishing fleet, and a big fire; also borrowed by the church in the fifteenth century as a way of imitating heavenly trumpets and pairs of angels; ballade form with a shorter refrain which always had the same words, specially chosen for their double meaning where possible.

Virelais were sung for dancing, but the other forms were often so complicated that it was impossible to dance to them. Singers delighted in rubato and syncopation (see folksong, page 14) and soon people would rather listen to them than dance; so the sung virelai lost its popularity. Concert dance music had come to stay in musical history, leading through the suites of Bach and the waltzes of Chopin to Stravinsky's Tango and the suites of Duke Ellington.

Every Renaissance composer had to be able to write all kinds of music. When he was writing a piece for church, he knew what combination of voices would sing it, but when he wrote a rondeau or a ballata he had to remember that it might be played on one, two or three instruments and/or sung by a soloist or in duet or as a trio. So he wrote one tune all the way through and harmonized it with two parts which could be played or sung by as many as were taking part; these added parts had to keep within the range of singers and instrumentalists, and must not all be essential to the harmony. Even though we know all this, we still do not know exactly what a fourteenth-century ballata sounded like. A modern piano copy of a popular song, played by an accurate but classically-trained pianist, does not sound like the music which a professional dance-band pianist will play from the same copy—and it is not uncommon for a singer, her pianist, and a rhythm section of bass, guitar and drums to read from the same copy. It is most likely that the three-part songs of the fourteenth and fifteenth centuries sometimes had a bass, lute and drum with them—and chime bells—without a written note surviving to indicate any of them.

Early madrigals were a peculiarly Italian invention and should not be confused with the international use of the term 'madrigal' in the sixteenth century. This meant a song 'in the mother tongue' and had two sections, but, unlike the songs which derived from French models, the time changed between the two sections from duple to triple. The top part was very much more richly ornamental, too, than any French song of the period. The words were often satirical rather than amorous, but there are also several examples of the most exquisite poetry, strictly formal or philosophical, by Petrarch, Boccaccio and their pupils.

Popular song: 1450 – 1600

In the fifteenth century all French songs, whatever their form, were called 'chansons'. The English again had a say in the refinement of techniques at the beginning of the century, as many French composers testified, but the main progress in elegant and precise popular songs of wit and polish took place in France. Rondeaux lengthened, ballades were shorter; musical phrases were made to balance, and poetry of charm and sweetness matched the music. Older terms disappeared and there was soon no distinction of time-signature between one form and another. Duple ousted triple time in the course of the century (as it has during the past sixty years). These chansons were usually in three parts, the top being written first, then the tenor, and finally the countertenor.

Italian songs about heroism, love affairs or less literary sides of life were all called 'frottole' between c. 1470 and 1530. The word *frottola* means, roughly, a hotch-potch, and they were composed speedily and to a stock pattern. The tune was small in range, full of repetition and sequence, like a folksong. The

composer wrote this to begin with, then the bass, and filled in
two middle parts as if he was making a musical sandwich. The
words, like a calypso, were often topical and new words were
often made up to stock tunes and harmonies. All the parts move
together to make a frottola sound like a gay hymn—if you
cannot hear or understand the words—specially lilting because
of the repeated rhythms. The most popular of these rhythms is
the 'long-short-short' pattern of most duple-time dances. This
may well be one of the rhythms which drummers added to
earlier popular songs, but singing with such a solid beat was
something new. Stock chords in this pattern lent themselves
readily to the strumming of a guitar or lute, and later trans-
scriptions for keyboard instruments managed to incorporate
both the tunes and the 'vamp'. By 1530, frottole had divided into
two types:

1. Canzona (*chanson*, put into Italian), very serious—a fusion
of the counterpoint of French chansons and close-harmony of
frottole, which became the sixteenth-century madrigal.

2. Villanesca or Villanella (= Street or Rustic Song), frivolous
—for carnivals and the like.

The villanella is a reminder that not every family could afford
to hear professional musical entertainers, either in their homes
or in the few theatres, and many had to make their own music.
Unison community songs and roughly-improvised part-singing
continued, but composers had begun to write specially for such
families in the simple harmony of the frottole. These songs had
the future of popular music in them, for (with religious words as
up-to-date laude) they led towards the chorales of the Protestant
church, and as sentimental love-songs their successors have been
heard in ballad-opera, pantomime, barber-shop and pier-
pavilion.

Sixteenth-century Madrigals

To most musicians, rightly, the late sixteenth century is the
age of the madrigal. The word 'madrigal' was first used again in
1533, after it had been buried for a hundred years and perhaps

shows more clearly than anything else how Italian composers felt about the Flemish composers' grip on Italian musical taste—and on the highest-paid posts. Madrigals were to be Italian part-songs written in Italian and in a style of their own. Poets rather than musicians were responsible for the form of the madrigal; their words were golden to an Italian composer. In madrigals, he tried to capture the actual meaning of the words, and, naturally, his songs became less repetitive. Each voice had to sing the words intelligibly and be equally compelling; whether you listened to the harmony or tried to follow the counterpoint, the poetry had to be enhanced if the music was to be justified. Madrigals were for solo singers and the composer wrote them in the same way as he would set about a motet for church, but passages of block chords emphasized important words far more often, and sliding, chromatic sequences reflected the emotions of the poetry in heart-searching phrases. This mixture of harmony and counterpoint was the ultimate solution of the problems raised by the canzona, but this was a peak of musical history, not a plateau; the world of the Renaissance was beginning to slope downwards even at its most splendid, and a new generation, also starting from the canzona but in a purely harmonic direction, was rising at its side.

Instrumental Dance Music

When the virelai died out in the second half of the fifteenth century, there were no singing dances left in high society. When they wanted to dance, wealthy citizens ordered a dance band. Popular songs were sung to the lute and the bands had a clear field—literally so, for much dancing was done in the open air.

Dance-band players educated themselves in the Renaissance just as Negro jazzmen have done in this century. In 1300, as among the Negroes in the United States of America in 1900, many dancers provided their own music by singing, unless by good luck one of their number could play an instrument—pipe and tabor, guitar or slide trumpet in the older period, and drum, banjo or cornet in modern times. Dance tunes were remembered and seldom written down. As long as only one instrument played the tune, this worked satisfactorily, for even if the tune was not traditional it would not take long for one player to pick up the latest virelai or carol. But as polyphony evolved so rapidly, dance musicians had to learn to play together on instruments which could all play tunes. The three they used were much the same in both 1400 and 1900:

FIFTEENTH CENTURY	TWENTIETH CENTURY
Small shawm (double-reed)	Clarinet (single reed)
Large shawm (very brassy)	Cornet
Large slide trumpet	Trombone (= large trumpet, in Italian)

All these instruments were at one time army instruments and it is just as likely that the Renaissance first used old instruments dumped by the military authorities just as the Negro did. In the fifteenth century, the large shawm played a well-known tune in the middle—he was the tenor—the trombone added a slow bass, and the little shawm invented quick figures to wind around the melody. Compare Dixieland music! Ex. 23 is one of the classics of the 1400s, with the skeleton which might well have become the basis of a motet, or of a later dance-tune.

The bigger the dance band became, the more written-out dance music was demanded. Arrangers found that it paid to revive old favourites in modern dress, but they saved time by using set sequences of chords—as frottola composers did—with new tunes on top. An old tune, in its cantus firmus form (see example 23) made a good bass and carried its own chords. In our time, the 'Blues' has a similar unchanging basic harmony and big bands frequently rely on such a set pattern, calling it a 'riff' (an unchanging refrain). Two famous riffs (corrupted 'passamezzo' from 'bassa-mezzo') came from the middle of the basse-danse in the sixteenth century. These harmonic grounds, on which hundreds of pavans were built, were the 'Measures' of Shakespeare's time (the nearest the English could get to 'Mezzo'). By taking the first ten bars of such a passamezzo, repeating bars 1-2, the 'Twelve-bar Blues' is revealed (see example 24, page 78).

Any music for dancing in the 1920s was called 'Jazz'; most music in the fifteenth century played by the dance band was called 'Basse-Danse'. There were two kinds of Basse-Danse:

1. Basse-danse Majeure, in duple time; what we could call 'Slow Foxtrot'.

2. Basse-danse Mineure, in triple time; what we think of as the Waltz.

Variations of step gave new names to kinds of basse-danse—as they have done to the 'old-fashioned' waltz—but the musical form did not change.

In the sixteenth century, two kinds of dance replaced the basse-danse:

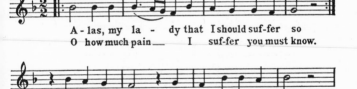

A - las, my la - dy that I should suf-fer so
O how much pain— I suf-fer you must know.

All of my life I'll live in sla-ver - y

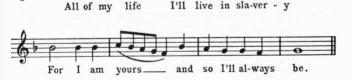

For I am yours— and so I'll al-ways be.

...... freely adapted from 'Hêlas, madame' in a manuscript from Bayeux.

As a Tenor  etc.

Example 23

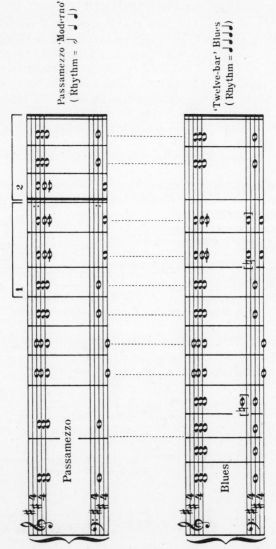

Example 24

1. Pavan (= dance from Padua or, more romantically, a dance which was as colourful as the peacock—in Italian, *pavo*—with tail outspread), in slow quadruple time; used for solemn parades at weddings, funerals or degree ceremonies, as well as at a ball; had the 'long-short-short' underlying rhythm of the frottola and was in square four-bar phrases.

2. Galliard, a quicker dance in triple time; later galliards use the same tune as the pavan before it, when the two were played as a pair.

Pavans and Galliards were soon the forms in which composers wrote more complicated pieces which were for an audience to listen to, not for dancing. Concert dance music—this time only for instruments—was leading to the suites and much symphonic music in the centuries to come. Whether music started with the dance (as dance experts claim) or not, the forms of the dance gave us most of the music which we hear in our concert halls today.

CHAPTER SIX

THE SOURCES:

1300—1500

The European Scene

It is easy to forget that the geography of Europe during these years looked nothing like the map of today. You have read of the supremacy of French music in Europe being challenged by Italian in the sixteenth century, but 'French' and 'Italian' are only convenient labels. Boundaries changed so much that we must define 'France' and 'Italy' more closely.

France was the largest united kingdom in 1300, but at one stage (1422–1429) in the Hundred Years' War, the Kingdom had diminished a good deal, and the English King Henry VI occupied half of it with his ally, the Duke of Burgundy. 'French' music is made up of English, Burgundian and Parisian sections during these 200 years.

Italy, meanwhile, was roughly divided into three sections: independent republics and principalities in the north; Papal states in the centre; and in the south the Kingdom of Naples, allied to France. Throughout the fourteenth century, the Popes were at Avignon and could do little about their possessions in and around Rome; not until the fifteenth century does the Papal Chapel in Rome become really important to musical history. Naples had to wait also until it came under Spanish Royalty at the end of the fifteenth century before becoming a great musical centre. The states which particularly interest us are marked on the map (page 82).

The musical geography of Europe in the later Middle Ages is complete if we add the four parts of Iberia (Portugal, Navarre,

Castile and Aragon); the conglomeration of German states under the two main houses (Hapsburg and Luxemburg) including the remnants of the Holy Roman Empire; Poland, Bohemia and Austria; the merchant towns of the Hanseatic League covering the whole coast north of Antwerp to Riga and beyond; and Scandinavia.

Composers could, of course, be classified by birthplace, but those we know most about travelled far afield, settling sometimes in other countries and becoming more 'native' to their adopted land than their own. As craftsmen, they lived where the work was good—round a great Cathedral or in a rich town—or found patrons with whom they travelled all round Europe. A very few seem to have become so famous that they could accept commissions as freelance musicians and their works appear in many collections.

Very few manuscripts have survived the hand of time; music was not printed until the last decade of the fifteenth century and even then it was a great luxury—there was no mass production as we know it. So the history of music in these times can only be pieced together from archives, a few writings, and paintings, tracked down by musical detectives to supplement the surviving musical evidence.

Church Archives

The Papal Church was teeming with heresies during this period and the great musical heresy was duly condemned by the Pope from Avignon in 1324. The musical effects of this heresy ('Ars Nova') have been described in the previous chapter. We know about it from a treatise probably written in Paris about 1320 by Phillippe de Vitry (1291–1361), then secretary to the King of France, but shortly to become a canon of Cambrai. He intended his fellow-composers to discuss it, and the heresy lay in his belief that church music needed a more personal approach, so that composers could express their worship freely in new Latin poems and in new music. This was obviously going to undermine the power of bishops and the Pope, and the 'New Art' was therefore banned.

Two collections present examples of the other types of
church music current at the beginning of the century: pieces of
English descant found in the binding leaves of some books in
Worcester Cathedral; and the Red Book (*Libre vermell*) belonging
to the monastery of Montserrat, containing a selection of Spanish
Pilgrim songs which, like the Italian Laude, were sung and
danced by ordinary folk on the way to the shrine of St. James at
Compostela (see map 2, page 46).

The Pope's ban on Ars Nova music did not, however, completely succeed in Italy, where settings of the Mass in the new
style have reached us in manuscripts from Ivrea, Turin and
Modena. There are also four early experiments in canon in the
Ivrea MS. In France the greatest musical genius of the fourteenth century, Guillaume de Machaut, wrote a complete and
very personal setting of the Mass some thirty years after the ban,
mixing the old style and the new with, apparently, full church

approval: the 'Messe Nôtre-Dame' (see page 85). By the end
of the century, the great cathedrals of Liège, Cambrai, Rheims
and Chartres, as well as Nôtre-Dame, had choirs of between
fifteen and twenty men and boys singing the complex new
music.

Fifteenth-century English music is kept alive for us in a
manuscript from St. George's Chapel, Windsor; the MS is
now housed in St. Edmund's College, Old Hall, off the Cambridge road near Ware. In this 'Old Hall' Manuscript are
works by more than twenty English composers of the late
fourteenth and early fifteenth centuries.

Many Englishmen, too, worked side by side with the Burgundians on visits to the English Court in France and were considered
throughout Europe to be the real masters of church composition.
Church records in Italy bear witness to this, especially collections
made for and preserved in the Cathedral of Trent, in the Italian
Tirol. The Trent Codices—seven huge, tightly packed volumes
of polyphony—show the popularity of the Anglo/Burgundians
on at least the northern part of the Italian scene: only two
Frenchmen and four Italians were thought worth including,
while there are twelve Englishmen and twelve brought up in
the northern Burgundian lands whom we would now call
Flemish. At Aosta, fifty more pieces, out of 180 re-discovered in
1947, are by Englishmen. The most frequent English name
found in these collections is John Dunstable (d. 1453).

The musical invasion of Italy by North French and English
musicians coincides with the period of great political power in
the two countries. The French-Burgundians penetrated deeper
into Italy with the return of the Pope from Avignon to Rome,
for the Papal Choir turned to the experienced choirmasters and
choirmen of Cambrai and other northern cathedrals in its years
or rehabilitation. The most admired of these was Guillaume
Dufay (c. 1400–1474) who went as a choirboy from Cambrai
Cathedral to Italy, later joining the Papal Choir as a choirman
and being rewarded with prebends at and around his old cathedral. For the last forty-five years of his life, the Cambrai

accounts show his increasing wealth and prestige as he became one of the few composers who could accept commissions all over Europe, yet retain his position at home. The English, with very few exceptions, retired home across the Channel after the end of the Hundred Years' War (1453).

Cambrai Cathedral records further reveal the names of two other famous composers: Johannes Okeghem and Jacob Obrecht. Okeghem studied there under Dufay, whilst Obrecht was choirmaster for a short time later. But by now the King of France had regained all his lands from the English and the Flemish part of Burgundy was not so powerful. We know more of Okeghem's life through the Abbey accounts at Tours where, with a chaplaincy from the King of France, he spent part of his life. Obrecht stayed mainly in the North where the records of Bruges and Antwerp Cathedrals reveal his fame, specially as a choirmaster. The two 'Os' represented the best of late fifteenth-century church music, consolidating the music of Dufay and concentrating on music for a choir rather than for soloists. Though they themselves did not aim at capturing the Papal Chapel with their music, Josquin Des Prez (1450–1521), their Flemish successor, was the wonder of Rome. He returned to direct the choir at Cambrai after eight years in the Papal Chapel, but his music remained the envy of Roman composers until his death.

Court and Civic Archives

The records of church administration and cathedral libraries are not the only sources of music with religious words. The Kings of England and France, the Holy Roman Emperor, dukes and counts throughout Europe maintained their own chapels who travelled around with them (or provided the civic organists from their servants). The account books, lists of establishment and private collections of music belonging to many of these patrons provide a panoramic view of musical Europe in the early Renaissance, though the detail is often indistinct.

Accounts tell us that an isorhythmic motet was almost invariably composed by a composer on the establishment (words and music together) to celebrate a particular occasion and not for general church use: hence their complexity. Royal marriages, funerals, the signing of treaties and all official ceremonies required motets, and the grander patrons of the fifteenth century commissioned them from foreign composers. These composers, the master craftsmen, were known personally through their travels as respected chaplains of a royal chapel, or through references given by one employer to another.

Lists of establishments give the musical detective clues to many a composer's career, from his first appearance—perhaps as assistant to an already famous musician—to his death.

The surviving private music collections contain a remarkable choice of all the kinds of music mentioned in Chapter V. There must have been scores of immensely rich patrons in the courts and cities of these centuries; indeed, Machaut had four successive employers beside the church, travelling to Italy, Poland, Lithuania, Austria, Spain and, possibly, Cyprus before settling down as a canon of Rheims. Here there is space to mention only those patrons associated with the master craftsmen.

Duke John of Berry (c. 1416), brother of the first Duke of Burgundy and a great book lover, ordered a collection of the works of Machaut and the manuscript, richly illuminated and decorated (complete with the composer's picture), was possibly made by Machaut himself. His selection shows clearly what he thought would appeal to a fashionable nobleman's taste. First he puts the unaccompanied songs which his patron could perhaps sing himself, looking nostalgically back to the chivalrous days of the troubadours; then comes the famous Mass (or, in other collections, a motet for his patrons) and finally ballades, rondeaux and chansons in three parts. Composers successful in their lifetime have always known when to be conservative in their style of writing and Machaut was no exception: in touch with fashion, he knew that patrons liked 'the good old ways' as well as the new. Tact such as this undoubtedly helped Machaut, the poet-musician, to become the friend and adviser of more than one ruler.

Collections of fifteenth-century Burgundian chansons can be seen in libraries from Copenhagen to Washington, D.C. These *chansonniers*, fashioned with all the care that miniaturists, poets and binders could lavish on them, are the beautiful memorials to the songs of Dufay and his fellow-chaplain, Gilles Binchois, and to the culture of the men who ordered them.

Court records for the time of Charles the Bold (d. 1477) leave a vivid impression of pageantry. From the time of his birth (celebrated in music by Binchois) this richest and most powerful of all the Dukes of Burgundy was used to the utmost splendour as he moved from place to place with his court. A typical journey would take him from Dijon (his capital) to Bruges, with a Mass sung under Dufay at Cambrai on the way, and back—perhaps with some more work from his servants the Van Eyck brothers to grace the walls of his palace at Dijon—by way of Lille and a great feast. After Charles the Bold died, the new Duke returned to the allegiance of the King of France, but in the new generation of northern composers only Okeghem was attracted southwards, serving three successive French Kings at Paris. Obrecht, though partly obliged by illness to stay in Flemish France, chose Ferrara when he could go abroad. By 1500, though, the great days of Cambrai Cathedral were over. Josquin had left to serve the King of France in Paris and although he returned to recruit singers, the Sistine Chapel in Rome became the last supreme training ground for Latin Church composers.

Rome reached its zenith under Pope Leo X in the early sixteenth century. Leo X was the son of Lorenzo de Medici, heir to a great family tradition of patronage.

The records of the great families in the city-states of Italy tell a social story that can explain many of the reasons for the differences between French and Italian music in the fourteenth century and for the success of the French-trained composers in the fifteenth. In the days of the Popes in exile at Avignon, Italian merchants built churches which were more their own parish churches than they had been under papal government. Painters and architects had considerable freedom in building and decorating, and when it came to music, the benefactors usually preferred the splendour of the organ to the sounds of a choir. In popular songs, however, composers had scope to experiment with new techniques not unlike the Parisian Ars Nova for the entertainment of these same benefactors at home, where they enjoyed listening to songs with instruments. So surviving Italian music of the 1300s (= *trecento*) is almost all secular.

There were hundreds of composers of Italian Trecento music, but we rely for what we know on very few collections of music. What the Berry Collection tells us of Machaut, the Squarcialupi Collection tells us of Italy. Squarcialupi (1416–1480), called 'Master Antony of the Organ' was the Medicis' organist in Florence and made a historical collection of some music sung in his city from 1325 to his own day. From these songs we get most of our present ideas about the early madrigal, the ballata and the caccia. The main composers were Giovanni 'from Florence', Jacopo 'from Bologna' and Francesco Landini 'the blind one'. Landini, who was blinded as a boy by smallpox, was the organist of San Lorenzo (the 'Parish Church' of the Medici family in the fifteenth century), and it may well be that the whole of Squarcialupi's collection was made from the Medici archives.

When Cosimo de Medici was elected to the leadership of Florence in 1434, the Pope had been back in Rome for seven years, and the sound of the Papal Choir was already becoming noted. Noble families began to wish for polyphonic singing in their own chapel, and its best composers were the Burgundians. So a two-way traffic of musical ideas begins. In rhythm, the Ars Nova of France and the Italian Trecento could merge fairly well, but the Burgundians had to assimilate the dance-like and florid lines of the Trecento, while the Italians learned to manipulate many voices and make them comparable in interest to the French music of men like Dufay. Eventually the result of this fusion returned to France and England as the later Italian madrigal. The vertical approach to music which the Italians had favoured in their songs was echoed in the experiments in depth and perspective of artists like Donatello, Botticelli and Leonardo, whose work must have affected the Burgundian visitor to Florence then as much as it does the tourist today. Motets began to have block chords in them; as the painter added a small portrait of his benefactor to the picture he painted, so the composer wrote his patron's name into the motet and set it to the richest sound.

If we add to the Papal Chapel and the Medicis the names of the cultured families of Sforza (Milan), Malatesta (Rimini) and d' Este (Ferrara), all of whom had political reasons to be friends of Burgundy as well as a cultured interest in *choral* church music, it becomes clear that the way to Italy was wide open for Burgundian composers.

The height of this kind of patronage was reached with the career of Heinrich Isaac, as this can be traced in court records. Isaac was born in Brabant, then a Burgundian Duchy but with strong connections with the Holy Roman Empire, where low German was the common language. Obviously highly gifted, he succeeded Squarcialupi as the Medicis' organist when he was twenty-five, and received commissions in Ferrara and Innsbruck a few years later. The rest of his life was divided between these three courts. When the Medicis were deposed, he went first to Innsbruck and then to Vienna with the Emperor Maximilian (who had a Burgundian wife). Later he was sent as a diplomat to Ferrara, while Josquin was there—like Machaut, Isaac had become his patron's trusted friend—and when the Medicis were restored to power he engineered his return to Florence to end his days there as a kind of special ambassador for Maximilian and a father-figure to all the young composers of Italy. He had to write music for French, Italian, Latin and German words to please audiences ranging from the revellers at a Florentine carnival to the highest church dignitaries in Austria, but the style of writing remained his own, so that he can reasonably be labelled the first 'international' composer.

Other records

Theorists, chroniclers, and poets (as distinct from poet-composers) must be read with caution. The first are expressing opinions, too often based on limited practical knowledge of music-making, the second have to rely on memory and frequently exaggerate to flatter an important reader or simply to make a good story; and the third have always been able to claim 'poetic licence' when charged with inaccuracy.

In France, Philippe de Vitry, with whom this chapter began, suggested two important changes to his fellow-composers: that they should 'measure' their music with time signatures; and that a smaller time-value should be allowed. His proposed signs for both innovations were adopted by most French composers—but without Vitry's original explanation of their meaning we should be hard put to it to glean the exact meaning of them. At about the same time (1325), Marchettus of Padua wrote down his ideas for Italian notation, specially suited to the more florid type of singing, which Landini and his fellows employed. Of the two systems, Vitry's seemed clearer at the time, but we today use an adaptation of the Italian.

Prosdocimo de Beldemandis, Professor of Astronomy in Padua, was the most constructive critic of Marchettus's system. Writing in 1410, apart from saying that its poor inventor was ignorant, he explains that Italian Trecento notation was incredibly complicated, but that the French was best for the kind of composition fashionable in his own day only if you added some Italian signs. He is also helpful in giving the meaning of the abbreviations which were used to make a written part longer or shorter in performance. These 'signs of proportion' could condense many pages of music into one.

Three late fifteenth century theorists remain, a Spaniard, an Italian, and a Fleming: Ramos de Pareja, who tells us how Spaniards tuned stringed instruments to accompany singers, and points out that tuning to mathematical ratios is all right for theorists but hard for singers who cannot even *see* their instrument. Gafori, who tabulates rules for writing good Italian counterpoint in 1496, keeps the explanations of proportions up to date, and 'corrects' a lot of statements about ancient music. The Fleming was Tinctoris.

Johannes Tinctoris (= John the Painter's son), born, like
Isaac, in Brabant, shown on the register of Cambrai Cathedral
in his twenties, serving six years in the Papal Chapel and many
years in an Italian court, followed the route of the greatest
Burgundian musicians of the fifteenth century. His Italian patron
was in the south: Ferdinand I, King of Naples and of most
of Spain. As teacher, historian, and composer, Tinctoris saw the
beginning of Neapolitan music and of real musical scholarship,
and he may well have had great influence on the bright future of
Spanish music during the following century. His *Summary of
Music* is the starting point for all research into the music of his
time, including a Dictionary of Musical Terms (probably the
first ever), how all the maze of rhythmic signs were invented and
what they meant, what he thinks of his contemporaries, why he
thinks music of his own time best, when music is used—a Teach-
Yourself book of the early Renaissance, but in Latin, and in
twelve volumes.

Poets contribute a little to what we know of composers in the
obituary verses which they wrote, usually for the late composer's
successor to set to music. We learn from these 'dirge' motets that
Machaut was a master of rhetoric, Binchois was a soldier in his
younger days and Okeghem was most popular with his colleagues:
the usual polite phrases after a short survey of the subject's
career. In referring to instruments, poets (and painters) often
have impossible combinations playing together and they have the
same trouble in trying to describe actual sounds as anyone else
attempting to say what a flute or an organ sounds like, but lists
of what are in use at any given time are helpful. Poets sometimes
mention popular tunes by name, which shows how well known
and liked that tune was (Chaucer makes Nicolas, the poor
scholar, sing the well-loved carol 'Angelus ad Virginem'). Most
revealing of all, 131 popular pieces complete with their music
were added to the French satirical novel, *le Roman de Fauvel* (1316).

Chroniclers describe the music at weddings or any ceremonial
procession in the style of much modern popular journalism;
there are usually 'hundreds' of trumpets, minstrels, organists

and the like with no distinction between them. As the average king employed thirty trumpeters or so according to the more precise account books, the chroniclers must come under the heading of 'romance' rather than 'history'.

The last important records are to be found in the archives of the Gilds of Minstrels and their successors as professional organizations. The word 'minstrel' can mean 'someone who ministers', and the fourteenth-century use of the word may mean that those minstrels were the heirs of the troubadours' assistants—the lesser fry—of the previous period. They were now attached to courts or cities and began to form themselves into trades unions comparable with those of, say, the shoemakers or tailors. These Gilds had different levels of craftsmen in them from the start. In the Burgundian and Italian courts, most minstrels were equal to standard bearers, but harpers and organists were a little higher, and trumpeters were high enough to have a special Gild to themselves.

Learning the craft began to involve learning to read music, and apprentices—both singers and instrumentalists—had to undergo long training. The higher ranks might become parish clerks, paid by wealthy businessmen to sing memorial services, to teach choristers in a choir school, or to perform sophisticated part-songs in private houses.

By the end of the fifteenth century, these musicians had regular church and civic duties: the gulf between them and the humble minstrels was the same as that today between a street fiddler and a concert violinist, a hot-gospel singer and a cathedral choirman, or the singer with the local dance band and Sinatra. So the most brilliant musicians—sometimes, like Machaut, of humble origin—could rise to fame, wealth, and honour, while the less gifted could still earn a living as 'Waits' (employees of the City Corporation), or as freelance instrumentalists, playing at dances, processions, funerals and even public executions. Only those with no talent at all were the wandering beggars of romantic poetry; the rest were craftsmen of different grades up to the remarkable masters who created the sublime polyphony of the sixteenth century.

CHAPTER SEVEN

THE SOURCES:

1500—1600

The European Scene

Continual wars, first political then religious, might well have destroyed most of our sources of sixteenth-century music had it not been for the invention of music printing. The three great powers in the first quarter of the century were France, Spain and Rome, and between them they controlled Europe.

By 1527, Rome was occupied by the Emperor Charles V, and the Spanish priests who were to lead the Counter-Reformation governed the Papal Court. The ideas of the Reformation, spreading rapidly in the North after Luther's declarations in 1517, were causing musical as well as religious strife. But the printing presses of Paris, Antwerp and Rome (the capitals of the powers) poured out music. Added to these, Venice (with Ferrara), Bavaria and, later, England—who kept out of the major wars—have left us a good deal of their output of printed music.

Owing to the cost of printing, patrons were still needed; so the ruling houses of Spain, France and England, the Pope and the Prince-Bishops were still the main source of a composer's income. In the Netherlands, Venice and Germany, however, prosperous merchant families provided more and more work. The long and invaluable patronage of the Medici family came to an end with the final flourish of the last 'worldly' Pope, Leo X, but the other renowned patrons of the fifteenth century in Italy— the d'Este family—continued to claim the services of the greatest composers in their palaces at Ferrara, Tivoli (near Rome) and Milan.

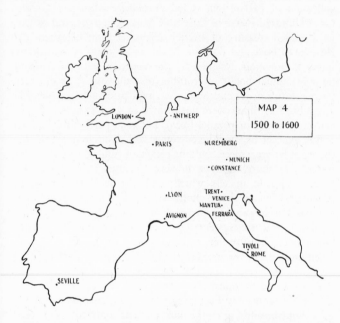

Many modern books contain short biographies of these composers and much of their music can now be bought in modern editions. Here there is space only to glance at the volumes of printed music as they appear from the press: the names of a few composers will crop up time and time again as their fame warrants reprinting or a new collection is made; dedications immortalize the names of enlightened patrons; and the dates and addresses of title-pages form a useful guide to the geography of peace and prosperity in the sixteenth century, for music was then, as now, a commodity to be bought and sold chiefly as a luxury. The richest of all European cities, and one of the most beautiful, was Venice.

Venetian Printers

Petrucci, the earliest music printer of all, produced his first collection of part-music, called *Harmonice Musices Odhecaton* (= A Hundred Pieces of Ensemble Music), in 1501, and so gave us a golden treasury of French chansons from Okeghem and Busnois to Isaac and Josquin. In the next twenty years, working under a monopoly assigned by the Venetian state government, he sold annual books of frottole (the 'top tunes' of the early 1500s), lute music, and laude—at high prices—to anyone who wished to buy. They were not printed in score (where each part can be followed in parallel lines), but each part was completed before another began. The customer had to be prepared to copy these out before a piece could be played or sung. Books of Masses for sale to churches were, however, printed in separate part-books and sold in sets which could be used straight away. Although it meant that a choirmaster had to make a score of all the parts if he wanted to know what was happening at any particular time, this system of printing became common practice. The modern musical detective knows this to his cost sometimes when only two or three of the original four or five partbooks can be found.

Petrucci's collections of frottole show clearly that Isabella d'Este of Mantua and Ferrara was the most generous patron, for Tromboncino and Cara—the most popular contributors for years —both worked for her, at the same time as the painter Titian and the poet Castiglione. Josquin was there, too.

The lutebooks, which began to appear in 1507, contained arrangements by well-known lutenists of pieces from the vocal collections, much dance music (mostly Pavans) and a few short Preludes. Lute notation looked something like the symbols for guitar in modern dance music, and, as with present-day sheet music, you could buy arrangements of all the popular songs for voice and instrument.

Petrucci's masses and motets declare Josquin des Prez as the grand master of Renaissance music. Three books of Josquin's masses were printed where no other composer had more than one to his name, and two of these books were re-printed when the firm moved to Fossombrone. Petrucci did not rely only on tried favourites: his motets in a series called *De la Corona* from 1514 onwards included work by Willaert, who was to head the next generation of composers in Venice, but was at that time in Paris as an unknown student.

In 1527, Willaert was appointed master of the chapel at St. Mark's, the most splendid church in Venice, and there, with two organs and a large choir to write for, he built up a style of massive motets for 'alternating' double choir. By then, Petrucci's monopoly had ended and others were adding to the store of part-books. Motets by Willaert and his Flemish companions at St. Mark's (Arcadelt and Rore), were in the lists of almost every Venetian printing house.

The new madrigals, by these composers and countless others, came on the market in 1533. Such was the furore they created that the most prolific madrigalist, another Fleming called Monte, had nearly 1,200 published. The foremost native Italian exponent, Marenzio—at last an Italian was the master of all madrigalists—addressed over 200 to his Italian patrons. The position is summed up in one firm's catalogue for 1591: of its 350 items, 170 were collections of madrigals.

Roman Printers

Antico, the first printer to the Papal court, began work in 1514, under the patronage of Leo X. Much of his music was pirated from Petrucci. Other publications reflect his patron's character: motets, mostly by Frenchmen, and two collections of French chansons underline the Pope's attachment to the Burgundian culture he had absorbed; books of canzone and frottole, some even by his own master of the chapel, were up to date in Italian fashion. Pope Leo de Medici, meticulous in his religious duties, could still enjoy a hand of cards and a few frivolous songs in a friend's house.

The Spanish conquest of 1527 soon changed the look of music coming from Roman printers. One of them, it is true, first used the title 'Madrigal' in a song collection in 1530, but there was nothing frivolous about these madrigals. The majority of them were written by another of the ubiquitous Flemings, Verdelot (lately of St. Mark's), but the master of the chapel—Festa, then the only Italian in charge of music at any of the larger Italian churches—contributed a few. Strangely perhaps, only Morales among Spanish composers became prominent, with two published books of masses.

After many years' deliberation on every aspect of religious life at the Council of Trent the church authorities delivered, in 1562, a musical ultimatum to church composers and singers: if these men wished to enjoy the patronage of the Church they should NOT:

1. Sing Mass too quickly;
2. Use profane melodies as a skeleton for the Mass;
3. Cover the words up with counterpoint which 'gives only empty pleasure to the ear';
4. Use any 'lascivious' or 'impure' harmonies.

Composers in Rome, however, had anticipated these requirements at least ten years before. Music printed in Rome in the 1550s shows that the organists of Roman churches, brought up as children in the shadow of the Spanish Inquisition, had no need of the Council's edicts. Among these organists in 1550 were Lassus and Palestrina, the two masters of Counter-Reformation music.

Palestrina's life can be traced in some detail by the dates on printed collections of his work. His first five masses appeared in 1554; in 1564 and 1567 dedications show that he was responsible for the concerts of the d'Este family at Tivoli; seven masses in 1567 were the fruits of directing music at a seminary formed to teach the principles of Trent; a gap of eight years occurs in printing dates during the epidemics and plagues when he was ill and lost most of his family—and a spate of publications in his last thirteen years coincides with his happy second marriage, when he combined a wealthy furrier's business with his solemn work as the guardian of 'pure' music in the Chapel. His genius matched the severity of the Trent edicts, which may even have been made with his music as a standard, and his lofty sounds bear no mark of a mind bound by uncongenial rules. He is almost as Spanish in his religious approach as his Spanish friend and contemporary Victoria, a Jesuit priest in Rome.

The music of Lassus, though published in Venice and dedicated in many cases to the Pope in Rome, leads us to the northern printers.

Flemish and German Printers

Flemish printers knew their best days under Spanish rule from about 1530 to the 1560s when the wars to regain the Netherlands from Charles V's successor began.

Susato of Antwerp was the chief pioneer of music-printing in Flanders and his first publications show the quality of the music at the Capilla Flamenca (= Flemish Chapel, in Spanish). There Clemens non Papa and Gombert were the leading musicians whose work justified the expense of printing. In 1545, Susato showed his business acumen by reprinting a complete book of chansons by Josquin which revived much interest in a composer who had been dead for almost a quarter of a century— an unheard of thing in those days of swiftly changing fashions. Six years later he marketed the first Netherlands lutebook of basse-danses, pavanes and galliards, together with the first of a series of *Little Music-Books* meant, as he wrote, 'to sing or play upon all musical instruments'; and in 1554 he started to print the works of Lassus, a long line of publications which were to spread throughout Europe.

Lassus, the last of the great Flemings, had published some villanescas in his youth when he was in Naples, but he affected to become ashamed of their 'light' character and nearly all his other printed works were religious. Susato's publication marked his return to Antwerp from Rome, but before long he took service with Albert, Duke of Bavaria and after 1557 the German printing-houses of Nuremberg and Munich were the first to receive his manuscripts.

Nuremberg printers had already contributed an outstanding collection to musical history in setting up the whole *Choralis Constantinus* by Isaac. This choirbook had been commissioned from the composer by the Cathedral Chapter of Constance and it contained Isaac's polyphonic arrangements of old plainsong tunes for all the Propers of the Mass throughout a Church year.

Adam Berg of Munich takes up the Lassus line, publishing the master's works for over twenty years under the insignia of the Duke of Bavaria. There is, however, a gap in the line from 1577 to 1582. At this time the composer seems to have been especially sought-after in Paris, where eighteen of his masses were published . . . and also the Bavarian Court was growing steadily poorer. Soon after the new Duke, William, succeeded his father, drastic cuts were made in the musical establishment, and the attitude to music became as severe as anywhere in the Counter-Reformation. Lassus, who had always been a good friend and firm favourite of the new Duke, became even more pious. The works printed after 1582 express the change: 'Seven Penitential Psalms', 'Lamentations', 'Spiritual Madrigals', and volumes of 'Sacred Songs'. The dedications and forewords are those of a sick, despairing penitent. The last collection of sacred songs needed a foreword on Michaelmas Day, 1593. Speaking in the true accent of the Counter-Reformation, the composer sent these words to his printer:

> 'As the light of the setting sun is more
> pleasing to the eye than at its rising,
> so may these graver songs of my closing
> days delight the mind and ear more than
> the gayer songs of my youth!'

French and English Printers

An immense amount of music was printed in France during the sixteenth century, but the names in the catalogues show that the composers were mainly local and none of them had the stature of Josquin, Palestrina or Lassus. The big Paris printers depended largely on the production of popular music: French chansons and lute music were their money-spinners.

Attaingnant, opening in 1529, published about 2,000 pieces which lasted no longer than the average popular song today. The pages, however, looked neater than most early music printing, partly because the French cared particularly about detail in language (so the words were more accurately placed under the music than usual), and partly because the composers made sparing use of counterpoint (so the lines of music could be printed with equal numbers of notes). The chansons were charmingly simple, occasionally naïve but more often sophisticated, and their composers were successful socially as well as financially. Three names would have been known everywhere: Claudin, Passereau and Jannequin. The last of these was particularly good at 'programme' songs. These songs, which were the heirs of the old Italian caccie and the French chace, described birds singing, women gossiping, street sellers crying their wares and—most famous of all—*La Bataille* telling (with appropriate sound effects) how the French beat the Swiss mercenaries in Milan at the battle of Marignano. The same composers wrote the church music which Attaingnant sold, taking as their models Mouton (a pupil of Josquin and the teacher of Willaert!), Gombert, Arcadelt and eventually Lassus.

LeRoy started business ten years after Attaingnant, who by that time was publishing a monthly series of motets and had a large catalogue of masses, songs, transcriptions for lute and keyboard, and dance music. Monsieur LeRoy was already famous as a lutenist and his first ventures were nearly all lute pieces—many of them on the stock passamezzo foundations—crowned by the very successful Lute Tutor of 1557. By this time, too, the House of LeRoy published the works of Arcadelt (the Fleming recently returned to Paris from the Papal Court), and perhaps through this connection LeRoy himself later brought Lassus to the notice of the King of France. Soon he was the sole agent for all the works of Lassus and continually printed editions and reprints of the Munich master. Pieces by Lassus became so popular that even the anti-Roman Huguenots added moral texts to his chansons (though the composer must have considered this a doubtful honour in his later years).

One provincial French printer did more for the future of music than the quality of the music he printed: Moderne of Lyon (called 'Grand Jacques' because he was so fat), who was probably the first to print two voice-parts on each page in such a way that the two singers could face each other on opposite sides of a table.

In England, everyone was about fifty years behind the continent. Composers like Fayrfax, Taverner, and Tye left beautiful old-fashioned music owing much to the Flemish style of the fifteenth century, but only in manuscript. Most of Tallis's work remained unprinted. Twenty songs were published in London in 1530, but they were probably printed by foreigners; a collection of psalms printed in 1540 was almost as soon banned as Lutheran; foreign lute tutors, including LeRoy's, were on sale by 1568; but music-printing in England, and with it the works of the last English Renaissance masters, really dates from 1575.

In that year, Queen Elizabeth granted a twenty-one-year monopoly for printing music and music paper to the two most eminent London composers, Tallis and his pupil Byrd. Neither of them was successful as a businessman and two years after Tallis died, Byrd assigned the patent to Thomas East.

East, commercially minded, bought new Dutch equipment and the stream of English printed music began to flow. Byrd was the first to benefit and collections of his *Psalms, Sonnets and Songs* in English, and *Sacred Songs* in Latin followed one another in quick succession during the first four years. At the same time, the first Italian madrigals were published in England. The first volume, *Musica Transalpina* (= music from across the Alps) in 1588 has become widely known for two remarks made by Yonge, the editor and translator, in the preface: that the book was for 'Gentlemen and merchants' to sing, and that Byrd was the 'great Maister of Musicke'. This foreword certainly proves that madrigals were sung by amateurs, but the inclusion of a madrigal by Byrd and the 'mention' may not have been unconnected with Byrd's position as holder of the publishing monopoly. The second volume was more ably translated and many of the pieces were by Marenzio, who was to influence English madrigalists in the books which rapidly followed.

Morley wrote the first two books of Canzonets (= small canzone: see page 74) and Madrigals by an Englishman to be printed. He was a pupil of Byrd, who was probably the finest teacher of the late English Renaissance. After two years of somewhat underhand lobbying he succeeded in obtaining a renewal of his master's patent, which had expired in 1596. Byrd, then only in his early fifties, was a devout Roman Catholic. He still remained a member of the Chapel Royal, and wrote much excellent Anglican music, but he was perhaps not thought a good proposition for sale to the 'gentlemen and merchants'. At all events, Morley published (with East and other printers) works by many other English madrigalists including Weelkes, Wilbye, and Kirbye, but little by Byrd. Morley's own works flourished and two have become highly prized: his *Plain and Easy Introduction to Practical Music* (1597) which remains invaluable today as a teaching book for sixteenth-century counterpoint, apart from its amusing and outspoken commentary on the music of his own day; and his *Consort Lessons* which added to the English reputation for instrumental music (see page 145). His last big venture was to collect a number of madrigals by all the well-known composers of his time (except Byrd), all having a refrain in praise of Queen Elizabeth, issued in 1601 as *The Triumphs of Oriana*.

In sixteenth-century England, information collected from printed books is not enough to judge the composers on, for Byrd was a master comparable with Palestrina and Lassus in the older generation and Monteverdi in the new. A few of his works were published after 1605, among them three remarkable masses as fine as any in the Renaissance, but manuscripts must be sought to justify Byrd's exalted place in musical history. Happily, many of these have survived, and you will read more of the 'English Maister' in the next chapter.

Spanish Printers

Sixteenth-century Spain still remains, musically, an enigmatic country. The first motets by Spaniards were printed about 1550 in Seville, but otherwise a couple of books of Villancicos and a collection of pieces by Victoria in 1600 make up the entire body of printed Spanish polyphony. Morales, and other Spaniards highly respected in Rome, seem not to have had anything published in their own country. Even the manuscripts of the travelling 'Capilla Flamenca' contain mostly compositions by Gombert and his fellow Flemings. Secular songs (Villancicos) survive in Venetian printing, and a few unoriginal motets have remained to gather dust in cathedral archives where the retiring organist-composers left them.

Yet Spain is incredibly rich in instrumental music. The astonishing series of lutebooks and lutesongs written by the so-called 'vihuelistas' (= Spanish lute or vihuela players) and two equally fascinating books of organ music, lead us headlong into the next 300 years of music—to the sounds of master performers.

CHAPTER EIGHT

VIRTUOSOS

THE master craftsman of the Renaissance had his assistants who worked fairly well to rule. The church choir sang the notes in front of them and only a few soloists could take liberties with the composer's text. The organist doubled the choir's notes during the service, and most instrumentalists had to be content to play pieces that were also part-songs and had been written by singer-composers. The solo singers, however, performing the works of lesser craftsmen—the frottole songs—with the lute or keyboard accompaniment had always added their own skill to the composer's and by 1600 they were writing their own music. In the same way, as instruments became easier to play and could compare with the voice for expression and range, highly skilled players first improvised, then *wrote* pieces to show them off. The virtuoso intrumentalist, because he had to learn the master craftsman's skill and apply it to several instruments, only overhauled the singer slowly on the road to musical fame and fortune. The two kinds of virtuoso—singer and instrumentalist—monopolized the seventeenth and eighteenth centuries, and the virtuoso composer of the nineteenth century took off on the highest flights from the runway they laid down.

Range

The years 1550–1800 show the biggest extension of range in melody, harmony and expression of any in musical history. In 1550, most types of voice or instrument performed within a narrow melodic range, in a set mode, and either loud or soft according to the instrument. In 1800, the virtuoso had an enormous range (even the singer spanned three octaves), could generally change key rapidly from one to another, and varied his dynamics from soft to loud as gradually as he wished. Rhythmically, perhaps, music became simpler, but in every other direction it became more and more complex.

The chorister and the lesser instrumentalist lagged behind as the range of the soloist grew. It is less difficult to sing in the choir in a Haydn than in a Josquin mass and it is as easy to play a Mozart dance as a LeRoy dance. But the number of lesser instrumentalists dwindled as the standard of playing increased and music became a crowded profession. The main stream of sound came from the soloists, and the higher and louder it was, the more successful.

Vocally, the 'tenor' of earlier music was what we would call a baritone, and the highest voice was, in our terms, a mezzo-soprano. In the seventeenth century three male voices covered the whole range from tenor to soprano: the counter-tenor whose low notes were strongest, the male alto whose best tone was in the higher register and the unnatural male soprano (castrato). If no castrati were available, boys would take the highest parts. The sound of the high male voice persisted in English cathedral choirs. Opera in the eighteenth century belonged to the castrato and the notorious 'prima donna' (a soprano of prodigious vocal and, generally, physical compass). By comparison with the high voices, bass, baritone, tenor and even mezzo-soprano fared badly for solo material until the second half of the century.

In most instrumental families only the highest and most agile interested the virtuosos—the violin, high trumpet and horn, flute, oboe and lastly, clarinet—but in the viol family two kinds of bass viol became the display members. These outstanding exceptions to the 'high' rule—lyra and division viol—are explained by their resonance, the richest in the sweet but weak-toned family. (A consort of viols sounds to modern ears rather like a thin harmonium.) Even when they died with the rest of their family and their old companions the lutes in the eighteenth century, their successors—cellos and guitars—retained their solo capabilities and still do. The middle strings (violas), the low brass (trombones) and woodwind (bassoons) were too cumbersome for the athletic new music and the rest of the sixteenth- and seventeenth-century families—the tenor violins, tenor oboes, alto trombones, shawms and cornetts—were thrown into the gutter by 1750. The clavichord, harpsichord and organ were all in the virtuoso's shop window, but before the end of the eighteenth century, pianofortes began to attract a good deal of attention from the virtuoso composers.

These last instruments, the keyboards, had also caused a revolution in the range of harmony composers used. If you play the cadences of example 26 on the piano, you will hear a definite progression of chords rather than the simultaneous movement of four or five melodies. The sixteenth-century listener had also become used to hearing sounds vertically and the relationship between chords like these two, built on a dominant and tonic (see page 57) was an accepted convention. The seventeenth century began to relate other chords to the tonic in the same way and even more important, one tonic chord to another. Two 'tonic' chords can only be different if you change from one mode to another (= modulate) and how could they tell the difference between modes any longer, if, by 1600, listeners heard the vertical sounds rather than the horizontal? In fact, the average listener could only hear the difference between two modes, our 'major' and 'minor', and this was the first relationship he recognized. Both could have the same tonic, in the new system, providing a sure relationship, but no one would mistake one for the other even if he only heard the tonic and dominant chords, particularly with a tune on top as example 25.

This way of working from chordal relationships rather than note relationships is called the 'diatonic' system, for you work 'through' (*dia* in Greek) the connection of tonic chords. If you try making up tonic chords on the white keys of the piano only, from one 'C' to the next, you will find that you can make three 'major' sounds: on 'C', 'F' and 'G', as at (a) in example 26.

Major

Minor

Example 25

(a)

(b)

(c)

F major
leading by
Cadence to
B flat
major

(d)

G
leading to
D
major

or
to
C
major

Example 26

These three chords must be related, says the theorist, and the ear will agree if you play them on the keyboard. Their basses are the tonic, subdominant and dominant notes of a scale starting on 'C'. If you now play perfect cadences to each of these three chords in turn, making each a new tonic, you will need two black notes ('B flat' for 'F' and 'F sharp' for 'G'): you have brought two extra *keys* into play if you change the tonic notes, as at (b) in the example. Finally, the tonics of 'F' and 'G' will give you a new set of subdominants and dominants which, in turn, will give more by the same relationships: you will have new sets of 'keys' to go to, as at (c) and (d) in example 26.

So composers began to explore this relationship of a tonic to the keys on its subdominant and dominant (and to the minor keys needing the same accidentals). One of the first tasks for the intelligent listener is to hear these key relationships clearly for himself; without this ability, no amount of analysing by eye will help towards an understanding of the subtler harmonic ideas of composers as far apart in time and style as Purcell and Mozart.

Rhythm and Accent

The beats of dance music must be regular and the grouping of them is always either in twos or threes throughout any one tune; the beats of church music in the late sixteenth century were equally regular but the grouping of them was always basically in twos (though with as few stresses as possible). Lute and keyboard music from Petrucci's presses showed the grouping of beats by bar lines, but the number of beats in each bar varied according to the type of piece. The grouping becomes regular throughout any piece of music by 1650, which then carries a time signature like ours. This has two main effects on the sounds of music: the first beat in the bar collects an extra strong accent as the 'down' beat; and syncopation (putting notes *off* the beat) becomes much clearer as the 'slipping' of the beat is made more obvious. Both these effects can be so over-emphasized in musical performances that the first becomes monotonous and the second irritating, but the formal strength which regular barring gives to music is undeniable. The least sophisticated listener, to whom key relationships may mean nothing, can usually grasp the eighteenth-century composer's rhythmic ideas.

The growth of performing technique, both vocal and instrumental, called for more complicated sub-division of the beats. 'Dotted' rhythms abound in music from 1650 onwards, adding a perkiness and sprightliness according to how they are played (the French in particular, were very fond of holding a dotted note until there was only just time to play the shorter one that followed it within the same beat). The medieval methods which divided any beat into two *or* three remained as 'simple' and 'compound' time. When duple time divided each beat in twos, the time signature remained 2; when each beat divided in threes the figure became $2 \times 3 = 6$. Similarly 3-time became 9, and 4-time 12, when the beat was compounded (just as it had done in the fourteenth-century Ars Nova).

Almost as soon as the regular barring was commonly used, composers began to dodge the implications by writing across the bar line and showing the grouping by phrase marks. In triple time, a dance with the underlying rhythm ♩♩ implied a strong second beat and this meant that the bar line did not precede a strong accent; in duple time, other dances began on the 'up' or second beat, which thereafter receives more attention than the first; and so on. These rhythmic subtleties were woven into concert music by the skilled fingers of the performer; the skilled voice in the early seventeenth-century lute songs and opera recitative followed the accent of the words and so sang all the intricate variations of accent which form metrical verse. The lines of verse became musical phrases and their length varied. By the eighteenth century, the passion for formal unity made most music 'four-square', dividing it into four-bar phrases. If the words did not fit into this scheme they could be repeated (or one syllable extended); if a melody did not flow for all four bars, part of its rhythm could easily be repeated to make it last the required length. Such conventions may make some of their music sound too obvious to us, or even (in repeated words or page-long syllables) too laughable, but they represent faithfully an age when what mattered was that everything should be complete as a whole; everything must add up. Artists call the period 'Baroque'. You do not notice first the nose, then the mouth, then the ears of a Rembrandt portrait, you see it all at once. You do not notice the steps then the pillars, then the statues, then the roof of St. Paul's; you see it all at once. You do not hear each Alexandrine in a line of Racine; you hear a whole line or even a verse as a whole. In all these, the rhythm (which is Greek, after all, for 'flow') is unbroken.

Melody

Unbroken melody is dull, for climax and anti-climax are essential in it and a piece as a whole must be divided into sections by cadences. The seventeenth century tried its best, however, to plan each piece as a whole by not allowing any particular phrase to stand out beside its companions. A lutenist song has, usually, two balancing halves and each phrase of melody is different but the effect on the hearer is of one long tune. You do not pick up 'snatches' of a lute song; you either know the whole tune or else you forget it. Early seventeenth-century recitative, for its part, sets out only to let the words be understood, and the melody must therefore be subservient. Songs in opera, however, could produce memorable melodies. Opera was created by groups of artists working for the one ideal: that all the arts should be combined to make one whole. In fact, this never worked. At first, words triumphed: melody was limited to isolated phrases which varied the monotony of unaccompanied recitative, movement was hardly allowed, and décor was sparse. With the aria, words suffered from repetition but melody gained strength from the shapely phrases which composers used in sequence after sequence. If you know one phrase of, say, a Scarlatti aria you can often guess the next. In the da capo aria (see page 119) the repetition of a whole section of melody brought formal balance to the music but wrecked the sense of the words. In France, after 1640 or so, dancing and décor were dazzling; words were trivial,

but melody was very delicately balanced. By the early eighteenth
century, ornamentation by the Italian castrati and prima donnas
was absurd and in their cadenzas (as well as in their 'da capo'
sections) melody had to give way to vocal acrobatics.

Professional instrumentalists have always wanted to show off
their instrument's capabilities and, to them, a simple melody
(however beautiful the sound may be) is not enough. Sometimes
the ornaments have been necessary: a virginals or harpsichord
cannot accent a note and stresses were therefore made apparent
by ornamental repercussions. Other ornaments were purely
decorative, adding elegance to an otherwise drab melody: these
were the 'grace-notes' which might, for example, provide a
'spring' for a note to bounce on. Dozens of ornament signs can
be found in early classical music, but a melody was always
decorated whether the signs were there or not. As the virtuoso
violinists and harpsichordists were their own composers, the
detailed decoration was put in at each performance spontaneously;
to play the most delicate embellishments while still retaining the
clarity of the melody was the greatest test for a musician. When the
instrumentalist began to imitate the opera singer he, too, fell
into the trap of losing the wood for the trees, however slender and
beautiful he made the trees.

Cadences

As early as the 1530s, lutenists and, later, bass violists knew
scores of ways to prettify their cadences, and the English
virginalists, too, added their finery. Here are only three of their
different formulas for the descant cadence (see example 27).

The old suspended discord essential to a cadence now figured
repeatedly in the detail of the ornament. To get these quicker
notes in without rushing, you had to slow up a little at cadences,
but only in cadences: anywhere else, the tempo remained unbroken. Here, though, is the beginning of that 'braking' at the
end of a piece which, if overdone, can make a mockery of a Bach
fugue or a Handel chorus.

When the opera singers, imitated by the violinists, drew out these cadential variations to what were virtually new pieces of throat or finger gymnastics, the cadenza was born. Here the Baroque principle fell to pieces, for the cadenza, coming as it did at the end, was bound to stand out from the whole. Again, the

Example 27

true Baroque artist made it fit by using only material which he drew directly from the rest of the piece, but the tiresome dood-lings of the Rococo fiddler and the clucking of a prima donna past her prime incensed many an eighteenth-century composer.

Harmony

You have already read how the keyboard player's way of modulating from key to key unlocked the gates of fresh fields for composers to romp in; and romp some of them did, using cadence after cadence in different keys as the basis of whole pieces, and revelling in sliding tunes (which they called chrom-atic). Sequences like this suited the Baroque temperament but the haphazard choice of keys did not; and the keyboard composer was always coming across a big snag. He tuned his chords by ear, but more accurately than we do today, so that he needed two slightly different pitches for each black note ('G sharp' and 'A flat', for example, were slightly apart), yet he only had five black keys in each octave, just as our piano has, so that he had to choose which set of notes to tune them to. Here is an example of the cart this could land him in!

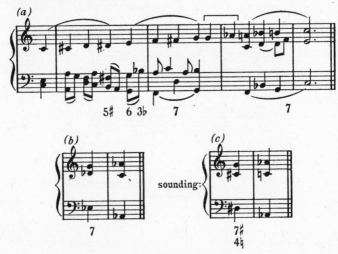

Example 28

To harmonize the two notes in square brackets he would need— as you can see at [a] 'E flat' and 'D flat' but these two keys are already tuned to D sharp and C sharp so that he would actually get sound [b]. This only *looks* odd to us, but it would have sounded badly out of tune to him. So his key changes (= modulations) were limited. First he tried building extra keys (on the organ) to have both 'D sharp' and 'E flat', but this was too clumsy. Soon, though, with the aid of the theorists, he created a compromise tuning in which both 'D sharp' and 'E flat' were slightly out of tune in absolute terms but at least made the same sound. This was called 'tempering' the notes and Bach was later to commemorate the event by writing preludes and fugues in all the possible keys (forty-eight) to be played, as his title says, or *The Well-Tempered Keyboard*.

Besides its three major chords (example 26), each major key has three minor chords (on the second, third and sixth degrees of the scale) and these gave Bach a set of 'relative minor' keys: the diatonic key range was extended as far as it could go.

Organists had been used to reading from a bass line and doubling the chorus parts with right-hand chords for some time before 1600, playing a précis of all the vocal parts; harpsichordists filled in harmonies from a written bass line to accompany singers. A bass like this went on, even if the voice rested, all through a piece and was called a Thorough Bass or, in Italian Basso Continuo—'continuo' for short. By 1600 the continuo-player had many chords to choose from and he had to be told of any that were not simply the third and fifth above the bass note. In example 28 the 'figured' bass line shows you the shorthand which helped him: in the fourth chord the fifth above the bass ('F') had to be played 'F sharp' (the 'D sharp' in the tune would be given anyway); you might like to work out the other figures yourself.

In the seventeenth and eighteenth centuries all ensemble music required not only a continuo keyboard but also a bass viol or, later, cello to draw the tune more firmly and occasionally, of course, to embellish it. So 'continuo' means at least two players. The virtuoso continuo was soon established as the organist or harpsichordist improvised an accompaniment within the figured framework, sometimes with full chords, sometimes in two parts and sometimes, in the singer's rests, in imitation of what the singer had just sung. With the cellist also embellishing the bass, small ensembles of this kind had to be very musical to make the sounds balance without focusing too much attention on any one part to the detriment of the others.

Form

It is dangerous to borrow terms from another art and though 'Baroque' and 'Rococo' can describe some parallels between music, architecture and painting, the two terms are so often difficult to choose between. The dividing haze usually has something to do with the amount and quality of the ornamentation. All the components you have just read about—range, rhythm, melody, cadence and harmony—belong to the most absorbing study of this period: the emergence of musical form as we still understand it in the opera house and concert hall. It is more convenient to parcel the words 'Baroque' and 'Rococo' together and label the package 'of the highest rank', the dictionary definition of 'Classical'.

You have already met troubadour forms, in particular virelai and rondeau, and mass forms from cantus firmus structure to fantasy. These were all based on tune patterns. Classical form uses them all but adds, because this is the harmonic age, the relationship of keys. Unity was difficult enough when the composer thought only in terms of melodies in one mode; when he also had to balance harmony in different keys the problems began all over again. Constant shifting of keys as in example 28 is as restless and ultimately boring as a melody which leaps about continually and never repeats a pattern. A key must be established in the ear and this takes time. First, then, how did the classical composer reconcile his new harmonic ideas with the old melodic formulae?

Form: Fugue

The fantasy structure of the polyphonic mass and motet, involving constant imitation of a tune 'subject' was transferred to instruments during the sixteenth century in pieces with names like 'ricercar', 'fancy', 'tiento' and 'canzona' for viols or keyboard and finally, for professional orchestras or keyboard, 'fugue'. The classical extension was to take the subject *as a whole* to new keys—dominant or relative minor first then home through the subdominant—in entry after entry. This had something of the restlessness mentioned in the previous paragraph, and the entries became separated by passages of comment on some part of the subject—called episodes—which, while maintaining the interest by using a snatch of tune carried the music to a new key. Moreover the experienced listener could hear it going to that new key.

Lastly, these episodes could be comments not on the subject but on what the listener first heard against it (the counter-subject). But by this time (Bach) a strict fugue was an academic exercise and the techniques of commenting (variation) and imitating (fugue) were one in the practical musician's mind.

Form: Prelude

Organ music from the fifteenth century onwards, lute items in Petrucci catalogues, parts of Spanish collections before 1550, and English virginal collections in the later sixteenth century: all contain pieces which grew from the practice figures which players made up either to test the tuning or to loosen the fingers before playing a service, a fantasy or a dance. Besides the name prelude, such pieces were called at various times: 'Preambulum', 'Fantasia', 'Toccata' (= touched) and, very confusingly as you will see, 'Sinfonia' or 'Overture'. They remained short and without any specific form throughout the classical period.

Form: Variations on a theme

Variations divide into those in which the theme is played at the same time as the variation; and those in which it is not. The first type derives from the cantus firmus technique, the second from lute and keyboard improvisation.

The plainsong cantus firmus motet or mass form was transferred direct to viols and organ in the sixteenth century as the 'In nomine' (after the plainsong used) and, in the Reformed Church, as the 'Chorale Prelude' (after the metrical hymn tune or chorale used). It was also used archaically for some movements of the Mass up to 1800. The constant repetition throughout a piece of part of a cantus firmus whether hymn or dance tune, returned in the early seventeenth and eighteenth centuries as the 'Chaconne' (= 'song dance') and 'Passacaglia' (= 'dance of the streets').

The harmonic grounds for dance-band improvisation such as the passamezzos (example 24) and many famous old basse-danse tenors became the foundations on which the virtuosos of the lute, virginals, recorders and harpsichord built pieces in as many separate sections of different variations as their ingenuity could devise. These 'divisions' (or 'diferencias' or 'partite' or 'variazioni') first needed two players, the virtuoso decorating while his assistant played the original tune (perhaps with stock filling-in chords) underneath. When only one player performed such divisions, the tune often disappeared partially when he could not manage two tunes *and* the harmony at once, or when his ornamentation carried him away. This kind of division leads to the technique of extending a short tune by continuous variation for a whole piece, first with well-known and then with freely-composed harmonies.

The second class of variation was usually associated with dance forms but you parodied a whole piece as the mass composers of the sixteenth century used to do, by altering its rhythms and by re-harmonizing it (transferring it, perhaps, to the minor). Pairs of dances like this, in which the second was a 'hotted-up' version of the first, began with the Pavan and Galliard. The technique was extended in dance music for concerts by the virginalists and Jacobean composers, who wrote long sets of variations which eventually keep only a tenuous connection with the original piece: such variations need an extremely experienced ear to follow the threads and even when you look at the music it is often very difficult to see, in places, how the composer felt the link with his theme.

Dance forms: 1550 – 1650

Dance tunes are usually short and catchy, and the usual way of lengthening them is merely to repeat the tune; in symbols, this is AA. This simple musical thought led to a maze of confused ideas which gradually took an orderly shape in the classical period. Music of the sixteenth century in dance form—but not meant to dance to—used the repetition for sets of variations upon the short tune which can still be lettered $AA^1A^2A^3A^4$, usually for lute or keyboard. Jacobean concert dances (or 'consort' dances in the older English term) for strings and wind instruments were, on the other hand, chains of repeated sections (usually three) each with different tunes, making a letter pattern AABBCC. Here the only formal connection between the sections was the four-bar metre of the original dance. Here are the main dances which the early seventeenth century used in consort music and keyboard variations:

1. Pavan and Galliard (see page 79), sometimes on a passamezzo ground but usually on the composer's own ideas.

2. Alman (*Allemande* in French = German dance), a sturdy four-in-a-bar, which often turns into a set of running quavers in music for solo viol or lute, and which later on has a dotted rhythm over a pair of beats somewhere.

3. Coranto (*Courante* in French = Running dance), with two triple beats in a bar (see compound time, page 108).

4. Jig (*Gigue* in French = Fiddle dance), with two or four triple beats in a bar.

The sections of the Coranto and the Jig—both gay dances— often end with the same snatch of tune or, at least, the identical rhythm.

Dance Forms: 1650 – 1750

The second half of the century saw these dances far removed from their origins as folk dances. Except for the ground bass technique in the chaconnes and passacaglias, the 'floor-pattern' was always AA^1 in a very sophisticated form. Section A now became little more than an initial idea which was extended by variation (see page 115) to a new key in which it was given a memorable cadence figure. The new key was usually the dominant, and the first section was repeated. The second section was a variation of the same tune idea (which makes the pattern AA^1) starting in the new key and coming home through the subdominant to end with the outstanding cadence figure in the tonic key. Key changes like this take time and the dances naturally lasted longer, so the old AABBCC formula lapsed. Taking our idea from the old example tune here is the sort of structure which a 'stock' dance-tune had between 1650 and 1750.

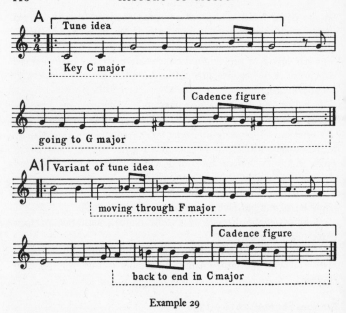

Example 29

If the tune idea was in a minor key, the first section would end in the relative major.

The difference between the dances was one of tempo, time, rhythm, and accent. Pavan and Galliard went out of fashion and the three remaining dances of the early seventeenth century were brought up to date and joined by others. The commonest eighteenth-century concert dances were:

   1. Allemande, now usually with eight quavers to a bar keeping the tune flowing and each section on an up-beat.

   2. Courante, which slowed down to a steady three-in-a-bar, sometimes with the accent shifted to a compound two (like many a *cantiga* in slow motion, see example 7); started on up-beat.

   3. Gigue, which now had two, three or four triple beats to a bar; the old identical section-endings of the Courante and Gigue

had, perhaps, given composers the notion of cadence figures to balance the harmony as in example 28.

4. Gavotte (= from the Gavots, who lived in the Pays de Gap, France), a stately two-in-a-bar, phrased across the bar line so that each section starts on the second beat.

5. Bourrée, a quicker Allemande, in two-time, each section starting on the last half of the second beat.

6. Minuet (= small step), a steady three-in-a-bar, in two-bar phrases.

7. Passepied (= pass-foot), a quicker Minuet with a warning up-beat; also called a hornpipe, after the instrument which originally played it.

8. Sarabande = English and Spani h sarabandes were often quick, but French, German and Italian were always slow, three-in-a-bar, and ended on the second beat, which carried a slight accent throughout.

These were, remember, all on one idea in two sections—AA¹ pieces. What about the ABA and ABACA formulae of the other old dances, the ballata/villancico/virelai and the rondeau? They, too, provided a frame which classical harmony opened out like an ever-widening trellis.

Form: Aria (= Air)

The most popular song form of the Medieval and Renaissance laude and cantigas was ABA. In the Classical period, aria form (the form of all 'set' songs in opera and of many slow instrumental movements) was also ABA. A was a complete section with a perfect cadence; B followed in a related key and was also completed by a perfect cadence in the new key; the singer then went back to the beginning ('da capo' in Italian and marked 'D. C.' in the score) and you heard A again but, of course, the virtuoso lady or gentleman disguised it under a new set of ornaments.

Form: Ritornello (= little return)

French keyboard composers kept the rondeau form alive

(ABACA . . .) in their rondeaux and chaconnes. The recurring refrain A was indispensable in concertos (see below) and operatic continuity was ensured by playing an orchestral 'chorus' before and after an aria; these repetitions were often cut short before the whole tune was finished and so were known as 'ritornelli'. The original dance-name itself returned in Italian ('Rondo') after 1750, in solo instrumental works. The all-powerful Classical invention of modulation saw to variety in the episodes *between* the ritornelli in concertos; the ritornelli (and the rondo theme in keyboard pieces) were played in the home key every time— so they kept the excursions into distant keys from roving too far by continually reminding the listener where he started from.

CHAPTER NINE

THE MASTER PLANS
OF COMPOSITION

THE basic lines of range, rhythm, melody and harmony formed the shapes of prelude, fugue, variations, eight main dances, and the two special dance-shapes which have become aria and ritornello. Of these shapes, virtuosos made six kinds of master-plans: suite, sonata, cantata, concerto, opera and symphony.

Suite (= followed)

Sets of pieces in contrasting rhythm and tempo were usually all written in the same key in the seventeenth century and often had one solemn 'abstract' piece to begin with, in prelude or fugue shape (or both); then followed a series of dances taken from the eight dance-shapes of which you have read. Some dances tended to group together like the Pavan-Galliard, or Allemande-Courante pairs. Sometimes the composer put two dances of the same kind in but wrote the second for solo instruments: a second minuet for three soloists was called 'Trio'; and a second gavotte or bourrée was called, after the sort of instrument it imitated, 'Musette' (=a bagpipe). In repetitions like this performers usually rounded off the section by repeating the first minuet or gavotte—back to the ever-popular ABA. Suites of this kind were called, variously, 'Ordre', or 'Partita' or (by composers borrowing from opera) 'Overture'.

By 1700 the commonest dance-tunes in suites were Allemande,

Courante, Sarabande and Gigue; any other fashionable dance—
the bold Polonaise, perhaps, from Poland or a wild Forlane from
Forli, near Venice—could be added, together with a choice of
minuets, gavottes, bourrées and passepieds. You could also put
in short, lyrical pieces with fancy names from the plain 'Air'
(not to be confused with aria-form which was not used in suites)
to 'Echo', having no special characteristic. At the beginning of the
century, composers still moved warily in changing key between
movements, though they had to change key within movements:
a piece or two in the tonic minor or (in the passionate Italian
manner) the relative minor was as much as they expected an
audience to comprehend. It was not until the last quarter of the
century that variety of keys between movements was common
and even then—in the suites called 'Serenade' or 'Divertimento'
—you always returned to the tonic key after each foreign expedi-
tion, making a rondo of key relationships between the numbers.

Sonata (= sounded)

The suite grew up as 'light' music; the sonata was always
highbrow. By its name, it meant something that was played rather
than sung (= *cantata*) and at the turn of the sixteenth century
when so much music was written to be played *or* sung, it had real
significance. Because of this, it is not surprising that the earliest
sonata sometimes used the fugal forms which voices had per-
fected. The new continuo type of harmony and the development
of modulation slowly changed their character.

In the seventeenth century the violin leapt to the top of the
orchestral tree. First came 'Trio' sonatas for two violins and
cello, then the solo violin sonata, but all sonatas had a keyboard
continuo player who filled in chords extempore and the bass line
of a solo sonata was also played on a cello or bass viol. So 'trio'
sonatas had four players, and 'solo' sonatas had three. The cellist
sometimes left his bass line and imitated the violin tune and the
other continuo instrument might be a harpsichord, an organ or a
lute; but the violinist was the director. Two titles differentiated
styles of sonata writing, one 'sonata da chiesa' and the other

'sonata da camera'. This did not mean, as *chiesa* and *camera* suggest, that some sonatas could only be played in church while others were for the drawing-room, but referred to the forms used in the movements. 'Church' sonatas never used dance forms and each movement has an abstract indication of its tempo; 'Chamber' sonatas invariably used dance forms and each movement carries a name of a dance.

By 1700, the two types of sonata had almost coalesced and the first genuinely 'solo' sonatas—for clavichord and, later, harpsichord—had emerged, in one to four movements using all the classical forms. For the first half of the eighteenth century 'Sonata' remained a loose description of any number of pieces up to five, for any instrumental ensemble up to five, that were not intended for the opera house. There were, however, signs that what we call 'chamber music' was settling down into a conventional pattern of three movements (quick-slow-quick) and that the first movement of such a sonata was evolving its own form as it grew longer and longer.

The term 'Sonata Form' coined by later nineteenth-century musical analysts should now be handed back to its academic mint, for it does *not* describe the form of any whole sonata and it is used in concertos and symphonies; nor is its alias 'First Movement Form' much better, because composers used and still use it in any movement. Historically, the formulas used by classical sonata composers are really all dance-forms and you have read how the ABA and ABACA forms lengthened into Aria and Ritornello form; the ultimate AA form outstripped both these in length and is quite adequately described if you think of it as the 'Long' form.

If you remind yourself of the AA¹ dance by looking at example 29 you will easily follow it as it becomes 'Long' form with four stretching devices:

1. Let the cadence figure develop into an idea comparable with the first tune idea, before writing the first double bar and repeat marks. This second idea will then, naturally, return at the end in the home key.

2. Plant your two ideas deep in the minds of the audience by making them complete tunes in themselves, and repeat the first tune before you bring back the second in the second half.

3. Take more time to get to the second tune in A^1 and so make the 'bridge' between the two have a design the listener can remember *on one repetition*.

4. Make the beginning of the second half as long as you can keep up interest by changing keys and reminding the listener of the tunes, particularly the first one.

The piece now has two tunes—one in the tonic and one in the dominant (or relative minor and major)—linked by a bridge, in a first section which is repeated; the second section has a development of some parts of the first, then all the first section is played again. The second section will have both tunes in the tonic (or major) key, and it is *not* repeated. Originally, therefore, the two sections balanced and the form was still AA^1. When you miss out the repeat of the first section, as all performers now do, you destroy this balance, for you only play half of Section A and Section A^1 becomes twice as long as A itself. The analyst accepts this and divides A^1 into *two*, calling the beginning of it the 'Development' section and the end—where the two original tunes are played again—'Recapitulation'. So you will find it easier to think of Long form now as in three sections. But we should be more honest with ourselves if we returned to the proper practice of repeating the first section—the 'Exposition'— in eighteenth-century music, so that a keen listener might at least have the same chance of remembering the material to be developed as a listener had when the music was first written.

The Long form was, then, even longer than we now play it and its design was very clearly emphasized by heralding the second tune in the exposition with a flourish or a momentary rest before it, by a complete break at the double bar, and often by a pause before the recapitulation. The virtuoso performer had to keep his audience's ears without a programme note or a miniature score to guide them: if he disguised the form too much he had only his gifts of dramatic sense, melody writing and finger virtuosity to rely on, and only the two virtuoso composers of the last quarter of the eighteenth century—Haydn and Mozart—could do that regularly. Even so, audiences found some of their pieces hard to understand.

The classical composer used all three dance forms in his sonatas. He used Long form whenever his ideas could sustain it, whatever the movement; Aria form was suited to the slowest movement; and Ritornello form, under its original dance name of Rondo, could provide him with a gay finale. If you add to these the possibility that he might still have chosen variation form or fugue, you will realize that to analyse a classical work by ear rather than by heart is much more difficult than it sounds. This kind of music needs an intelligent audience familiar with all the conventions of the period, and this is why the young 'Promenader', for example, usually finds most of his or her favourites among later music.

Cantata (= sung)

The continuo style of the early sonatas was also, of course, used for the solo and duet cantata, but the forms were very different; there were also the two divisions *cantate da chiesa* and *cantate da camera*, distinguished by their words, however, rather than by their music.

In the seventeenth century, the new 'madrigals' for one or two mezzo-sopranos and continuo, which had become fashionable in the late sixteenth century in Italy, were allied to the revolutionary recitative and called 'cantatas'. Like the madrigal, Recitative was the creation of poets rather than musicians and was very much part of the longing to return to the ways of classical Greece. The ideal was to sing words not to any set melody but merely rising and falling with the inflection and accent of speech, as its creators imagined Greek song had been performed. In its purest form it was said to be *secco* (= dry) and was strung out over a few 'props' of chords on the harpsichord or lute; if, in the later seventeenth-century cantatas, an orchestra provided a harmonic 'cushion' underneath it was, in Italian, *stromentato* (= instrumented). However workaday this might seem, the virtuoso singers declaimed with such passion that the more poetical minds in the audience were greatly moved, but the very long solo cantatas, in recitative throughout, were not generally popular. Composers had to learn to use recitative more practically, to set the atmosphere for a song. The second generation of cantata composers kept the long rhapsodical recitatives but gave them more melodic freedom and a steadier rhythmic pattern on parts of the 'cushion'. This kind of writing was known as 'arioso' (= 'like an air'). When these passages were separated by full-scale songs (in aria form for a soloist, in fugal or short dance forms for up to five soloists) or by short refrains in ritornello fashion (for singer or orchestra), the cantata was, in fact, a vocal suite or sonata with an arioso narrative linking the set numbers.

By 1700, Italian chamber cantatas were fairly uniform in design: two recitatives, each followed by an aria. Church cantatas, however, were in a turmoil of forms and terms. The Roman church cantata had begun by linking polyphonic and continuo motets to recitative and the name 'motet' was still used to describe even a solo cantata in 1700. Protestant countries had meanwhile allied, first, motets in their own language (called 'anthems' in England), then hymn tunes (called 'chorales' in Germany) to recitative in their cantatas. When soloists alternated with a choir these cantatas were also called 'Verse Anthems' and 'Sacred Concertos' or, if very long, 'Passions' or 'Oratorio'. As oratorio had also lost its stage setting in Italy by this time (see 'Opera' below), you are pretty safe in calling any long eighteenth-century church cantata an 'oratorio', any short oratorio a 'church cantata', and any oratorio about the Crucifixion a 'passion', or even 'passion-cantata'! As every church or princely feast was celebrated with a motet in the Renaissance, so priests, noblemen and city fathers celebrated with a cantata in the Baroque.

Concerto (= 'consort')

The word was first used during the last decade of the sixteenth century to describe church pieces for two choirs (see page 95) singing together, or as an alternative title to 'church cantata' (see above). In the seventeenth century it meant any collection of instruments playing together; and during the eighteenth it was given only to a collection of movements in which a soloist or small group of soloists (*concertino* = the little consort) was contrasted with the main body of the orchestra (*ripieno* = padding). It was really, then, a showcase in which the virtuoso could be displayed against a pleasant, recurring background pattern. In form it closely followed the development of the sonata; in sound, its contrasts helped the symphony (and the orchestra) to grow up.

The late seventeenth century was almost the monopoly of the solo violinist and for fifty years after 1685 or so, concertos generally contrasted one, two and three stringed instruments with the ripieno string band. Around 1735, however, there came a change: continuo-players began to branch out as solo harpsi-chordists and organists; later, as their instruments became surer to play, flautists and oboists followed this lead. In thirty years' time, certain technicians on the bassoon, horn, trumpet—and even the double bass—could command concertos from even the greatest composers, while wealthy amateurs, too, were provided with solos to play on their gentlemanly flutes (or lady-like harps) with their private bands. If you had the money you could buy your own concerto to play on any instrument you specified, new or old. The violin and cello still kept their solo places and many older fiddle concertos were revived as arrangements for oboe, flute, or up to four harpsichords.

There was, by 1750, an orthodox form for the solo concerto: three movements, quick-slow-quick. Before then, a composer chose as many movements as he liked, including some for the soloist(s) alone, or pauses when the soloist(s) could improvise in each performance. The later composer kept something of these extra solo movements within his strict three-fold design. The first movement was usually in Long form with the soloist and orches-tra sharing the tunes, but it was even longer than before. First the orchestra 'introduced' the soloist before he began the move-ment proper, and repeated the introduction in the recapitulation;

then, just before the final cadence, there was space for the soloist to improvise on his own (called the *cadenza* = cadencing) as a 'parting shot'; finally, everyone came together (= *tutti*) to play some of the first tune as a tailpiece (= *coda*). This gave a triumphant ending and perfect formal balance.

After such a long movement—the first section was not, by the way, repeated in the concerto as it was in the sonata—the slow movement was usually merely a continuous tune which the soloist, accompanied discreetly by the band, decorated as he went along. Sometimes the tune was shared between the orchestra and soloist, and sometimes the soloist might play a few short variations *after* the orchestra had begun the tune. The last movement takes us back to the singing origin of the term 'concerto' for it is usually a rondo. The earliest rondeaux were sung alternately by soloists and chorus, the early concerto rondo used the band as 'chorus' (which might change key between tonic, sub-dominant and dominant or related major and minor) alternated with the soloists who played the different 'verses'— called 'episodes'—in between. In the later classical concertos the return of the chorus is often shortened (ritornello), the division of work between concerto and ripieno involves them both in 'verse' and 'chorus' material, and there may be a short cadenza before the final ritornello.

Symphony (= sounding together)

This word was restricted to instruments throughout the classical period. It was often found above orchestra passages in early opera and cantata scores, and music-hall comedians still used it to ask for the ad-lib introduction to their songs as late as the nineteen-thirties. In this sense it was a short instrumental prelude but, before an opera act, it soon collected more sections (usually two) and could also use fugue and dance-forms. By the eighteenth century there were always three movements in the Italian opera 'sinfonia' (quick-slow-quick). Meanwhile the sonata and the concerto were finding audiences outside the opera house. In the concerto, the ripieno players were in much the same position as continuo players in an early trio sonata: they were 'fillers-in'. The weaker members did not object, for the ritornelli were usually easy and many a gentleman had been known to saw his way through a ripieno part to impress his musical skill upon his friends; but the better players—those who were nearly but not quite in the virtuoso rank—had to carry the others through with the help of the keyboard continuo. So the best orchestral violinists, the continuo harpsichordists and the organists began to write orchestral pieces which needed only the best players. During the eighteenth century all three instrumental skills were often found in the same man, and by 1740 the best classical composers were at work. They called their orchestral pieces 'symphonies' and the opera dropped the name in favour of an earlier alias, 'overture'.

The mid-eighteenth century saw all the stretching devices of the Long dance-form (page 118) tried by symphonic composers, who experimented with them in all movements except the third of their four-movement work. The second movement was always slow (and sometimes in aria form), the third usually a minuet and trio, and the fourth, if not experimental, might be ritornello variations, or (very seldom) a fugue. By 1770 the evolution of the classical Long dance-forms was complete and further harmonic experiments had begun. Ten years later, orchestras were on occasion expected to play in remote keys involving as many as six sharps, and audiences had to be very intelligent to follow the composer in his wayward modulations.

Not all members of the audiences were so knowledgeable or keen-eared and the most admirable composers realized it. If you cannot follow a modulation you can still enjoy good tunes, lively rhythms, and varied instrumental noises—soft, loud, high, low, wind or string—and the best composers gave you all these. The structure was firm but only the expert was expected to be aware of it.

The art of orchestration owed a good deal to the contrasts which concertos had taught. The first symphonies outside the opera house were for strings only, with organ or harpsichord, and the composer secured variety by using loud and soft contrasts for some solo passages for violin. As you might expect, these pieces were a cross between a sonata and a concerto. When other reliable instrumentalists joined in, however, more attention had to be paid to balance within the orchestra. Wind instruments were admitted in pairs: flutes and oboes came first but—as it was usually the same player who played both instruments—you used one pair or the other, never both; the same players could probably 'double' on clarinets after 1750 if you needed them; bassoons joined the continuo bass line; horns, the most limited of any instruments at the time, were best used for long notes in the middle where they could help smooth out the harmonies; and only for special occasions did trumpets and drums come from the military barracks.

With all these available, the keyboard-playing composer first transferred his work to the wind to sustain the harmony, and then to the cellos, basses and bassoons to play not a continuous but an independent bass which could allow for contrasts between high and low instruments playing separately. Now, as he only had to preside at the keyboard in case of an emergency he could concentrate on grading *crescendos* and *diminuendos* in a performance and become a non-playing conductor. Finally, as the number of his string players grew, he could take some of his wind players off 'filling-in' work, to play solo phrases and still be able to keep a full sound, and here the experiments of contrasting different instruments in concertos came in useful. Indeed, some composers openly called such a symphony a 'sinfonia concertante', but the general classification 'symphony' remained to describe any sonata for full orchestra.

Opera (= Works)

This modest, almost off-hand title introduces the most ambitious invention of the classical age in music. All the elements of music you have read about in this chapter combine to make opera; you can also maintain that opera discovered all these elements. Consider the forms: recitative, arioso and aria cover the whole ground of singing; prelude, fugue and dance-forms contributed to and were demanded by the orchestral symphony before an opera; ritornelli held the 'works' together, unifying the action and music while letting the singers change costumes and get their breath back, drowning the noise as the stagehands changed scenery, and keeping the audience amused. The only basic form missing is the theme-and-variations. But this was continually happening in the virtuoso singing—and in the plots librettists worked overtime to vary the themes of Greek legend, classical history, or the lives of the Saints.

The sight and sounds of opera grew in length, height, depth and number. The earliest opera was almost entirely dry recitative with, perhaps, the odd chorus and a final dance. Characters sang dialogues (but never duets) within a small range of notes, declaiming the words clearly, but unless you understood Italian you would find it hard to keep awake, for the music alone was too monotonous. Even the composers of these pieces realized that their enthusiasm for the wedding of music and poetry would meet opposition from the parents of both parties, as well as from their friends. Singers and their audiences enjoy the beauty of melody, poets and their audiences the beauty of thought and language; and both enjoy the beauty of form; so the match-makers gradually stopped trying to please poetry at the expense of music and concentrated on this last common ground. Recitative had neither verse nor balanced melody and was therefore relegated to dialogue which could move the plot along without using particularly beautiful thoughts or language. If the composer wanted to highlight a striking thought, he made the music underneath it regular for a few bars so that it sounded like the beginning of a melody. Arioso passages like this at least relieved the monotony and, with the orchestral ritornelli, made the opera considerably longer.

There was no difference at first between secular and sacred music-dramas. As the theatre soloists took charge, the operas contained more and longer arias and duets in place of recitative and arioso; on the other hand sacred works (which had to use the church choir) acquired more choruses at the expense of recitative, and the difference between opera and oratorio (as the sacred music-drama was called) was duly marked. During the seventeenth century stage sets became more and more elaborate. The Heavens (which were usually represented at some stage in opera *and* oratorio) had to be made higher to match the soloists' roulades as they soared to the top of their compass and church performances could not compare with the theatre. It was difficult, too, to control choruses if they were always on the move, so oratorio became static and by the eighteenth century was no longer acted. Opera, meanwhile, was to become longer and higher still, with even greater depths of acting and dancing.

By the 1670s, opera was a vast entertainment and the old intellectual ideas about the marriage of words and music were well tempered by ideas of what went to make up an aristocratic entertainment. The overture was lengthened until it resembled the concerto in Italy (quick-slow-quick) and the suite (slow-quick-series of dances) in France. Audiences might well arrive late and this overture gave them a chance to settle down, but it had nothing to do with the opera so it needed only such attention as they wished to pay. Ballet—a French word—was all the rage

in France, and French opera allowed for this by interpolating dream sequences and pastoral dances at most unlikely places in the still classical plots. In eighteenth-century Italy, castrati were backed like racehorses, and da capo arias sent the audiences into almost hysterical delight when their favourite began to let himself go in the repeat as the winning post came in sight. In every operatic country stage-managers carried out the most formidable requirements of the designers, to keep all eyes riveted on the stage. Against all these attractions, how could recitative compete? Nobody wanted to listen to 'sung' speech. If they had to know what the words were for the sake of the plot, people preferred either to have those words sung on one or two notes clearly but quickly and for the singer to make any joke or prophecy by putting his own inflections in, or for the music to stop altogether while the actors spoke. The first style, 'recitativo parlante', was kept for serious opera until German opera houses broke away from it in the late eighteenth century; spoken dialogue was usual for ballad opera (see below) and much comic opera. Again, what chance had unstaged oratorios against the opera? Shortened (i.e., as cantatas) they survived in eighteenth-century Europe, but only in England did the full-scale oratorio live on, thanks to Handel. Even he used to play organ concertos from time to time in his oratorios to give the audiences some extra entertainment.

The extravaganza opera, also, was too serious for many opera-goers who felt the need for some light refreshment in between the heavy courses which the tragic and high-minded classical plots offered. Intermezzos (= 'in the middles') were common in the sixteenth century during the intervals of literary plays, and comic musical turns in between the acts of opera or ballet adopted the name in the eighteenth century. Most composers wrote them, and as there were usually two intervals, they began to write them as two-act comic operas. If you went to the opera house you saw two operas with very different plots for the price of one. This state of affairs offended some persons of good taste and the farcial intermezzos began a life of their own as Opera Buffa (= works for buffoons). In Italy, composers used the same techniques in these comic operas as in their grand works, includ-ing quick-fire recitative, but the rest of Europe retained the

spoken dialogue. Their immense popularity resulted in one highly
important feature of serious opera: the farcical plots often entailed
three, four or five characters all singing together and there was
always a final 'chorus' in which all the soloists took part. From
these beginnings, grand opera became a continual mixture of
recitative, aria, duet, trio, quartet and chorus, with orchestral
overtures and ritornelli—and intermezzi.

One further attempt to revive the ideals of 1600 was made by
intellectuals in about 1770. Starting with the orchestra, the new
pundits said that all ritornelli which had nothing to do with the
plot were superfluous; the overture should set the mood for the
opera and should be listened to as part of the whole piece; and the
composer should use orchestration with as much variety as the
librettists used words—all important sentences should have
attention drawn to them in the orchestration. Turning their
gaze on the self-important singers they demanded that all undue
display should be banned and that any repeats which slowed up
the pace of the plot (as in da capo arias) were to go as well.
Austerity is always a dangerous subject for sermons, and to ask
Italians to limit their vocal passions is to preach anarchy, for
singers and audience adore singing. In France and Germany,
however, the virtuoso singer had to lay his or her art at the
composer's feet by the nineteenth century. The composer had
become master of operatic music, but the designer and librettist
were still there to be reckoned with and audiences had still to be
won over.

Popular Music

Church music was free for everyone to hear, whether Roman
or Protestant. Cantatas, anthems, masses and motets mirrored
the development of opera and there was much more opportunity
of hearing small orchestras with the local organist than we are
used to now. The old polyphonic forms survived longest in the
mass and motets, but few composers could free them from the
infirmities of their old age.

Much more important was the development of congregational

music in the Reformed Church countries. Carols, popular songs and a few plainsong hymns which had formerly been sung between the scenes of mystery-plays or at some festival—particularly Christmas: these were the starting point in the early sixteenth century. The tunes were usually in a regular metre; the words were translated first into German (Chorales), then as Metrical Psalms into French and English. Harmony stuck round the tunes was meant for a choir only and if the congregation joined in, the song was unaccompanied. Latin hymns did not fit well in English translation and in the seventeenth century English hymns appeared in a few collections for the first time. The tune was still set in the tenor. Eighteenth-century Nonconformity brought with it a host of hymns, grave and (mostly) gay, for the roaring bass and determined mezzo-soprano of every English parish to sing: in all of these the tune was at the top and the organ played the harmonies.

Theatres were expensive and the greater part of the population of Europe probably knew of grand opera and ballet only from the impersonations of great stars which they might see in a ballad opera at a fairground, or from vivid descriptions given by servants who waited for their masters in a special gallery while the performance was going on. Taverns and open-air cafés had their tiny bands and some of them (particularly in the seventeenth century, when the waits still favoured their fathers' and grandfathers' shawms and trombones) were quite good. The pipe-and-tabor man and the fiddler still played for open-air dancing and polite circles adopted hundreds of English country dances (calling them, in French snobbery, 'contredanses') and Austrian *ländler* to make up their programmes. The old singing folk-dances with chorus were still made up by rustic poets in the Common Metre of Protestant hymns, and street singers were forever making up new political or scandalous variations on them (a relic of the troubadour news, this!) in their ballads. Touched up a little or in a composer's sophisticated fashion, these ballads (called 'broadsheets' or 'broadsides' from the shape of the paper) found their way into comic or sentimental plays to become 'Ballad Operas' in England, Opéra Comique in France, or Singspiel in Germany.

Music for virtuosos, music for beginners; for aristocrats and errand boys; to praise God, or Mammon: the same composers wrote it all. As a master architect could house a whole community in one overall design of a monastery or a palace like Versailles, so the classical composer drew up the plans which all musical communities have lived in ever since. All that remained to do was to build bigger and bigger movements on his plans.

CHAPTER TEN

THE SOURCES:

1550—1756

The European Scene

The Treaty of Westphalia in 1648 finally settled a hundred years of religious wars. France, Germany and Austria had been in the thick of the fight, but England, Spain and Italy were territorially not involved and musically they prospered. England's finest hours of music and literature were between 1560 and 1640, before the Civil Wars or 'The English Revolution'. Spain made the most of her new material riches from America and the musical dividends—lute and keyboard music—which she declared as early as the 1530s were shared by the rest of Europe (especially England and Italy) between 1550 and 1600; in the seventeenth century Cervantes (the Spanish 'Shakespeare'), Lope de Vega and Calderón, and the three most honoured of all Spanish painters Velasquez, Murillo and El Greco shone on the duller north in brilliant reflections of the power of the Spanish Empire. Italy, which Lorenzo de Medici had likened to a 'five-stringed lute' (Milan, Venice, Florence, the Papacy and Naples) began, after 1600, to blaze with the new music which made her the centre of musical ideas for almost two hundred years.

By 1648, Flemings were no longer rulers of the musical world and indeed had not even a princeling to match against the Italians. North of Flanders, the United Provinces were at the height of their powers but though they gave us Rembrandt and the long list of great Baroque painters, in music they were silent. There remained the three centres whose struggles had just been brought to an end.

Politically, the Treaty of Westphalia saw the emergence of France as the most powerful Kingdom in Europe, and before long the rays of the 'Roi Soleil' were being felt in many countries. Paris and Versailles produced not only opera and ballet but the theatre of Molière (the French 'Shakespeare') and the verse of Racine and Corneille.

The years of material peace soon brought the 'national' styles of playing and composing into open warfare: within ten years of the treaty, French and Italian styles of music had become so different that the whole of musical Europe began to take sides as to which was the better taste, and most up-to-date. By 1700 some kind of peace was made between the two musical sides—French and Italian composers wrote in each other's 'language'—on a basis of co-existence; but only towards the middle of the eighteenth century did the two sides really make peace and join up with each other to speak the same language . . . and by then composers foreign to both France and Italy were beginning to speak the language best.

These 'foreigners' came from the great new powers of eighteenth-century German lands: Austria and Prussia. After Westphalia, the Austrian Hapsburg dominions gradually annexed the whole of South Eastern Europe to the borders of Russia, while Brandenburg, when Frederick the Great died in 1786, ruled Europe north-east of Bavaria. The western borders of Prussia and Austria in 1800 roughly corresponded to the 'Iron Curtain' line of 1960. The other powerful German states of Hanover, Hesse, and Saxony were united with these major powers and the Franco-Italian musical alliance was short-lived. As the English Revolution had cut short England's finest musical days, so the French Revolution and Napoleon saw the end of French musical power. The Italian fire, too, was spent by 1800, save for a last flicker of resistance in nineteenth-century opera.

The years 1550–1800 were marked in politics and geography only by confusion; in music they were undeniably marked by the successful occupation of the whole of Europe by Italy.

All occupied countries, however, produce their notorious men and women either as heroes of a resistance movement or leading collaborators or, most exciting and subtle, leading collaborators who turn out to be leaders of the resistance. This was as true musically in the Classical period as it was politically in Norman England and may yet be in the Soviet Union, and it does not imply that Italian music was oppressive: some loved it; some despised it; many took it for granted; a few thought it funny; and most of the population did not know it existed. Composers and virtuosos, however, were nearly all willing collaborators, and the subtlest of these—Handel, Haydn and Mozart—finally led the resistance successfully, and in turn, prepared the German occupation of the nineteenth century.

MAP 5
1550 to 1815

Here, then, in three phases is a short account of the progress of the most powerful Italian musicians in England, Spain, France, Germany and Austria. The first phase takes us to the Treaty of Westphalia.

Vocal Music: 1550 – 1648

Two 'Ms', Marenzio (1553–1599) in Rome and Ferrara and Monteverdi (1567–1643) in Venice, broke the Flemish spell cast over Italian vocal music. Marenzio became a model for most English madrigalists after the second volume of *Musica Trans-alpina* had made a collection of his works widely known, while Monteverdi's title 'Canzonets' served Thomas Morley in his first volumes of English 'Canzonets' (1593 onwards). Some of these madrigals and canzonets clearly followed the line laid down by their Flemish precursors, but some of them pointed clearly to the harmonic and monodic style of seventeenth-century opera.

Others claim a place in history books as the first composers of opera—Caccini and Peri in Florence, Cavalieri and Landi in Rome—but they were more the slaves of an intellectual ideal than masters of a new and exciting medium. Monteverdi was its master. In his *Scherzi musicali* (= Musical Jokes: 1607), he had insisted that the words of his poems were important and that setting them to music was only having fun with them: the words mattered most, as indeed they still do in comic songs. In the same year he wrote *Orfeo* for the local Academy (= Club) of poets and musicians in Mantua. He had practised writing for many different mixtures of voices and instruments in the Scherzi, and in *Orfeo* he showed his ear for orchestration, using thirteen different *kinds* of instruments in all sorts of combinations. (Wagner only uses fifteen kinds in the whole of *The Ring*.) The recitative pioneered by Caccini and Cavalieri, dramatic choral writing reminiscent of the earlier Venetians like Gabrieli, the da capo aria, the orchestral ritornello: *Orfeo* has them all.

This was the first of nineteen operas and ballets, but neither Monteverdi's nor Mantua's finances would run to publishing complete operas and only three (which were on such a small scale that they could be included in madrigal collections) were actually printed. His last opera, *The Coronation of Poppea*, has survived in two manuscript copies at Venice and Naples. It was performed in 1642 in the still new Venetian opera house, the first ever open to the public. The changes of thirty-five years were many. Now the orchestra's various timbres played little part and the romantic collection of thirteen kinds of instrument was reduced to strings and continuo; recitatives were almost all secco and short; all arias were da capo, and the singers were all soloists who could put the repeated section to good use, for there was no chorus. By 1648, when *Poppea* was still in the regular repertory at Venice, the singer ruled the composer in Italian opera.

In church music, and still in Venice, Monteverdi's Vespers (1610) had crowned the work begun by Willaert at St. Mark's half a century before and carried on by the Italian organists of that church from 1584, Andrea and Giovanni Gabrieli. Its dramatic choruses for one and two choirs, solos florid with ornaments and big contrasts in orchestration pre-echoed the sounds which were to break into oratorio, passion music and the concert mass in the eighteenth century, but after this one outburst the composer seemed to lose most of his interest in writing for choirs. Out of over seventy religious works he is now known to have written after 1610, only four are called 'choral'; the rest are all 'chamber' size.

Resistance to this Italian emphasis on solos with simple accompaniment was strongest in England and Germany. Byrd and Gibbons in London and Tomkins in Worcester worked the old polyphonic seams in their verse anthems for strings, soloists and choir and brought up fresh gold. Of the three, Orlando Gibbons (1583–1625) has left us most—twenty-five anthems in which strings (or organ) and solo voice break up passages for the full choir—but Byrd, who had already made his place in history safe with his polyphonic masses and madrigals to overshadow the Italians, must count as their leader. In these English anthems the soloist is not all-important but stands out from an inner part amongst the surrounding strings simply by the beauty of his melody compared with theirs. For melody accompanied by subsidiary harmony we must look to the lutenists.

The ayres of the Jacobean lutenists from 1597 onwards brought a brief late flowering of English song, delicate blossoms by the side of the flamboyant Italian aria, but perfectly-formed and on a firm stem. They grew from the same stock as the Spanish *villancico* of the vihuelistas Milan and Narvaez in the 1530s (an equally strange and short-lived bloom) and the French *air de cour* of Tessier and Bataille, which was popular at the same time. The soloist sang a simple but very emotional melody while underneath, a lute, lute and viols, or two or three other singers, pointed the tune with harmony that hardly ever sounded like the 'main' tune. In form many airs made use of 'short' dance repeated sections (see page 116) and the accompaniment was a mixture of polyphony and strummed chords. English songwriters were led by Dowland (whose First Book of Ayres in 1597 contained twenty-one of his eighty-seven surviving songs) and Campion.

They were enormously popular and their songs were printed as economically as possible, not in partbooks (as were all madrigals) but in an ingenious arrangement of a double page so that everyone taking part could read a line without looking over someone else's shoulder (see illustration p. 100). Any light music other than a madrigal was called 'air' in England and France and 'villancico'

in Spain. The composers of these simple but charming songs—often their own poets—formed the nucleus of the movement which grew, by way of the masque, into French opéra comique, English ballad opera and the Spanish zarzuela in the eighteenth century.

The Lutherans Walther in Dresden, Tunder at Lubeck and Hieronymus Praetorius in Hamburg continued to set the regularized tunes of the chorales, simply for their soloists, and with 'block' chords for their choirs. Their highest representative was to be Schütz (1585–1672).

Lucky enough to be born in the principality of Hesse, where the prince (the Landgrave Maurice) was the foremost patron of music in seventeenth-century Protestant German lands, Schütz was taught music in the court chapel choir, law in the University of Marburg, and then sent to Venice to learn the Italian music under Giovanni Gabrieli . . . all at the Landgrave's expense. The conditions were, of course, that he should introduce the Italian style in chapel and court when he returned. So, naturally, the first publications of work by Schütz were a set of madrigals in five parts (Venice: 1611) and, when he returned to Germany, a collection of Psalms set to German words in the Gabrieli style, called 'motets or concertos' for eight or more voices, three or four choirs, with basso continuo and a large assortment of instruments (Dresden: 1619). At intervals during the rest of his long life Schütz returned constantly to the Psalms for inspiration and his settings varied from the polychoral to simple note-against-note harmonization of the entire metrical Psalter. When he next visited Italy (1628) the new Monteverdi style was all-conquering and in the same year Schütz's technique changed with the titles of his music: 'Sacred Symphonies' for various combinations of voices and instruments (up to six) to Latin texts were dedicated to his new patron, the Elector of Saxony. The combinations show the tremendous gifts of his orchestral ear—two violins comment delicately on a duet for tenor and bass about the beauty of woman, three bassoons set the scene for a song about the darkness of night, and four trombones accompany David's lament for Absalom—and the truly dramatic way in which he thought.

By 1648, though, Schütz was beginning to draw back from the Italian style. He had already set *The Seven Words from the Cross* for small-scale forces using a chorale text for his choruses (which reflect on the story of the Passion), straightforward chorale harmony for the orchestral symphonies, and a dramatic but never showy part for the Evangelist narrator. His second set of Sacred Symphonies had German, not Latin, words and nearly all were accompanied by two violins and a bass only. In a preface to some choir music in 1649 he writes openly that the Italian manner is not an end in itself but can only be useful to someone who has a thorough grounding in the old contrapuntal style: it should be used to fortify, not destroy, the German tradition.

Instrumental Music: 1550 – 1648

Ganassi, an Italian intrumentalist, had published tutors for the recorder and viols as early as 1535 and 1542 in which various ways of improvising on a tune were shown. Ortiz, a Spaniard working in Italy, had codified rules for viol variations in a famous book of divisions (Rome: 1553). The books of *diferencias* by the

Spanish Vihuelistas had explored the fantasy structure thoroughly and contain many sets of variations on popular tunes and passa-mezzo grounds. But Italian violists like the Lupo and Ferra-bosco families amazed Europe with their technique in the second half of the century, and Italians reigned supreme in violin music. Keyboard music was not so dominated by Italians. In England, as long before as the early 1540s, Hugh Aston had prepared the way for the Elizabethan virginalists, and by the end of the century there was an enormous repertory of keyboard music by Bull, Byrd, Farnaby and the rest. Much of it is pre-served for us in the 297 pieces which make up the Fitzwilliam Virginal Book. Collected in the early seventeenth century, these preludes, fancies, airs, pavans, galliards, almans, corantos and jigs used techniques that Jacobean composers like Brade, Holborne and (again) John Dowland and Orlando Gibbons soon learned to adapt for viols or recorders with, perhaps, lute, organ or harpsichord all playing together (or, as it was called, 'in consort'). The Italian methods were copied before the end of the sixteenth century by Thomas Morley, the man who had already introduced English ears to the Italian canzonet in his own compositions. His collection of 'Consort Lessons' (1599) uses a violin, a bass viol, two kinds of guitar, a large flute, and a lute. The music is fit for virtuosos to teach on, for the lute divisions are unplayable by any but the finest artists today—yet it was designed for the use of civic bandsmen.

In the early seventeenth century, the undisputed pride of the English court was Coperario, writer of 'incomparable Fantasies' for viol, which King Charles I himself is said to have played. Born plain John Cooper, 'Coperario' journeyed to Italy in or about 1604, and returned to join Holborne and Dowland as a master of music for viol and violin in the year of Dowland's beautiful *Lachrimae* ('Seven Teares, figured in seven passionate pavans'), perhaps the finest example of all early chamber music for violins or viols.

English virtuosos—some of them Roman Catholic refugees—also began to settle and find great honour in Northern Europe.

The Royal organist, Dr. Bull himself, left for Brussels in 1613 never to return. As organist of Antwerp Cathedral his techniques of composition had their effects on many a Northern organist, including the last of the Flemish leaders of European music, Sweelinck, organist of Amsterdam Cathedral. Sweelinck, in turn, passed on this blend of Flemish polyphony (in his chorale-preludes) with English virginalist manners (in his variations on secular tunes) to his pupils in North Germany, notably Scheidt of Halle.

If we follow this 'S' line of organists across Europe we come up against Schütz again, and two other 'Sch's': Scheidemann of Hamburg and Schein of Leipzig. Note the towns! These three, with Scheidt, circulated the Frenchified dance suites, sometimes for 'broken' consorts (that is, many different *kinds* of instrument: *cf.* Monteverdi above), and the style of keyboard fugues which was to lead to the German 'preludes and fugues' of the eighteenth century.

As you may guess, Venice—and the organ loft of St. Mark's—was the Italian headquarters from which many instrumental forms set out: Willaert in his ricercars for viols or 'any instrument you like', G. Gabrieli in his sonatas for various specified instruments alternating in concerto style, Merulo and Gabrieli in toccatas for organ, and many lesser composers with their suites of dances for violins beginning with a Padovana (= Pavan) led the way. Mantua and Ferrara were still the training ground for Italian composers but gradually towns further south became important. In Bologna, Banchieri provided an early textbook on how to play from a figured bass in 1605 and the town became a teaching centre. In Rome, Frescobaldi (1583–1643) was in the organ loft of St. Peter's and many thought him the finest organist in the world. Frescobaldi brought in the northern Italian training of Ferrara, and the rest of Europe heard his music through his personal visits as virtuoso to the Netherlands. His most apt pupil—the second 'F'—Froberger, organist at Vienna and international artist of the two post-Westphalian decades, began a German-speaking line of development in keyboard music which runs through Kuhnau, Telemann and C. P. E. Bach to the sonatas of Haydn and Mozart.

To sum up this first virtuoso period of the 'new' harmonic music, you may like to remember these composers' names alphabetically: in Italy, Marenzio and Monteverdi; in England and North Europe, Byrd and Bull; in Northern Europe, Sweelinck and Schütz; and in Italy and Central Europe, Frescobaldi and Froberger. The second phase of the classical period takes us from Westphalia in 1648 to the outbreak of the Seven Years' War in 1756, a period of almost continual wars which was to end the power of the French monarchy and leave Europe to an uneasy peace. In Italy, the four great cities of music—Venice, Rome, Bologna and Naples—remained untouched by fighting and free to develop opera, oratorio, cantata, sonata and concerto. Louis XIV, as master of Europe, poured money into the arts until, by the time England and France were at war (1689–97), bankruptcy took its toll of French musical influence. We must, therefore, only expect France to be musically outstanding between 1648 and 1689 (long enough, however, to cause a short period of fruitful collaboration in England after the Restoration in 1660). Hanover, Prussia, Bavaria, Saxony and Austria each assume musical power in the first half of the eighteenth century as musicians took advantage of their patrons' prosperity. Wars, however, mean that international artists must suffer and only the Italians, at war with no one, could travel freely to any European country and receive freely the most promising musicians of the continent.

Italy: 1648–1756

Venice continued to lead the operatic field, through yet another alphabetical pair, Cavalli and Cesti, until the 1670s. Cavalli, a pupil of Monteverdi, wrote over forty operas, only one of which was written for performance outside Italy. This was about Hercules and, being for the French court (1662), he could write for large choruses; in Venice, where the choruses were weak, he seldom used them and his operas are continually arioso for soloists broken up by short dramatic recitatives which would hardly keep us interested today. Cesti carried Venetian opera further both musically and geographically: musically he preferred the formal aria to arioso; geographically he seems (understandably) to have preferred the splendour which the Viennese court could provide to the strained resources of Venice, and eight of his fifteen operas were first performed either in Vienna or Innsbruck.

Meanwhile, in Rome, a third 'C' composer—Carissimi—takes us into the 1670s but in the fields of oratorio and cantata. Words were still important and he prefers the lyrical arioso to recitative or aria. In his chamber cantatas the result is a continuous flow of melody which, although many individual phrases are very moving, wanders too much for our 'formal' ears. In the oratorios a chorus may take the part of a crowd (with various anonymous solo voices penetrating from time to time) or may echo what a soloist has just sung and the block writing which Carissimi uses gives them a loose formal structure. Indeed, like many a composer before and since, Carissimi paves more of the path of music through his vision of the whole ground to be covered than in the detail of his actual craftsmanship.

In the north of Italy lived the violin makers. At Cremona, Nicolo Amati (representing the third generation of a famous family) had no rival and his pupil, Stradivari, continued and enhanced the reputation of Cremona until his death in 1737. It is not surprising that the earliest of the great Italian violinist-composers, Vitali, should also have come from Cremona; but he learnt his composition at Bologna, and it is there that we must look for the development of the sonata and concerto. Vitali already distinguished between sonata da camera and da chiesa; Torelli, in 1686, published a concerto da camera which led to the solo violin concertos a quarter of a century later; and the trio sonata was finally established firmly by the finest of all the Bolognese, Corelli. Corelli was first taught the violin and composition at the Philharmonic Academy in Bologna, but he settled in Rome and there pupils flocked to his side. His works circulated all over Europe, and among his pupils Geminiani (who wrote the first Violin Tutor in English about 1740) and Castrucci (who led the band at the King's and Covent Garden theatres in London) led the Italian conquest of London, after the wars with France had killed any taste for French music which the English might have cultivated. Any composer visiting Rome was bound to meet Corelli and would have been received courteously at his Monday concerts; if the visitor wanted to know more of Italian opera, Corelli would doubtless have recommended him south to Naples.

Naples, capital of the Kingdom of the Two Sicilies, was, musically, the Kingdom of Alessandro Scarlatti nicknamed 'Il Siciliano'. He had been trained in Rome with Corelli, who would remember the first of his seventy-odd operas and where most of his twenty-four oratorios had their premieres. During Corelli's last years Scarlatti was again in Rome, but in 1713 the Sicilian returned to Naples and there reached the highest peak of his fame. Corelli, and his players in Naples, had shown him what violinists could do and he began to use violins to accompany the singers instead of playing only the ritornelli and overture. The result was a much more integrated opera with the orchestra playing a full part in the modern style. Tune-ideas in his arias had longer and longer developments, specially in the second half before the da capo, and dance rhythms, particularly the *Siciliano*, pervaded them. He finally moulded the 'Italian' overture, and left behind him all the material which could fill in the master-plans of which you read in Chapter IX, in form, melodic variation, sequence and balance using a complete vocabulary of diatonic harmony. Scarlatti's house in Naples became almost a place of pilgrimage, and his name a household word even amongst those who could not see his operas or hear his oratorios, through his chamber cantatas (over 700), sonatas and suites for recorder, strings and continuo. Another European celebrity from Naples was Durante, noted for his church music. Between them, these two Neapolitan masters numbered most of the successful Italian opera composers of the late eighteenth century among their pupils. One further Neapolitan concerns us as we return to Venice: the master of the keyboard sonata, Domenico Scarlatti, son of 'Il Siciliano'.

Venice, in 1700, was no less an operatic centre than a forcing ground for violinists. When Domenico Scarlatti arrived there to study opera in 1708 he went to his father's erstwhile rival, Gasparini, a pupil of Corelli and head of one of the four big music schools for orphan girls, the Ospedale della Pietà: There, however, he also found Vivaldi (as violin teacher), and another visitor—Handel. In this year 1708, Venice harboured for a very short time Italy's last two great instrumental composers and the first of the international German line which was to oust even the Italian opera! Scarlatti and Handel went off together to Rome and Naples before the end of the year, while Vivaldi was constantly coming and going as befitted a great violinist. Each ended his days away from his homeland, and each adopted country went far towards naturalizing its settlers: Scarlatti died in Madrid, Handel in London, and Vivaldi in Vienna.

Spain: 1648 – 1706

Domenico Scarlatti's Madrid (from 1729-1757) had once been a centre of keyboard music. You have already read of the Spanish influence on the technique of earlier Romans like Frescobaldi; now Scarlatti amply repaid this loan of technique in more than 500 keyboard sonatas, most of them written during the last fifteen years of his life. Many were called 'Exercises' and they may have begun as lesson-pieces for his pupil, the Princess of Asturias. Scarlatti's sonatas make a curious dent in the line of German-speaking composers of keyboard music. As in England, Spain had a promising school of organists in the sixteenth century headed by Cabezón, but neither country developed its keyboard music in the seventeenth, and the Italian Scarlatti is an isolated figure in eighteenth-century Spanish harpsichord music. In his day, Scarlatti's music was almost unknown outside Spanish court circles—yet some present-day critics hear echoes of his sonatas even in Mendelssohn's *Songs without Words* and the piano pieces of Liszt. Whether living for years in Spain really affected Scarlatti is difficult to tell—who can say just which traits are 'English' in a naturalized Englishman?—but certainly the old string 'division' figures, the large leaps which need crossed hands on the piano but which are easy and effective on the guitar, and the emphasis on a major-minor contrast with the same keynote give some of Scarlatti's Italian dance-forms a Spanish step or two. By 1713 the Spanish Empire in Europe had crumbled away and although the Two Sicilies reverted to the Spanish Bourbon house in 1735, the Jesuit-ridden country retired from continental progress and no follower of Scarlatti arose save his pupil Soler. In the royal monastery Soler took over the teaching of the Royal family and wrote a great deal for them, chiefly—like his master—sonatas.

England: 1648 – 1756

Handel's London (1720–1759) had an international culture but until the open quarrel with France in 1689, English culture (at least as far as its music was concerned) had survived the Civil Wars and even produced a native composer to rank with the world. 'Honest' John Playford, bookseller and publisher during the Commonwealth, printed airs by such men as Lawes and Wilson to the words of Shakespeare and Herrick (in 1653) and began a long line of editions of *The English Dancing Master* which house a vast collection of English tunes for country dancing. Lawes had written music for Milton's *Comus* at Ludlow Castle in 1634 which approached an operatic setting, and Locke's *Cupid and Death* has the arioso declamation and dances of Italian opera already highly developed, with a masque in the French manner at the end. The Jacobean string suites also found a champion in Locke, who kept the English polyphonic fancy alive. After the Restoration, naturally, French and Italian ideas poured into the country, but one man, only a baby when the King enjoyed his own again, lived his short life long enough to keep the English idiom alive: Purcell.

Purcell was educated in the re-founded Chapel Royal, went to work as a copyist when his voice broke and was appointed organist of Westminster Abbey in 1679. It seemed that he had only to collect a copy of someone else's music, new or old, and he immediately became master of the other's language and absorbed it in his own musical speech. His two teachers, Humfrey and Blow, had made him 'bi-lingual' to begin with, for whereas Humfrey had been sent abroad and had presumably learnt the new French and Italian styles, Blow had never been out of England. Purcell, however, was an individual genius: archaic fantasies and even old plainsong variations called In Nomines, full anthems and verse anthems after the style of Tomkins, Lawes and Locke, all came as easily to him as solo songs, duets and catches in the French style, and just as easily he stamped them all with his own name. Over forty Restoration plays had songs by Henry Purcell and after the break with France in 1689 he provided five 'musicals' including Shakespeare's *Midsummer Night's Dream* adapted as *The Fairy Queen*.

One specifically English style which Purcell extended was the 'Ode', a sort of joyful verse-anthem with full band to welcome Royalty to a feast, a birthday, or a marriage or simply as a welcome home after a week or two in the country. Here French overtures, Italian arioso and duet and English verse-anthem chorus made a musically brilliant affair of poetically dim material. Three fine odes were also written to celebrate the patron saint of music on St. Cecilia's Day.

Purcell's importance to the future of English music is greatest in the opera *Dido and Aeneas* and in his songs. *Dido* was written (like so much Venetian music) for a girls' school and first performed in 1689, a year after the first French grand opera had been seen in London and the year in which many Italians had left

England upon the coronation of the Protestant William and Mary. It is partially French in style but many features are faithfully Italian and English. All three long airs are built on ground basses (the last, 'Dido's Lament' slides chromatically down in a way which had been practically an unwritten law for Italian opera laments since Cavalli). The choruses are usually in block harmony with some fugal entries, and on the whole resemble the canzonets and airs of the earlier English type; the recitative and arioso is very emotional and more chromatic than most Italians would normally have preferred. This experiment with dissonance characterizes above all his twenty-two trio-sonatas for violins, bass viol and continuo which are at times almost bizarre in their effects: like many young composers searching for new sounds, Purcell has his successes and failures in these sonatas but they are for the most part far more interesting than the Italian models he said he used.

Purcell died while the war with France was still bitter. After three years' peace in which no one yet wanted anything French came the other war, this time over the Netherlands. By the time peace was made at Utrecht in 1713, Handel was already in London and wrote the ceremonial *Te Deum*.

Handel (1685-1759) first brought Saxony to the notice of the musical world, for he was born at Halle (now in East Germany). By the age of eleven he had begun to learn organ, harpsichord, violin, oboe, harmony and counterpoint; at eighteen, he had finished reading Law in the University and he could speak German (his native tongue), French (the polite way of writing to someone) and Italian (for talking to musicians); so he entered the opera house at Hamburg . . . in the orchestra pit as a violinist. Within two years he had his first opera produced and he had an introduction to the Medici family in Florence. For four years he travelled in Italy (where you have already met him with Scarlatti and Vivaldi) and knew everyone who was anyone. In 1710 he first saw London and by 1712 he had come to stay, especially as his old patron became George I of England in 1714. Six years later he was ready to storm London with his Italian opera: he had Italian singers like Senesino (see illustration p. 270), an Italian band headed by Castrucci, and his own genius. For twenty-one years (1720–41) London had Handel operas every year. As any public stage figure must be, Handel was involved in scenes between actors and actresses, backstage plots between his and others' supporters, and personal rivalry; in his case, prima donnas, the King and the Prince of Wales fought over his music, but the public loved it and his friends were the 'top people'. He was as at home in a country house, or taking the waters at Tunbridge Wells, as in his London house with his German cook and copyists, for English was now his adopted language. His statue stood in the Vauxhall Pleasure Gardens and but for illness he must surely have been the happiest composer of all time. The last twenty-two years were spent struggling against paralysis and eventually blindness.

Yet it was in this last score of years that he wrote the oratorios by which millions of English musicians have known and know his music: *Saul*, *Israel in Egypt*, *Judas Maccabeus* and *Messiah* are amongst them. These are 'English' works, for no other country has produced their like and Handel himself acknowledged, in his earlier 'Chandos' anthems, his debt to Blow, Purcell and the line of English choral music. As you have read, audiences needed relief from the solemn oratorio and Handel used to put in organ concertos to amuse them. He had previously written nearly a score of Italian concertos contrasting groups of instruments with a full band and various other orchestral 'concertos' which were only short pieces to include in suites like the *Water* and *Fireworks* music, but with the long oratorios came the solo organ concertos which Handel used to play himself. Most of them require no pedals and could well still be used by school orchestras with piano.

These oratorios and virtuoso keyboard concertos were the mature Handel and it seemed that no other forms interested him in the last twenty years of his life. His considerable output of harpsichord music (pieces called variously Lessons, Fugues, Partita, Sonata and Sonatinas, and arrangements of his other music), sonatas, trio sonatas (for various instruments, not always violins), Italian cantatas, English, French and German songs was complete by 1739. After that date only special occasions brought forth any work other than oratorios with keyboard concertos. Two choral pieces for the victory at Dettingen, a Hornpipe for Vauxhall Gardens, a suite for the Royal Fireworks, an anthem for his charity the Foundling Hospital, odd pieces for visiting artists to play or sing, and three hymns to words by the new evangelist Charles Wesley reflect the life of the ailing but still fashionable and kindly George Frederic Handel. Never, before or since, has a naturalized Englishman received such honour during and after his lifetime: at his funeral in Westminster Abbey, the three great choirs of London sang; in 1784, over 500 professional musicians in the same Abbey sang a concert to his memory, the first of many monster Handel Festivals; and to this day, at every *Messiah*, audiences stand for the 'Hallelujah' chorus just as George II had done at its first London performance.

This is surely the best known congregational 'Hallelu' of all time.

France: 1648 – 1756

Handel, a naturalized Englishman, had conquered his adopted land with Italian music, but the English choral tradition gave that Italian music a new look. Lully, a naturalized Frenchman, also won the day for Italian music but, in Paris, the French dancing tradition transformed the musical scene.

Lully was born in Florence but he could hardly have known a great deal about the new Italian style when he was brought to France, for he was then only about eleven years old. His wonderful violin playing, however, got him a job four years later in the King's band, 'The Twenty-four Violins', and he became such a favourite with Louis XV that when a new band 'The Little Violins' was formed, Lully was appointed its trainer. He was not, however, brilliant at the keyboard, so to his Italian training on the violin he added French training on the harpsichord. Ever since 1620 France had been, above all, the country for lute and harpsichord music, and the three musicians Denis Gaultier,

Chambonnières and Louis Couperin (the Elder) were at the height of their powers in the late 1650s. From their music Lully learnt the elegant and formal style of French dance music and song. Ten years after the Peace of Westphalia (1648), Louis's sumptuous court ballets were the envy of Europe and Lully provided the music. The first Italian opera—one of Cavalli's—was performed in Paris in 1660 but the French wanted their own divertissements added. Lully provided them.

For the next decade Lully continued to write ballets and although he was the darling of the court he was popular mostly as a dancer and wit. By 1672 he had found a librettist to produce words for him, and within the next fourteen years the team of Lully and Quinault put on twenty operas and became as linked in the public's mind as Gilbert and Sullivan or Rodgers and Hammerstein are today. The operas faithfully reflected Lully's bilingual upbringing. The airs were modelled closely on Cavalli and he quickened up the stately French dancing songs, putting women on the stage to perform them. But neither Lully nor his French public would stomach recitative secco and he always accompanied the narrative in arioso fashion—the choruses and dances ensured that the arioso should not become as monotonous as in much early Italian opera. Everything was consummately poised and in good taste; nothing was unduly emotional or harshly dissonant. In England Purcell could rend the heart with his experiments with discord, but in France Lully stood by his own well-established conventions. As long as he could please the King and so buy privilege and position, Lully was happy. At his death he left four houses in the most fashionable Parisian districts and a considerable fortune.

Lully's rule over French opera was as great as Handel's in England half a century later, and he became as much a monument to future generations in Paris. Right up to the French Revolution, serious opera to any Parisian meant either Lully or his ultimate French successor Rameau though, to tell the truth, by 1756 many people yawned and laughed in the wrong places: they went only for the dancing and the spectacular sets. Nowadays, Lully is remembered most for his incidental music to Molière's plays, particularly *Le Bourgeois Gentilhomme*, and Rameau's best opera *Les Indes Galantes* sometimes turns up in the repertory of the Paris Opera for its scenic display.

François Couperin (1668-1733) was nineteen when Lully died. A member of the famous family, at the age of eleven he had inherited his father's job as organist of a fashionable parish church but he did not take up the duties until he was seventeen. In the meantime, another musician ten years his senior, who had fallen foul of Lully—Lalande—took his place. After Lully's death in 1681 his duties were shared out. Lalande (1657–1726) now had his opportunity and in forty-five years' service at the court wrote various ballets, 'Music for the King's suppers', and motets for the Royal Chapel. Opera became the chief occupation first of Campra then of Rameau. Couperin was appointed first as an organist and then as harpsichord teacher to the Royal family. Soon Couperin's name became a household word outside as well as inside Versailles. Knighted in 1696 he lived in great style in Paris, conversing and corresponding with most of the eminent musicians of his day. Some of his works are lost but he will always find a place in history books for his hundreds of pieces of harpsichord music.

Couperin's pieces were arranged in Ordres (or suites), each in a single key and were published between 1713 and 1730, in four large volumes. In them you will find all the standard dances, as well as more airs with charming titles not unlike those which composers still use in teaching pieces: *The Bees*, *The Enchantress*, *The Nightingale in love*, *Sweet Nothings* and even *Happy Thoughts*! The decorations in all the pieces are most carefully indicated and in his book on harpsichord-playing, Couperin says a good deal about how to play them; he gives us a very good survey of what all French music must have been like in the eighteenth century and, by saying how the French differ from Italian performers, how we should play other music of the period. This book and a later treatise by C. P. E. Bach reveal the keyboard styles of their age almost as well as if they had put the sounds on to records. Geminiani and Leopold Mozart did the same for the violin, and Quantz (1697–1773) for the flute. When Couperin was writing, the lute had had its day, even in France, but his suites transferred many of its happiest inventions to the harpsichord and gave them new life.

Austria and Germany: 1648 – 1756

The Venetian companion of Handel and Scarlatti, Vivaldi (1675–1741) died in the third capital of eighteenth-century music, Vienna. There, and all over Europe, his concertos—not only for the violin but for bassoon, flute, oboe, viola d'amore—transformed the sound of instrumental music between 1700 and 1750 more than any other collection of works by a single composer. One sphere of Vivaldi's influence was in Saxony, where J. S. Bach arranged no less than nine of his violin concertos for one to four harpsichords and one of his pupils was solo violinist at the Saxon court. But no Saxon wanted only to imitate Italian music, for Germany had a flourishing instrumental style of its own. One man brought the two styles together, and brought in the French style to point the way to the common ground of the late eighteenth-century sonata, symphony and concerto: Johann Sebastian Bach.

The Saxon family of Bachs had been musicians for well over a century before Johann Sebastian's birth, and music continued to run in the family until the death of his grandchild, W. F. E. Bach, in 1845. Johann Sebastian's career contrasts remarkably with that of his fellow-Saxon, Handel. At the age of ten, like any other intelligent schoolboy, he knew his Catechism and Psalter and a little Latin; from eleven to fifteen he studied Latin, Greek, History and Geography; as a choirboy he learned to read music; his elder brother (J. J. Bach, who settled in Sweden) taught him to play the clavichord and harpsichord in his spare time; and he copied all the keyboard works he could lay his hands on. In 1700, still as a choirboy, he was sent north to Lüneburg, near Hanover. There he became a reasonable violinist, practised hardest at the organ, and started to write his first keyboard pieces. True to the

tradition of Sweelinck and the 'S' composers, these were variations on chorales and chorale-preludes, for not far away was the
stronghold of German Protestantism, Hamburg. Equally near
though, at Celle, was an orchestra and court musicians almost
entirely made up of Frenchmen. When Handel joined the
Hamburg Opera orchestra as a violinist in 1703, Bach was on his
way back to work in Saxony also as a violinist, in the court band
at Weimar. Later in the same year he moved to Arnstadt as a
church organist, but the few months at Weimar had given him
first-hand knowledge of Italian instrumental music. German
organ preludes, French keyboard airs and Italian string trios had,
by 1705, become second-nature to him, and his years as a choirboy meant that German chorales, motets and cantatas in the style
of Schütz were also part of his nature. One more visit to a
reigning musician completed his education at outside hands:
in 1705 he journeyed further north than ever before, to hear the
celebrated Danish organist Buxtehude at Lübeck, and perhaps in
the hope of succeeding him.

Buxtehude had succeeded Tunder (see page 143) and so
inherited the north German technique of the chorale-prelude for
organ, but he became famous for breaking away from the
chorale foundation and writing truly 'free' works for organ and,
above all, instruments. His cantatas for the five Sundays before
Christmas also became things which no aspiring composer would
want to miss. So Bach became up-to-date in the German
cantata.

With all these qualifications, Bach should have been ideally
suited to running the music at a wealthy court or, if he wanted to
concentrate solely on church music, at a wealthy town church.
First he went to the Saxon court at Weimar as a kind of second-
in-command of the music: he had already discovered that he had
not the gifts of a brilliant choir-trainer and the Weimar post
saved him from having to deal directly with choir discipline.
Perhaps because he found it hard to keep discipline, he was not
promoted to Kapellmeister when his senior died and he had to
find a 'Reformed' court (where there was no big choir) before he

was finally in charge of all music for the Prince. The court where
he succeeded was in the small capital of Cöthen and he stayed
there from 1717 to 1723, providing occasional cantatas and
almost continual chamber music. In these Calvinistic surround-
ings musicians first played the Bach violin concertos, the unaccompanied violin and 'cello sonatas, the French suites and the
first book of the 'Forty Eight' Preludes and Fugues for keyboard,
and the six Brandenburg Concertos. No organ pieces seem to
have been written at Cöthen, and he must even have put the
Orgelbüchlein collection of chorale preludes on one side while he
was there, though it is hard to believe that such a fine organist
would not have exercised his pen on a little organ music during
the six years. Whether this is true or not, we assume that Bach's
life as a composer divided neatly into the 'organ' period at
Weimar; the 'instrumental' period at Cöthen; and a third,
'choral', period at Leipzig.

At Cöthen, Bach was fully occupied with daily duties for his
employer, but he found time to put together a set of six concertos
to find favour with another eminent patron, the Marquis of
Brandenburg in Prussia. These 'Brandenburg' Concertos show
superbly how Bach found completely new ways (for a German)
of combining instruments. He knew something of the Italian
style, but his own musical nature was based on organ stops and
keys when it came to orchestration. How well he succeeded we
can fortunately still hear in concert programmes today, though
new theories about the range and quality of the instruments
Bach wanted may yet uncover even clearer evidence. The last
work he wrote at Cöthen was a 'test-piece' for the post of Cantor
at St. Thomas's, the historic choir-school in Leipzig.

The Leipzig authorities, true to German tradition, demanded a
setting of the Passion and gave Bach ten weeks in which to write
it. After six years of secular work, the old ambition welled up in
the devout organist. For years he had dreamed of setting the
Passion and he had almost decided on his libretto in detail;
well within the ten weeks, the St. John Passion was down on
paper. Yet even this inspired piece was not enough for the

Council of St. Thomas's: only when they had failed to get Telemann (the renowned organist and director of music at Hamburg), and the court organist from the fashionable and glittering chapel at Darmstadt had also refused to move, did they offer the position to Bach. Grateful though musicians today may be that Bach was appointed, the city fathers of Leipzig had cause to wonder about their mixed blessing of a genius for twenty-five years and more. Quarrels and controversy surrounded the new cantor, who was still (by decree) honorary Kapellmeister of Cöthen. With the best intentions but little administrative skill, Bach sought to bring together all the finest players and singers in his school, the town and the University to form a body which would perform music to the glory of the Lord such as had never been heard before. But the town, gown and surplice did not care for change, and preferred the school to go on as it always had before.

St. Thomas's School had its old traditions and they were housed in old buildings under an old rector. Hardly an alluring prospect for a famous organist nearing the age of forty! Still, he had two choirs to write for, his pay was augmented by wedding and funeral fees, living was rent-free and he had status in the town. Slowly he trained boys (privately on the violin, in class for singing) until they could perform the sort of music which takes choirs weeks to learn today, but after ten years even Bach was no longer able to keep up his enthusiasm. Those ten years gave us the Magnificat, the motets *Be not afraid* and *Jesu, priceless treasure*, the big Psalm settings, the St. Matthew Passion, and the B minor Mass; if we add to this work the direction of nearly 1,500 cantata performances, it is small wonder that he was tired. By 1735 Bach needed a practical and spiritual refuge and he found it in the 'chorale' cantatas, the short Lutheran Masses and his beloved organ preludes. In the last fifteen years of his life, he withdrew from as much practical work as he could and became almost mystically immersed in the arts of counterpoint and fugue. The second volume of the 'Forty-Eight' and the Goldberg Variations for keyboard, the instrumental *Musical*

Offering (for Frederick the Great) and the last three works (all fugues) for organ retrace the three 'periods' of Bach's work. Finally, and fittingly, the work he left unfinished was called simple 'The Art of Fugue'.

After his death the life and work of J. S. Bach was soon forgotten. In those days, as for many centuries before, contemporary music and musicians were all important. The old masters were seldom revered by their sons and Bach was no exception. His sons in the family and his 'sons' in the musical world revered the memory of his playing but not of his work. After all, his music had not even been fashionable or 'contemporary' when he wrote it. What had fugues and old-style variations to do with the opera, the concerto or the symphony? Even the manuscripts of the orchestral suites and the Brandenburg Concertos, which could have taught Bach's successors a good deal, were tucked away and forgotten about, for they were 'occasional' pieces and the occasion itself had passed.

Italians ruled German musical fashion before 1756, except at Hamburg. There Keiser (1674–1739) wrote scores of German operas which kept the Hamburg Opera going for most of its sixty years' life; there, too, Telemann (1681–1767) wrote out more compositions than even he himself could count, and Mattheson (1681–1764) began the first musical magazine in Europe. Mattheson's book *The Complete Musical Director*, Rameau's *Textbook of Harmony* and the books on playing by Couperin, Quantz and C. P. E. Bach will give any reader today all he needs to follow the history of sounds in music from J. S. Bach's day to the break-up of harmony in the late nineteenth century.

CHAPTER ELEVEN

THE SOURCES:

1756—1815

The European Scene

Frederick the Great invaded Saxony in 1756 and brought about the Seven Years' War. Some Saxon musicians, such as Hasse in Dresden, found themselves in the middle of the battle between France and Prussia and fled south to Vienna; others, like C. P. E. Bach, already worked for the Emperor in Berlin. French musical manners had become very frivolous but Paris, the centre of fashion, continued to attract many of the best composers from Italy, Austria and Germany up to the Revolution (1789). London and Dublin were also on the circuit of international virtuosos until the Napoleonic Wars thrust all the arts into the background. When music began to emerge again after Napoleon's downfall, the revolutionary ideas (which had seized people far more than the personality of the French dictator) remained to affect many composers in the nineteenth century.

Berlin

The court of Frederick the Great has attracted too much attention in musical history, partly because of the romantic picture of the flute-loving Emperor playing chamber music with his servants and teachers, and partly because of the descriptions of the fabulous new Opera-House which was opened in 1742. In fact, however, Frederick's musical tastes were restricted and his two favourite composers, Quantz (who wrote his chamber music) and Graun (who wrote his operas) are far less important to the study of musical history than the comparatively humble court harpsichordist, Carl Philipp Emanuel Bach (1714–1788), second son of J. S. Bach.

Appointed to Potsdam (the palace suburb of Berlin) in 1740, he soon tired of its claustrophobic atmosphere, and by 1750 he was desperate to get away. But he was too good an accompanist to lose . . . and his wife was a Prussian subject; Frederick refused to let him go and only by pleading ill-health after twenty-seven years' service did Carl Philipp manage to reverse Frederick's decison. In 1767 he moved to Hamburg to succeed Telemann as musical director to the city, but by then the great glories of the Hamburg opera and North German music were faded; as he said himself, he arrived fifty years too late. Yet there he remained for twenty-one years, receiving visits from most of the younger generation. He did not care for counterpoint, and thought his father a dry composer; for Carl Philipp, straightforward, easily recognizable harmony should support a beautifully-balanced set of phrases which added up to a pretty tune. C. P. E. Bach's sonatas, symphonies and keyboard concertos went far towards the new German instrumental style, which drew together the best in older Italian, French and German music. No less a composer than Mozart said of Carl Philipp, 'He is the father of us all, and we are his children'. By the time of C. P. E. Bach's death (1788) the symphony could stand beside opera as a long art-form of its own, but by then it had moved from its North German birthplace southwards, first to Mannheim then to Vienna.

Prague, Mannheim, Vienna and Paris

Johann Stamitz, the eldest of a large family of musicians, moved to Mannheim from Prague in 1741. There he worked very much along the same lines as C. P. E. Bach, counting harmony more important than counterpoint, but emphasizing the need for contrasting melodies (especially in Long form) and dramatic dynamics more than his contemporaries. His orchestra was famous throughout Europe for its disciplined playing and increased its reputation under his successors, Cannabich and Toeschi, though his compositions—novel in their day—had been turned into a formula by the 1760s. Stamitz, of course, visited Paris (1754–1755) and added his Bohemian symphonic recipes to the bowl of fashion, which already contained ingredients from Italy, Austria and North Germany. The final mixture, however, came from Vienna, with the later symphonies of Haydn and Mozart.

Vienna was the city of the symphony by the end of the Seven Years' War (1763) and it remained the capital right up to 1914, from Haydn and Mozart through the days of Beethoven, Brahms and Bruckner to Mahler. The court of the Austrian Emperors held innumerable concerts and no virtuoso could fail to earn a living in Vienna; but a composer had to keep to the customs of his day and it was not so easy to experiment. Some princes, however, had large country estates and there a resident composer might skilfully carry his patron's appreciation along with his own taste. These patrons became as well-known as the Italian philanthropists of the Renaissance and Austro-Hungary found its 'Medici' family in the Esterhazy line.

Haydn (1732–1809) joined the family of Esterhazy in 1761 and served it continually until 1790. The usual training in violin and harpsichord, combined with a choir-school education in the cathedral choir of St. Stephen's, fitted Haydn for a household appointment at an early age, but the noble families preferred their musicians to have a reputation before they employed them. So the young man had to earn that reputation. He started to earn his living as a street musician, playing in and writing music for the various bands who were constantly busy at 'serenading parties' with opera excerpts and dance music. For eight years, too, he went round the city giving music lessons to children in their own homes (as so many worthy teachers did in England not so long ago). Neither of these occupations was good training for a virtuoso and Haydn became much more interested in composition, playing and studying the 'modern' C. P. E. Bach as a composer will, to give himself new ideas. His teaching did, however, bring him useful contacts. Among these were Metastasio, the court poet and king of opera librettists, whose adopted

children were Haydn's pupils; and the Neapolitan teacher of
operatic singing, Porpora, who also taught the same little girls.
With Porpora, Haydn appeared in a few exalted circles as
accompanist, met more of the musical *élite*, and slowly built up
his reputation as a performer as well as a teacher. Pieces which he
had written for his pupils were also becoming widely known. At
last, in 1759 he landed his first household job as director of music
to Count Morzin, only to see his orchestra disbanded within
two years when his patron had to economize. Fortunately for the
young director, Prince Paul Esterhazy remembered the excellence
of the Morzin band and immediately offered him a contract as
assistant to his aged director.

The Hungarian house of Esterhazy had their castle at Eisenstadt, and the Prince divided his time between this country town
in the hills and the glittering round of Viennese life. Haydn's
contract made him responsible for writing and rehearsing any
music which the Prince commanded, for the welfare and discipline of all the musicians in the Prince's employment, and for
the upkeep of all music and instruments. For 400 florins a year
the middle-aged prince had bought himself a new servant, who
was to hand the family name down to more generations than any
member of the family was to know.

Less than a year after he had appointed Haydn, Prince Paul
died and was succeeded by his brother, Nicolas, a discriminating
listener who played the baryton (an odd cross between a guitar
and a big viola da gamba). For the first few years of Nicolas's
patronage, Haydn was worried by family affairs and the Prince
was not too pleased. The turning point in their relationship came
in 1766, when the Hungarian's version of Versailles was ready—
the palace of Esterhaz, resplendent in the middle of a marsh, well
situated for duck-shooting—and Haydn succeeded to the
directorship. Haydn quartets had already been published in
Paris and Amsterdam; he had written over thirty symphonies;
his collection of Masses and operas had steadily grown; and he
had passed his half-century of piano sonatas. The new director
of music was, however, by his own admission, not a quick

writer and with full command over the Prince's musical establishment, he had little enough time for all he had to do. The
household went less and less to Vienna as years went by and
Haydn was always too busy with the domestic music at Esterhaz
to see or hear much of the world outside. Every other year he
produced a new opera—including a comedy *The World of, the
Moon* which has been revived recently—for the estate Carnival;
he composed dozens of symphonies and sonatas for the evening
concerts, quartets, piano trios and divertimenti to amuse the family
and their guests; and for nearly twenty years he developed entirely
at the hands of his own genius and his faith in God's gifts to him.

From 1784 to 1785 the Esterhaz establishment spent more time
than usual in Vienna and Haydn, to his surprise, found that he
was famous there. Players who had left Esterhazy had taken his
training with them . . . often copies of the scores of his works as
well. Through their travels, 'Father' Haydn (as they all knew him)
was known in England, France, Holland and Spain. He had, of
course, met most of the famous Viennese musicians on his
fleeting visits before, but in these two years he had time to make
real friends, amongst them Mozart.

Mozart (1756–1791) had been settled in Vienna as a virtuoso
of the keyboard for four years, with an astonishing career as a
child prodigy and a heart-breaking period of service in the
household of the Archbishop of Salzburg behind him. With his
father he had left Salzburg, his birth-place, to tour the nearest
musical cities which it was safe to visit during the Seven Years'
War, when he was only six years old. The following year (1763),
after the war ended, father and son went further afield: to his
conquest of Munich, Linz and Vienna, the boy added Paris,
London and Amsterdam. Not only did his playing astound and
delight the connoisseurs but in each place he presented to the
court a group of violin sonatas which he had composed himself.
In London, aged nine, the public even paid half-a-crown daily
from noon till three in the afternoon to see and hear him.
Wherever he went he made friends, and one who meant a lot to
him in later life was J. C. Bach, in London.

Johann Christian Bach had spent six years working with his elder brother Carl Philipp in Berlin, but afterwards went to the wise professor of Bologna, called 'Father' Martini, and when Mozart knew him he was in charge of Italian opera at Handel's old theatre, the King's in Haymarket. So, in 1770, Mozart went to Italy for Martini's approval and within two years was writing only music in the Italian fashion. Two other significant visits remained: to Vienna in 1773, where Gluck reigned at the Opera with his mixture of French and Italian styles; and to Mannheim in 1777. These two visits, perhaps more than anything else, guided Mozart's operatic and symphonic imagination until he became friends with the Austrian 'Father' Haydn, in 1784.

Haydn and Mozart had first met three years earlier, when Mozart was beginning to earn a precarious living in Vienna as a keyboard virtuoso and opera composer, but as Haydn had to be away so much in Esterhaz and Mozart had, on the average, four concerts a week, they had little chance of seeing each other frequently. The two years 1784 and 1785 meant a great deal to the two composers as friends and as musicians. They were both married, Haydn to a shrew and Mozart to a spendthrift; Haydn had no children but was always 'adopting' them and the Mozarts had a new-born son. Mozart had known continental admiration but was then, in Vienna, valued only for his stunning virtuosity in his own piano concertos; Haydn had never toured at all and was no great virtuoso, but his symphonies and, particularly, his string quartets were then admired all over the continent. Mozart had one great advantage over Haydn in their friendship: he knew the other's music before they met. For both composers, the years after their time together in Vienna show an extraordinary change in their fortunes. Mozart's first Italian comic opera *The Marriage of Figaro* was given in Vienna in 1786, and Haydn's first 'commissioned' symphonies for a foreign city were played in Paris in the same year.

Opera had travelled like a shuttlecock between Vienna and Paris in the person of Gluck (1714–1787), a Czech brought up on the Italian operas of Hasse in Prague and Vienna. He had conducted in all the best opera houses of Europe during the first half of the century, and been knighted by the Pope in the year Mozart was born. This extraordinary figure was to play Caccini to Mozart's Monteverdi. In seventeenth-century Florence Caccini had fought for an intellectual ideal in opera which was only fully realized by Monteverdi's music in Venice; in eighteenth-century Paris Gluck fought for similar ideals, only to be eclipsed by their fulfilment in Mozart's *Figaro* in Vienna and—in the year of Gluck's death—*Don Giovanni* in Prague. The ideals of all four composers were roughly the same: painters, poets and musicians should combine in exactly equal parts to produce a whole. But the details had changed in the 150-odd years between Monteverdi's *Orfeo* and Gluck's *Orpheus*. By 1762 Gluck had shown that accompanied recitative (French-style) was to supersede the *secco* Italian recitative; choruses should be properly catered for in the plot; and the overture should be part of the opera, warning the audience in music of what they would later see in the sets and hear in the words. So much for the detailed differences. The rest of Gluck's ideas were reactions to such abuses of the 1607 standard as the singers' extravagances which ruined the text, and pointless ritornelli and da capos which destroyed the sense. Dances remained (Gluck was writing for Paris, where—action or no action—ballet was sacred to opera) and the other accepted convention—the male soprano—still played the main part. When *Orpheus* was performed in Vienna even the castrato was dropped in favour of a tenor. A quarter of a century later Mozart completed the reform by adding a modern rather than a classical plot and by writing the exquisite music of *Figaro* and *Don Giovanni*.

The Italian trio-sonata and overture, C. P. E. Bach's keyboard sonatas and the Mannheim symphonists provided the form of the classical symphony to which Haydn was born: three movements ending with a dance. By 1765 Haydn had begun to use four movements always, but Mozart wrote his first symphony in London in the same year in the old Italian style of his friend J. C. Bach. By 1773 Mozart had 'caught up' with Haydn's style and

when the two finally met the older man found much to learn
from his more brilliant—and subtler—young friend. Nowhere
is this more obvious than in Haydn's 'Paris' symphonies of 1786:
his old fondness for contrapuntal devices and rumbustious
rhythms is replaced by a new preoccupation with changing keys
(a harmonic rather than polyphonic exercise) and a vitality in
rhythm which is much more controlled; and his whole approach
to the use of dynamic contrast is restrained, so that any sharp
change from say, soft to loud is exciting without being bizarre
or shocking.

Mozart's music was a refiner's fire to Haydn, but it had itself
undergone many refinements. The first striking change came with
his first symphony in a minor key, written in the year that he first
heard Haydn quartets (1773), when he broke away from the
Italian overture type; the next four years show him using every
musical *cliché* of his century but always with an unmistakable
Mozartian pronunciation which somehow makes each a *bon
mot*. You may recognize a formula immediately, but you can
never be sure how Mozart is going to end it. The last refinements
began in 1782 with the *Haffner* symphony: the first movement
takes a tune which Haydn would have loved and uses *only* that
tune, in so many effortless ways that the old polyphonic form is
transformed beyond anything the Esterhazys would have dared
to expect from their musical director. The 'serenading song' of
the slow movement and the simple minuet and trio have tunes
which would have been undistinguished in any hands other than
Mozart's, but are actually embroidered in pure musical gold;
and the Finale is a brilliant piece of comic-opera writing almost
as good as the *Figaro* overture. Symphonies played first in Linz
(1783) and Prague (1787) also reflect this growing mastery of
opera, which had its dramatic moments of tragedy as well as
farce. In his last symphonies Mozart composed three of the
masterpieces of music in one year, 1788. Over the years, writers
have exhausted all the possible adjectives to describe them and
their differences: here they can take only their pre-eminent place
in musical history.

After the symphonies of 1788, Mozart the virtuoso had but three years of touring left: to Dresden, Leipzig, Berlin, Mannheim, Munich, Prague and Vienna, names already on the roll of musical history. Two new works above all looked towards the future: the first—the fantasy of *The Magic Flute*—towards opera in this world; and the last—the unfinished Requiem Mass—to his own life in the next world. The writing of music was to Mozart a mechanical task. The ideas which were constantly pouring into his mind were always carefully sifted by his genius before he ever took up his pen and he would usually rather have gone dancing or played billiards than write, unless he needed money so badly that a commission was urgent. As a travelling keyboard virtuoso, he knew the value of leaving behind keyboard pieces for his audience to try to play while he was away—over a score of full concertos and of sonatas have survived—and as a dancer he was always ready with music for the latest fashions, whether minuets, French country dances or German dances heralding the waltz. Together with all these, his songs for prima donnas and showpieces for other virtuosos (such as the Clarinet Quintet), quartets, and chamber music for all sorts of the oddest combinations of instruments Mozart's fortune should have been guaranteed. But nearly all were for special occasions (and therefore no good to a publisher for general sale), or too 'modern' to be palatable, or simply 'pirated' by publishers who never paid a penny for them. He died, worn out, in 1791, and was buried in a pauper's grave.

Haydn began his travels as an international figure in the year Mozart died. Prince Nicolas Esterhazy, who died in 1790, had left him a reasonable pension; the new prince paid him a small salary as long as Haydn agreed to be called his *Kapellmeister*, and asked no more. Back in Vienna as a freelance—and famous—musician, offers flooded in: would he be Director to the Count X? The King of Y would like some duets and would Haydn join his court? Lord Z wished he would visit England and write something for . . . ? In the end, the astute London impresario Salomon tempted him with a promise of £1,200 for twenty concerts of new works, a new opera, and six symphonies. Georgian London in the days of Sheridan, Reynolds and Pitt was a flourishing society in which music was a commercial proposition as much as a patron's hobby. Haydn was a celebrity in the public concert halls and in the private drawing-rooms. For the 'Salomon Concerts' he composed (and conducted at the piano) his agreed six symphonies during 1791–2; his opera for London—yet another setting of the story of Orpheus in the Italian style—never reached the stage owing to some business wrangling and a royal feud; but he was a most welcome guest at the music parties of the highly successful musical historian and amateur organist, Dr. Charles Burney.

Burney knew everyone in Europe through his 'musical tours', to France and Italy in 1770, and to Belgium, Holland and Germany in 1772. His diaries of these tours will give you an enchanting picture of the social side of music to set beside the textbooks, the letters written by composers, and their printed music. In London, Burney was eager to help the eminent director from Esterhaz: through him Haydn first heard *Messiah* at one of the Handel Commemorations in Westminster Abbey and received an honorary doctorate of music at Oxford. Both events were important to him; for after his Oxford visit he had the *entrée* to the highest society even more easily than when he arrived, and after listening to *Messiah* he resolved to turn his mind to the peculiarly English Handelian oratorio, which resulted in *The Creation* (1796–8) and *The Seasons* (1798–1801).

Esterhazy required Haydn to re-join him at the coronation of Francis II of Austria as Emperor in 1792. War had just broken out between Austria and Revolutionary France, and to get to the ceremony at Frankfurt, Haydn had to go through the Netherlands to West Germany. At Bonn he was asked to see a local seventeen-year-old boy who was already a most original musician, the young Beethoven, and the acquaintance was renewed when Beethoven became his pupil and friend in Vienna. But Haydn, now in his sixties, was restless, and returned to London in 1794 with a further five symphonies for Salomon. As with Mozart, these last symphonies are still the most widely played of all; they include the 'Military', the 'Clock', the 'Drum Roll' and the last of all, the *pièce de résistance* of many a school orchestra today, the 'London'.

The war with the French was now going badly on land for the Austrians and worse at sea for Britain. The Salomon season for 1795 was cancelled and Haydn took his last leave of the country in August, burdened with a good many generous presents, including a talking parrot. Yet another Esterhazy prince—Haydn's fourth—was at the head of the house when he returned to Vienna: Nicholas II. His chief interest was in church music, so he preferred his choir to any instrumental combination; and he had no thought of using the palace at Esterhaz. So Haydn, as he had begun, divided the next ten years between Eisenstadt and Vienna, writing annual masses—among them the 'Imperial' and 'Teresa'—for performance in the Parish church on the Princess's birthday, two last groups of quartets (making over eighty in all) . . . and his two fine oratorios. In Leipzig, Breitkopf and Härtel published a printed collection of his works which took six years to complete and in far-away Edinburgh, a Scottish folk-song collector, Thomson, received a steady stream of Haydn's arrangements of Scottish, Irish and Welsh songs over the same period. By 1806, at seventy-four, Haydn's weakness approached senility and a younger man had taken over the Esterhaz work. Beethoven had succeeded to the work for Thomson, as the new leading light of Vienna who had already set down on paper his only opera, four symphonies, four piano concertos, the Violin Concerto and almost a score of piano sonatas (including the 'Moonlight', 'Waldstein' and 'Appassionata'). History marched cruelly past 'Father' Haydn. The second occupation of Vienna by the French finally brought on the end. Unharmed and even protected though he was by the enemy, events were too much for the patriotic old man: three times on his last day of life he played his own Austrian national anthem 'The Emperor's Hymn', each time more emotionally than the last. His body now lies in the parish church of Eisenstadt, where the visitor can read on the wall these simple words: 'Here lies a great man'.

In the same bombardment of Vienna which hastened Haydn's death, Beethoven was hard at work creating the 'Emperor' concerto in the cellar of a house only a few miles away. As with Mozart and Haydn, we can imagine a great deal about 'The Lion of Music' from his letters, for all three were devoted correspondents—Mozart to his sister Marianne, Haydn to his brother Michael, and Beethoven to his brother Johann. By this time, too, critics and scholars wrote biographies of fashionable composers in the form of extended obituaries within a short time of their deaths; many portraits were painted to tell us many different stories of their looks, while busts made from death masks give us an equally unreliable picture of their features; and the printers, with the collected works of Purcell, Handel, Haydn and Mozart already in type, were providing us with evidence of their genius in black and white, which—when we can sort out what has been added or taken out by editors—we can still study.

From all this it is clear that these were considered, above all, the master virtuosos before Beethoven. (Bach was virtually unremembered.) Handel, Haydn, Mozart and Bach were primarily concerned with writing for a specific public in court, church, opera, concert hall or drawing-room. Beethoven also had his patrons and dedicated much of his music to them, but he was principally concerned with writing *for himself* regardless of his music's reception. Here we reach the musical crossroads at which many audiences still lose their way. The road to Beethoven was covered by the composer and his audience together. Occasionally a composer might have moved slightly ahead of his audience— Caccini, Monteverdi, Mozart—but the listener usually caught up fairly quickly and could understand what was happening. But beyond the crossroads of Beethoven, understanding is difficult: follow him blindly, with faith which comes from heart and not mind, and the road leads to the open country of romantic music; stop, to decide rationally which road Beethoven was taking, and the music is so inconsistent that you will be most likely to turn back. You can seldom tell, by ear, what Beethoven is going to do next; you can only analyse the printed page and no amount of that is going to speak to the heart. He is the master composer and you must put your own signpost at the crossroads: it may read 'to Heaven' or 'to Chaos' according to your view of the music written after Beethoven.

By 1810 Napoleon ruled Europe, and not even the diplomats who planned the treaty at the Congress of Vienna could restore anything remotely like the number of countries that were on the map before his domination; Beethoven ruled musical Europe at the same time, and no patron—state or private person—has been able to put back the clock.

CHAPTER TWELVE

MASTER COMPOSERS

THE virtuoso instrumentalists and singers of the early eighteenth century demanded fairly straightforward music from their composers so that they could show off their skill in decorating the simple music; but virtuosos who were also composers could afford to write fewer skeletons like these and could do their decorating on paper as they went along. By the last decades of the century singers had little chance to improvise, for their scenas had as many fireworks in the written notes as they could manage, particularly in the 'presto' closing sections. Instrumentalists had such detailed parts in symphonies and concertos that the notes had to be played exactly as they were written. The sounds of music were now created by the composer single-handed; the performer became no more than a mechanic, serving the composer's reputation, not his own.

Range

The enormous compass of the virtuoso singer and the agility of most musical instruments had been exploited to the full by Mozart and his contemporaries. Beethoven and his successors took these for granted, and concentrated on exploring ways of making the whole range effective rather than the extremes. Opera sopranos still had a few extremely high coloratura arias which exploited the upper reaches, but during the nineteenth century it was the mezzo-soprano—the middle voice—and the tenor who declared their passions (often in duet) for all the world to hear. Most tenors could sing as low as most of our baritones can today. The real bass was kept for villainous or clownish parts until Russian opera composers came on the scene.

Mixed choirs settled down in the nineteenth century to a stock 'S.A.T.B.' pattern, though three-part male and female choruses remained popular in clubs and families. Opera choruses divided in the same way with a wider gap between the highest soprano and lowest bass notes.

Orchestral extremes were catered for in the more regular use of the piccolo, bass clarinet and double bassoon, but in general the nineteenth-century sound is a 'middle' one with violas, horns, cor anglais, and the mellow centre of the trombones' and cellos' compass providing the richness which we associate with Romantic music. The range of excitement in orchestral sound was also increased by adding exotic percussion instruments of all kinds: triangle, side drum and bass drum had appeared occasionally since Gluck first used them in his opera orchestra, but cymbals (modern and antique), gong, tambourine, castanets, the rattle and the anvil all made their débuts in the orchestra between 1790 and 1876.

The range of tonality which had evolved in the eighteenth century was so extended in the nineteenth that the old 'tonic-subdominant-dominant' key contrast often disappeared. You could follow the track of modulations between tunes in most of the earlier music, but when composers found ways of moving smoothly to the strangest 'away' keys one after another, you could not even remember—by ear—what the 'home' key was. Usually a composer before 1876 *did* return to the home key— after wandering through a dozen different keys—as a matter of form, but few members of his audience would have known (or cared) if he had ended in G flat a piece that started in C. The commonest way in which this wandering happened was called 'enharmonic change', which means changing a note's relationship to its key (the family to which it belongs) by calling it something else. The simplest enharmonic modulation worked like this: the note 'G' is the dominant (fifth note) in the key of C major but the leading note (seventh note) in the key of A flat major; so if you harmonize the note 'G' first as the dominant of C and then as the leading note of A flat you can change enharmonically from the key of C (no flats or sharps) to that of A flat (four flats). Sometimes the changing dominant might also have to be given a new letter-name to make it a leading note (E flat, as in example 29 here, being called 'D sharp'); and ultimately any note of a scale may change its name to become a leading note of a new scale. Here is the first phrase of our all-purpose tune, modulating enharmonically until it finally comes 'home' again to C major.

Example 30

To Schubert this type of modulation—to a key on the 'flat side' six notes higher—became a *cliché*; Berlioz continually flits from key to key by calling any note of the scale the leading note of something else; Mendelssohn and Brahms continued to think of modulation as from one 'set' key to another; Liszt and Wagner found less and less satisfaction in any set key. So the range of harmony stretched and stretched into experiments with new sets of keys in new orders of tones and semitones, that have led us to serial music . . . of which more, later.

Rhythm and Accent

The eighteenth century grouped all its beats into bars of two or three and their multiples. In terms of time signatures Mozart and Haydn used mostly: 2/4 3/4 4/4 6/8. Beethoven normally keeps to these, too, but later composers occasionally tried 5/4 and other irregular additions of three and two. From Beethoven onwards, more syncopation (dragging the beat) and many sudden strong accents (sforzando) were used to make music more dramatic. Notation, therefore, became more involved. The strong beat implied after a bar-line was still 'slipped', particularly in the music of Berlioz and Brahms, by deliberately phrasing across the barline. In general, though, this was not an inventive age in time or rhythm but rather a consolidating and probing of earlier customs: as they strengthened the middle registers of voices and instruments, so Romantic composers re-arranged the 'middle' times of 3/4 and 4/4, changing time within a piece, or varied the division of beats to increase the emotional tension.

Melody

Baroque composers tried to avoid highlighting particular figures in their music; the Romantics went from one highlight to another. Compare a group of figures by Delacroix with a group by, say, Watteau: each of Delacroix's figures is in a different spotlight: Watteau's figures are in different positions, each beautiful, but under the 'flood' lighting of a stage set with no spotlights. Each of Delacroix's figures could make a striking picture; Watteau's live only in relation to each other.

Musically these plays of light are conveyed in various ways. A line of a song may suddenly be emphasized by a dramatic change of key, dynamic or tempo; an unexpected dissonance in the harmony, left momentarily unresolved, will check the ear at that spot in the melody. These moments are just as effective in music as sudden splashes of an unlooked-for colour in a painting. The sung melodies of Schubert, Schumann, Mendelssohn, Brahms or Wagner are 'middle' melodies, governed by the mood of the words as the composer feels them, not necessarily by their poetic accent or metre: the highest note (the centre 'spot') is usually only used once; the other spotlights pick out now the accompaniment now the melody, so that sometimes the melody will fade into the background; the light may keep returning with increasing intensity to one particular figure in the tune; a sudden dramatic pause in the melody has the startling effect of a stage 'blackout'. Romantic melody has, in fact, a complete theatrical lighting plot.

Harmony may convey the composer's mood even better than melody, and many nineteenth-century melodies grew from the harmonic (and particularly the enharmonic) changes. Harmony had become the master both of words and melody, and so melodic ornament became scarce. Yet one of the old ornaments—the appoggiatura (= leaning note)—was truly overworked to screw up the tension in a Romantic melody. Such an ornament alone makes our old tune right up-to-date in the nineteenth-century. Play the melody of this example first on its own, then with the harmony (which is as simple in its chords as any Bach chorale). No German composer, setting the word 'Liebe', could ever resist the appoggiatura.

Example 31

Cadences

Appoggiaturas of this kind had started in the days of Bach and Handel in cadences and especially at the ends of recitative. There, the harpsichordist left them to the singer before he played his own perfect cadence. Mozart and Haydn often used them too, in keyboard pieces, but they usually 'prepared' them so that the appoggiatura was, in fact, a repetition. Nevertheless, their use in a cadence was always frankly emotional. Beethoven knew they were far too effective to keep only for cadences and would often use 'double' appoggiaturas (like that in the last example).

Perfect cadences provided a summary ending, often repeated many times, for most Romantic pieces. The archaic 'plagal' cadence without a leading note took on a new harmonic life in the form in which both examples 30 and 31 show it. Again, in cadences, you see the process of consolidating, of rearranging and strengthening old positions.

Cadenzas, the outcrop of eighteenth-century virtuosos' cadences, were kept short and to the point by Romantic composers from Beethoven onwards. Even in opera (and even in Italy) prima donnas had their wings of fancy clipped so that by 1870 or so, no composer need find himself listening to his own song 'arranged' by the singer or feel obliged, as Rossini did, to say to the singer of one of his own arias 'A very pretty song! Who wrote it?'

Harmony

It had taken a long time for musicians to think in terms of chords and not in lines of melody. Even when the old polyphonic counterpoint disintegrated you still thought of the tune and bass as two well-shaped melodic lines and filled in the gap between the two with harmony. When the bass stopped being continuous—and the *continuo* thus disappeared—you finally had to think in terms of a piece which progressed chordally. Mozart and Haydn knew this in their late works, and it was left to Beethoven and his successors to use their chordal vocabulary and, again, to consolidate it. But the re-arranging of chords, however familiar each individual chord may be, completely alters the sound of the music. Taken individually, the basic chords which Brahms used are only those which Mozart and Haydn knew, but their rearrangement and their frieze of appoggiaturas makes them seem much more complicated. In the figured terms which you met on page 113 the eighteenth century had only five 'common' chords

which they used, eventually, interchangeably. Taking 'C' as the
lowest note of each chord they were:

'Common' Chords: on 'C'

Chromatic Chords:

Neapolitan
Sixth

Augmented
Sixths

Diminished
Sevenths

Example 32

They were used within the framework of related keys and to them
you could add, under strict rule of ear, the five 'chromatic'
chords which you see above. Of these chromatic chords, the first
two belonged to a key and were always on the fourth and flat
sixth of that key respectively; the last three became common to
all keys by re-christening their components enharmonically.
The nineteenth century stripped these chromatic chords of their
last connection with the old counterpoint by *not* resolving as a
matter of course all notes which were discordant with the bass.
Appoggiaturas added to any of these chords did resolve but the
chords themselves became 'common' (plain) rather than 'chromatic' (coloured). Analysing like this, any wonderful effect of
Romantic harmony becomes on paper quite logical; the marvel
lies in the ears of men like Berlioz, Liszt and above all Wagner
who heard such harmony unwritten. They were not concerned
with its logic by cold analysis; they knew of its power to penetrate
men's hearts.

Forms

Musical history must nevertheless be written by analysis and, as far as form goes, Romantic music sets a nasty problem. We take refuge in words like 'through-composed' (meaning 'formless'), 'modified sonata form' (when the keys are wrong or the composer leaves out much that we would expect or adds an equal amount that we would not) or 'sonata-rondo' (when we cannot quite make up our minds on the balance). The form of Romantic music is like a dream: it is a passing show of incidents which are in perfect order as long as you are asleep but often hard to link up when you try to reconstruct the dream some time afterwards.

The only forms in eighteenth-century terms which allowed the composer to move where his fancy led him were the fantasy and the prelude, and these two words appeared on countless title pages throughout the 1800s. When a piece was purely descriptive, reflecting the eye of the composer as he picked out certain parts of a story or points in a landscape and tried to translate them into music, the name gave you a clue to follow in the notes. There was no argument to pursue, no central idea to track down in several disguises; such collections of pieces (usually for piano) were short and ephemeral; they gave intense but short-lived emotional satisfaction at their best and a purposeless delight at their weakest. But anyone giving full attention to a piece likes to know where he is from time to time, and longer pieces—even if they were frankly descriptive—often adopted the Aria form. As a composer you went back and had another look at the beginning of the book, or your eye went back to the first spot you noticed in the landscape and the music was duly repeated. Second time round, you may have taken a slightly different view but the image remained the same. Such were the Nocturnes of Chopin.

Songs were hardly ever in aria form, from Schubert onwards in the drawing-room, or after Mozart in the opera house. Long dramatic settings following the mood of the poem or the libretto were musically formless; short songs with several verses used the same music for each verse and the earliest form of all—simple repetition—had returned. This 'formlessness' extended to the opera overture which became a pot-pourri of tunes which were to be heard in the next act or which were the most important dramatically in the whole piece. These overtures were called 'Preludes' or 'Intermezzos'—quite correctly from a dramatic point of view but unfortunately for the musical analyst, who knows these names in earlier contexts.

But can any musical work be formless which continually uses the same material? The nineteenth-century masters treated form as they treated rhythm melody and harmony: they re-arranged old customs. To them the only valid musical form was, therefore, 'variation' on as many tunes as the situation—dramatic or lyrical—called for. So Romantic Long (or Sonata) form may have many more than two subjects as it grows longer and longer. On the other hand, one 'connecting' tune which keeps returning between episodes in a musical story (Rondo form) may itself vary in key or some other way; and one tune may serve in disguise for a long series of short pieces (the original Fantasia form). The old forms are still there, but the composer may treat them as he likes and you, the audience, need not be aware of any of them. You do not any longer know what *should* happen, formally, and you can only follow the light as the composer shines it on his different characters. Because the Romantic composer's characters are so appealing, his setting so dramatic, and his lighting so colourful, most concert-goers start their listening in this period; and like the romantic novelist, his characters make the piece alive.

Fugue was an academic subject, though canon remained a useful starting place for variations. Ground bass and passacaglia returned in the second half of the nineteenth century but only in short sections, usually triumphant endings to a set of variations (as in Brahms' Variations on the St. Antony Chorale), repeated at the same pitch like a long pedal note in so much organ music. Dance-forms were ruled by the waltz.

The Waltz appeared as a concert item in opera as early as 1786, in its future capital, Vienna, and was the first Austrian national dance to come into the repertory. It was short and catchy—eight bars—and you repeated the tune in the dominant key to form a second half. When composers began to write concert waltzes never intended for dancing (1808 onwards) the first half naturally grew longer and the keys in the second half varied. Eventually, like the minuets before them, waltzes were written in contrasting pairs (the second a trio making aria form), or in whole collections (rondo form); and they acquired an introduction and coda. The tempo and rhythm took time to settle down into the Viennese lilt of what is now the old-fashioned waltz. French waltzes usually got faster and faster in the course of the piece and were written in 3/8 or 6/8 whereas Germans generally preferred a slow, steady, '*one*-two-three'. The two finally compromised and the Viennese waltz swept through Europe. In its train followed other three-time national dances, all in the same form but with their special rhythmic characteristics:

Viennese Waltz, fairly quick 3/4 ♩♪♪ ♩ beginning ♪♪|♩

or ♩♩|♩

Polonaise and Mazurka, stately 3/4 ♪♪♩ ♩

Polka, originally slow 2/4 ♫ ♫.♪|♫ ♩ but quickened up later.

* * * * * *

Romantic composers made the sound of their music inseparable from its source. They gave you three choices: you could try to guess what they were trying to say or stress in their music from the titles they chose; you could sit back and worship them as heroes or magicians; or you could hate their music passionately because of its association with free behaviour and the Bohemian life. The one thing they would never have forgiven was to be ignored. This lay beyond the crossroads marked by Beethoven and from now on the historian must first quote the source and then write of the sounds coming from the source. He can no longer write about 'the Symphony' or 'Opera', it must be Beethoven and the Symphony, or Verdi and Opera.

CHAPTER THIRTEEN

CONCERT HALL

The European Scene

When Frederick the Great died in 1786, the French Monarchy had three years left. Six years later Napoleon had begun his attempt at the conquest of Europe in Savoy, the Rhineland and the Austrian Netherlands. Milanese at La Scala Opera House saw their last important first night for nearly forty years—Cimarosa's *Secret Marriage*—in 1793; all over the Rhineland, Electors and Princes prepared to spend their resources on defence and musical directors were shorn of their choirs and orchestras; Parisians rejoiced at their unexpected victories but had time for little music except patriotic songs; only in Vienna and Prague, the two great cities of Austria and Bohemia, did the threat seem remote. For thirty years, the history of music was carried on almost entirely in Vienna, through Haydn, Beethoven and Schubert.

After the defeat of Napoleon, the Congress of Vienna (1814–15) tried to sort out the chaos by returning to something like the pre-war balance of power. But both Germany and Italy had known something of the benefits of small states in a 'national' union, even under the dictatorship of a foreigner like Napoleon, and they were no longer prepared to return to the old dependence on a local landowner's temperament. Prussia grew enormously westwards, and not unnaturally Berlin was one of the first of the big capitals to re-start its musical life with a new generation of composers in the early 1820s. Weber produced the first Romantic opera (*Der Freischütz*: 1821) and Mendelssohn the first Romantic symphony (1824) in Berlin, while Beethoven was finishing his last symphony and Schubert his last two quartets in Vienna. England, too, had a secure outlook across the Channel once more, with friendly neighbours in the Netherlands and a France who had been remarkably leniently treated at the Congress, due in large part to English pressure. Londoners in the twenties saw Liszt and Mendelssohn for themselves, and the London Philharmonic Society commissioned Beethoven's last symphony.

Meanwhile the Italians had, of course, taken their operatic costumes out again, and the mercurial Rossini was carrying on the line of Italian opera interrupted so abruptly after Mozart's *Marriage of Figaro* (1786) and *Cosi fan tutte* (1790) had changed its direction. Rossini's 'Figaro' story, *The Barber of Seville*, was given in Rome in 1816 and the pantomime story of *Cinderella* followed in the next year.

Within ten years of her surrender, Paris was a gay city once more. Comic opera reigned there in 1825, and romantic opera by the most fashionable Italian—Rossini himself—reached the Paris Opera in 1829. The following year, Berlioz's *Fantastic Symphony* drew attention to the Artist with a capital 'A', in commanding terms. French grand opera resumed on an even grander scale with Meyerbeer's *Robert the Devil* in 1831. Liszt was now teaching and playing in Paris and the refugee Chopin had arrived. From that time, for a hundred years (surviving even the First World War), Paris was the fashionable centre of the world. Her own composers—Berlioz, Gounod, Bizet, César Franck, Saint-Saëns, Délibes—all contributed masterpieces (at least as far as present concert, ballet and opera-goers are concerned) between 1840 and 1876, and hardly a single new craze or lasting discovery passed her by.

The Scala in Milan, the San Carlo Opera in Naples and the Fenice theatre in Venice shared after 1830 the first nights of Bellini, Donizetti and the incomparable Verdi, losing only a few operas to Paris, St. Petersburg and Cairo who commissioned them, and a couple which Verdi had performed in Rome for diplomatic reasons. But no important Italian symphony or concerto is heard in the nineteenth century: Italy was living in dramatic times and the work of Garibaldi and his followers needed dramatic music. It took eleven years (from 1860 to 1871) to unite the three main divisions of Northern States, Papal States, and the Two Sicilies, divisions that had existed for eleven centuries. During these years no famous opera appeared in Italy. Even Verdi was silent. His operas had helped to pave the way to unification, and once this national ideal had been achieved a new kind of opera was needed, with up-to-date plots that would reflect the lives of ordinary people realistically.

Tsarist Russia had been given a position of great power by the Congress of Vienna and her western borders were much more a part of Europe than they had ever been before, particularly after she annexed Poland and Finland. St. Petersburg had begun to attract Italian opera composers and singers in the eighteenth century and received virtuosos from all over Europe in the early nineteenth. The glory of her power became, musically, the court opera at St. Petersburg, which performed the epic stories of past Tsars and fairytales (looking towards the East, still) as the poet Pushkin re-told them. Political and fairy-tale opera developed side by side and the symbolism in both, as in Verdi's earlier operas, was eagerly sought by the restless spirits who were to overthrow the Tsars. But St. Petersburg still had plenty of time to go, before it became Petrograd and then Leningrad: pageantry at the opera kept many people happy; the Imperial Ballet School was preparing its first full-length ballet (Tchaikovsky's *Swan Lake*) in 1876, for performance at the Bolshoi in Moscow; and Russian symphonies by Rimsky-Korsakov, Tchaikovsky and Borodin fill in what would otherwise be a gap in the chronicle of symphonies between 1851 (Schumann's last) and 1876 (Brahms's first).

Berlin, as we have seen, was among the first capitals to recover its music after the Napoleonic wars. In 1833 the Saxon states joined in a custom union with Prussia, and Leipzig lay along the path of musical history again, with Schumann in residence, Lortzing at the opera house and Mendelssohn in charge of the famous *Gewandhaus* concerts. The firm of Breitkopf and Härtel continued to make Leipzig the centre of the publishing trade. In the forties Dresden, just over the old border between Saxony and Prussia which had been swept away, mounted Wagner's first three operas. In the fifties Weimar (the 'German Athens', which had once housed J. S. Bach for a short time), became a magnet to attract all lovers of opera as the Court's Director of Music, Liszt, produced Berlioz and Wagner, Cornelius and Saint-Saëns. The sixties saw the three wars planned by Bismarck to complete German unity, and Vienna temporarily provided German composers with their first performances (save for the 'premières of the year' in 1865 and 1868, Wagner's *Tristan* and *Meistersinger*, in Munich). In 1876 all musical ears and eyes were turned to the ultimate symbol of German dreams of grandeur, Bayreuth, and the opening cycle of *The Ring*.

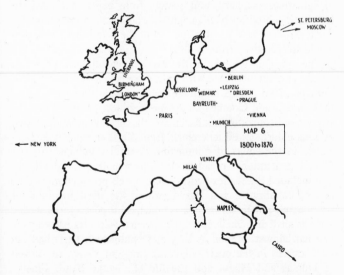

These were some of the political and geographical changes which affected musical history in the nineteenth century. The literary circles and family gatherings of the nineteenth century lived through them all. On the one hand the poets and the new writers ('novelists') of prose went from one emotional crisis to another in society drawing-rooms; on the other, solid commercial fathers listened with pride to their wives and children singing or playing sonatas on the violin and pianoforte at musical evenings in their homes. Composers were welcome everywhere, if not in person at least in their music. They wrote in diaries and magazines, and their correspondence alone would fill thousands of attics; many of them still played or conducted for a living; most of them accepted some regular job either in playing or teaching at some time in their lives. Many tried to follow the 'Lion' Beethoven and determined to write music for their own release or delight, but almost as many were soon disillusioned. To be truly 'Romantic', the dictionary tells us, a man must be 'imaginative, visionary, and remote from experience'. All the Romantic composers were imaginative (as any composer must be) but few indeed could match the rest of the definition, try as they would to 'get away from it all'.

The court of Weimar in the early nineteenth century commanded the literary stage with its two poets Goethe and Schiller. Both provided poems to which Beethoven and Schubert added their music, and Goethe's *Faust* was a subject to attract practically every Romantic composer. In the next generation Heine of Düsseldorf, and Eichendorff from Ratibor were linked together in the songs of Schumann. A similar influence of two literary generations spread to the continent from England: the first included Sir Walter Scott (whose novels provided more than one opera libretto) and Byron (whose life itself inspired the passionate Frenchman Berlioz as much as his poetry); the second was headed by Shelley, whose poems were translated into German almost as soon as they were published. Paris had her own sources in the poetry of Lamartine and Vigny, the novels of Dumas and Hugo, and the life of George Sand. Finally, available to all, were the myths, tales and legends of every country.

Symphonies: Beethoven

With his third symphony, the 'Eroica', Beethoven wrote music not just for any hero, but for Napoleon and his ideals. Despite the fact that he scratched out the dedication when Napoleon accepted a crown, the music has the 'outside' connection of all Romantic music: Beethoven is expressing his feelings about a specific man, yet we must accept that we are hearing music which is Beethoven himself and *not* a musical portrait of Napoleon's life. There are no programmatic touches like the few bars of the 'Marseillaise' or booming of cannon in Tchaikovsky's overture '1812' which is a representational piece about Napoleon. The 'Eroica' is a symphony—abstract music, in the sense that Beethoven's own feelings must be abstract to us, classical only in its formal balance.

The form of the 'Eroica' illustrates clearly many of the things you have read about in Chapter XII. The first movement has groups of tunes which still show a contrast of tonic and dominant in the exposition, but which travel through immensely remote territory in the development section and are pushed off their homeward course in the recapitulation by deliberately contradictory keys until the huge coda sums up in the main key. The second, a very long funeral march, has for its main tune the usual underlying long-short-short rhythm but it is a perfect romantic melody, full of appoggiaturas, reaching its climaxes on the highest note in the phrase (which often has an additional 'spotlight' in a *sf* sign) and changing the division of beats in the bar almost ceaselessly. When it repeats a section the ending goes where Beethoven wishes, always in a different direction, with as many new twists as he likes. Above all, it is a 'middle' melody in the richest string register. The third movement of a Romantic symphony could hardly remain a Minuet in the age of the Waltz and Beethoven had already quickened up the older dance in his second symphony, using the old Italian word for his little game, 'Scherzo'. In this third symphony the Scherzo acquires an element which the minuet never possessed: drama, a guiding principle to the Romantic. Listening to the contrast in dynamics at the beginning, no one could escape the effect of the sudden strong phrase, or be untouched by it. Drums, too, play a big part in the tension at the end. The last movement is in the all-embracing term 'Variation-form' on a tune *and* its bass, sometimes like a fugue, sometimes in division, sometimes as a ground—with big changes of tempo between sections. The final coda is a summing-up not for our benefit, but for Beethoven's. His mood is completely new, perhaps showing a side of Napoleon that had not occurred to the composer before, but which must obviously be mentioned before Beethoven's original admiration for his triumphal hero ends the tribute.

There is no space here even to summarize the other Beethoven symphonies. If you will listen to, say, Mozart's last symphony, the 'Jupiter', (nicknamed by a publisher and not by the composer) and this third symphony of Beethoven written only fifteen years later, no more summarizing is needed to point the difference in sound between the classical and the romantic symphony. The sixth symphony, 'Pastoral', must be mentioned if we are to understand the trend of the times. The titles of the movements which include *By the brook*, *Merry meeting of peasants*, and *Thunderstorm*, say what the scenes in his plot are, but just as two painters would produce different pictures of such scenes, so each listener can imagine his own picture. Beethoven's intention is not pictorial, but, as he himself said, an expression of his own feelings. We are not meant to imagine scenes but to listen to Beethoven's reaction to several brooks, country gatherings and thunderstorms, and imagine, if we will, his emotions. Things which we have all seen are only a stimulus to writing (or listening to) pure music, and we do not (or should not) need a detailed 'programme'. Nature is a universal inspiration and we must be inspired, or not, by Beethoven's music alone in his symphony, considered *as a symphony*.

Hero-worship and Nature are two of the Romantic composer's 'outside' influences: the words of the poet make a third, and Schiller's 'Ode to Joy' provided Beethoven with the last movement of his ninth and last symphony. It is not a setting of the words only, but a song with a commentary on itself. Again, though we hear Schiller's words, it is Beethoven's expression of joy which the music gives us. Listening to a performance in German, no man need understand any language but that of the music.

Symphonies: Schubert (1797 – 1828)

Of Schubert's early symphonies, you may still hear the fifth, in B flat, fairly often. From our present viewpoint, this is a four-movement work for small orchestra which is modelled formally on Mozart, but it has those enharmonic changes of key you have read about, which assign it firmly to the nineteenth century. Listen particularly to those in the slow movement. This was the only one of his symphonies which Schubert ever heard; over ten years after he died Schumann brought to Mendelssohn in Leipzig the score of 'The Great' C Major, sometimes called 'No. 7', sometimes 'No. 9', and there it was first heard at a Gewandhaus concert. Its length is that of a romantic symphony and it might well be called Schubert's 'Eroica', for its first movement introduction is a hero's entrance, its slow movement (even to the very rhythm of Beethoven's in the first bar) is a lament with words of comfort in its broad second subject, its scherzo has the long strides of a powerful figure, and the four repeated notes of the last movement leave a terrifying impression of the fall of a giant.

So this symphony affects me, and I have written down my feelings as best I can in order to emphasize that the way to judge romantic music is through your own emotional reaction. This is not an age in which knowledge of conventions will help you to listen: the symphony has the usual first movement form; its slow movement and scherzo with trio are both in 'aria' form; it has a 'long' last movement with a coda—but it does not matter a scrap whether you analyse it like this or not.

The Sixth Symphony (in B minor) had to wait until 1865 for its first performance. It has only two movements, quick and slow, which produce two copybook examples of the change in outlook after 1800 that was summarized in the previous chapter. The second tune of the first movement is in G major (on the flat sixth of the home key) and Schubert reaches it by holding a 'D' hardly long enough until he can decently re-christen it the 'dominant' of G major; such an abrupt change would have hurt the ears of a tonic-dominant minded eighteenth-century listener, but to our ears it may be enchanting. In the second movement the big tune is given to the clarinet, the new 'middle' instrument, and the enharmonic changes in the coda which lead from E major to A flat major and back are perfect examples of the wonder which the opening-out of key relationships brought to music. Why Schubert never finished this symphony no-one knows, for he wrote a great deal of music after these two movements, but many romantic guesses have been made to add to the mystery of 'The Unfinished'.

Symphonies: Mendelssohn (1809 – 1847)

Four of Mendelssohn's five published symphonies have titles and one—the 'Reformation', written in 1830 to commemorate the tercentenary of the Protestant declaration at Augsburg—uses actual quotations to help the listener to understand what he is trying to express. In this case, Mendelssohn uses the 'Dresden Amen' and the tune *Ein' feste Burg* both of which every Saxon churchgoer would know and many English hymn books include. 'Musical programme notes' like these led later composers to base whole symphonies on folk tunes, and so express their feelings in language that their countrymen could immediately understand. This type of symphony in turn descended to the 'symphonic fantasies' on national themes which used such familiar language that they became, in many cases, musical slang.

The other three symphonies are more genuinely romantic, in the sense of being 'remote experience'. The 'Italian' and 'Scottish' symphonies have no tunes which the composer or listener might have heard on a visit to Italy or Scotland. They are musical accounts of what the composer felt on his visits, and as a result of them. Romantic painters would begin a landscape on the site but preferred to finish it at home, where their imagination would be unchecked by prosaic reminders of the actual scene every time they looked up. Composers might begin with a tune-idea or rhythm which came to them in a certain town (or on a particular road, or at some specific point in a book or poem) but wrote the movement on this idea months later when imagination was freed, perhaps, by nostalgia and not fettered by memory. So the only immediately recognizably 'Italian' feature in Mendelssohn's symphony is the rhythm of a tarantella in the last movement, and his 'Scottish' symphony has only a hint of a Scotch snap in its Scherzo. Yet neither symphony would have been written exactly as it is if the composer had never visited the country and you may perhaps understand the mood better if you have paid a similar visit yourself. If not, there is still the pure music with its romantic scoring, and abundance of singable tunes, some subtle and some openly dramatic shifts of key, to appeal directly to your heart.

The so-called 'symphony-cantata' *Lobgesang* (Hymn of Praise) is Mendelssohn's pale attempt to write something like Beethoven's Choral Symphony, using soloists and a chorus in the last movement on the same pattern. Again, as it was a piece written for a festival to honour Gutenberg, the inventor of printing, he uses a tune familiar to all in his finale—the hymn 'Now thank we all our God'—which was calculated, by its associations for each member of the audience, to attune the listener to the composer's feelings of admiration. Such calculation is really cheating, and the music suffers unless it is played when mass emotions can be relied on to move in the same channel; it might, perhaps, go well in a large church at a Festival of Remembrance, but not in a routine choral concert.

Symphonies: Schumann (1810 – 1856)

The mere length of a classical symphony defeats any composer whose emotions are intense but short-lived, for the demands of a 'long' form are that a theme should develop and grow. If your tune is itself emotionally full-grown, you cannot do anything with it except repeat it and hope to maintain the intensity by altering its key; take each part of it and work on it, and the emotion of the whole tune is ruined. Schumann's inspiration was as intense as any romantic composer's.

In the first movement of his First Symphony he tried to make a single, short deeply-felt theme last for a 'long' movement by keeping its rhythm going almost throughout and repeating snatches of the tune time and time again in sequence; his second subject, the entire development and the coda stem from the same little nervous idea. Only a master of orchestration can keep the same idea interesting for over five minutes and Schumann was too inexperienced for this movement to be a success.

The slow movement in waltz-time with a syncopated accompaniment, is again on one melody but this time one of the richest in all romantic symphonies, twenty-three bars long with telling appoggiaturas on to chromatic chords and intriguing dynamic changes. Schumann plays it first on the violins in octaves, modulates (by sequence through two keys a sixth apart and finally on an enharmonically changed leading note) to the dominant and plays it again, this time on the cellos (marked 'cantabile') singing in the middle register round about middle C. More modulation on a development of the first modulation interrupts his tune and climbs to the climax of the whole movement (on the highest note, of course) and the tune is played a third time in the home key, in octaves on the oboe and horn. The finest magical touch of romantic orchestral imagination is left for the last twelve bars, when three trombones (playing pianissimo) echo the opening of the tune and prepare the way for the Scherzo to follow without a break. For this movement, if for nothing else, Schumann must keep his place in the romantic repertory of symphonies, and anyone who wants to explain what romantic music sounds like has only to put on this quarter of a long-playing record.

The Scherzo has two contrasting trios—the first in two-time to counteract the swift three of the rest—and the coda mixes up both speeds and accents in quick succession. The Finale is a perfect example of the classical Long form with the key changes of the romantic. Its two main tunes are well contrasted in rhythm with the second broader (on the strings in octaves), but the first wanders from tonic to dominant keys in four bars and the second from the relative *minor* of the tonic to that of the dominant in eight. After that the exposition closes 'satisfactorily' on repeated perfect cadences in the dominant. All the extensions of the tonic-and-dominant pattern are easy to analyse on paper and seem quite logical, but even straightforward variations of this kind are hard to track with the ear. For the rest, a short development of the broad tune roams through the 'flat sixth' key to a series of sequences, and the recapitulation has the second tune ending up firmly in the home key. The work ends with four perfect cadences in the home key and *sixteen* bars of the key chord.

This is the finest of Schumann's four symphonies and I have gone into its form in some detail to show how one romantic composer, at least, struggled hard to make classical form of romantic shapes against his nature. It is ironical that Schumann should have been inspired to write so against his own nature in what he called his 'Spring' symphony, and astounding that he did it so well. The whole work was sketched in four days: how white-hot the composer's mind must have been . . . and what side of Spring did he express? The opening horn call may well be the 'call of Springtime' and Schumann makes the beginning of it even more urgent in the heat of the rushing last movement? A flute cadenza must, surely, mean bird-song recalled at his desk, just before the last recapitulation? Woe betide anyone who hopes to follow such a programme in this symphony; far better, call it '*the* Schumann symphony'.

Symphonies: Berlioz (1803 – 1869)

It must now be clear that all romantic symphonies are, to some extent, self-portraits. You first listen to the music of a man as if you meet someone for the first time; you do not and cannot know his inner feelings at once; you may not even know whether you like him or not. Only after several meetings can you begin to know how he reacts to things; so you should listen several times to a romantic composer's music before you can begin to know anything about it. Some composers are, naturally, more sociable and easier to get to know than others: one who would never fail to make a first impression—in person or in his music—was Berlioz; nor is he reticent about himself, in his letters or his music.

Berlioz's *Fantastic Symphony* is sub-titled *Episode in the life of an artist*, and the composer went to great pains to point out whenever he could that it was intended to be autobiographical, even though his original thoughts were stimulated by reading De Quincey's *Confessions of an English Opium Eater* (in a very bad translation). Not for Berlioz any attempt at conforming to the 'long' classical pattern: he was portraying *his* life and *his* feelings and he therefore made any laws himself. He realized that no one could understand what he was at unless he could, nevertheless, provide some unity for his long movements. Schumann had tackled the same problem, within 'sonata' form, by deriving everything he could from a single idea, and he tried to give all four movements unity by referring in some way to that tune (as in the 'nature call' in his 'Spring' symphony). Berlioz, unfettered by any conventional idea of 'exposition' and 'development', adopted the same process in his *idée fixe*. But whereas Schumann had to develop his *idée*, Berlioz wrote a succession of small pieces and linked them or broke them up whenever he wished with his *idée*. The *Fantastic* is therefore a sort of vast rondo in which the refrain can come in at any time, in any sort of transformation.

The narrative of the symphony was outlined in a detailed programme which had to be read during the performance; without this—in 1830, one of the earliest 'programme notes'—no one could understand it. There were five movements in place of the usual four, each connected by the *idée fixe* which itself represented Berlioz's obsession with love for an actress. This love (which in the programme of the symphony leads the Artist hero to suicide) had cooled down before the work was performed, and though he contemplated suicide after another love affair, Berlioz had many years of impassioned, self-pitying life ahead.

His next symphony was even more a suite than the *Fantastic*.

Harold in Italy had Byron for its literary 'parent', and 'Childe Harold' was represented by the middle instrument of the violin family, the viola. Here Berlioz returned to four movements but they had no unity other than the *idée* of the viola and were only four separate scenes attempting to show how the composer felt after reading the poem. The *Romeo and Juliet* symphony 'after Shakespeare's tragedy' had soloists and chorus, the orchestra playing four movements roughly in a symphonic pattern (including the 'Queen Mab' Scherzo) in between choral and solo items. The old idea of a symphony was gone and the way was open for 'symphonic' poems, legends, suites and variations.

Berlioz required his audience to read programme notes and his instructions to conductors were minutely detailed. The art of conducting with a baton was still fairly primitive, so Berlioz wrote down exactly how to beat any awkward time or tempo, and he had such a keen ear for the balance of instruments that he told his interpreter just how many strings should play each part. His expression marks, too, left the individual player in no doubt as to the composer's intentions and some of Berlioz's scoring is so unexpected that unless these dynamics are strictly observed either the tune or the bass may disappear altogether. So the romantic composer dictated to his conductor, to his players and to his audience. One more principle laid down by Berlioz even dictated the future course of some French and Russian composers: that composers should be concerned with sound *as* sound, and not necessarily as part of a melody or harmony. This was the spur to his *Treatise on Instrumentation*, published in Paris (1844). Its masterly descriptions of orchestral instruments, of what they could and could not do, and of how they could combine has made this book a set work for generations of music students; in its own century it led to the experiments by Rimsky-Korsakov and Debussy which anticipate sounds now so familiar through the lush arrangements of light music for large orchestras.

One of the first composers to come under the spell of Berlioz was Liszt, who was teaching and playing in Paris at the time of the *Fantastic* and *Harold in Italy*. His three symphonies all have a poetic background and all have names: the *Mountain*, after Victor Hugo; a *Faust* symphony, after Goethe; and the *Dante*. The second was dedicated to Berlioz and it becomes obvious that the boundary line between symphony and opera was naturally narrowing. It may be comparatively simple to write a short piece of music to capture the atmosphere of words (as in the scores of 'symphonic poems' after Shakespeare, Byron or Lamartine) but how much easier in a long piece inspired by a play or a legend to sing some words as well! Beethoven had felt the need of Schiller's ode to convey its own meaning—aided by the music— in his Choral Symphony, and Liszt used Goethe's words in the final movement of his *Faust* symphony. Berlioz used everything of opera except scenery and costume in his symphonic 'dramatic legend', *The Damnation of Faust*, with solos, choruses and even recitative between long orchestral passages of great descriptive power like the Hungarian March or the Ride to the Abyss and charming ballet sequences like the Dance of the Sylphs; and by these standards Wagner's cycle of 'dramatic legends' in the *Ring of the Nibelungs* is really a colossal four-movement symphony for orchestra with voices. At the other end of the scale the *Siegfried Idyll*, the charming little work for small orchestra which Wagner wrote for his second son, is also called, on its title page, 'symphony'. By 1876 the term 'symphonic' covers as wide a field as ever the word 'sinfonia' did two hundred years before.

Other Symphonic works

The smaller symphonic works of the eighteenth century were the serenades, divertimenti and ceremonial overtures. The term 'serenade' returns only in the last decade of the nineteenth century; divertimenti were confined to the stage as short ballet pieces; and the ceremonial overtures become the concert overture.

Many overtures originally intended for operas are performed in the concert hall, including Beethoven's *Leonora* overtures (for *Fidelio*), Berlioz's *Roman Carnival* (for *Benvenuto Cellini*) and many by Weber and Wagner. Mendelssohn carried this one stage further in deliberately writing concert overtures which were never meant to 'open' anything. The title is misleading but it tells you that the form of these pieces is that of an opera overture: 'long' like the first movement of a symphony but without repeating the exposition. The most well-known is *The Hebrides*, a perfect landscape painting in music which has for its second subject one of Mendelssohn's finest tunes, played first on cellos and finally on clarinets. The doubling of these two instruments in the overture *Ruy Blas* (which has no connection with Hugo's play other than its title) for another 'cantabile' second subject has the essence of romantic orchestration about it. Most romantic of all, though, is probably Tchaikovsky's *Romeo and Juliet* overture (1869-70).

Incidental music for plays and numbers for the ballet provided 'symphonic suites' in the concert hall long after the performances for which they were written were forgotten. They took the place of the serenades and usually had an overture followed by a few shorter pieces including dances and openly descriptive 'scenery' music. Mendelssohn's music for *A Midsummer Night's Dream* (1843) is typical: a grand overture (written in this case a long time before the rest, when the composer was seventeen); a scherzo; a nocturne (the lovely horn solo); and the famous Wedding March. Bizet's music for *L'Arlésienne* (1872) provides two suites which include the Carillon and Farandole.

'Symphonic' poems, ballads and sketches began with Liszt's *Les Préludes* (1848) on Lamartine's poem, but by 1876 the terms were used for any short work for the concert hall which had a programme, from Smetana's *My Country* (six pieces depicting Bohemian scenery and legends) to Franck's *Redemption* for a soprano solo, chorus and orchestra.

Concertos

Between 1786 and 1876 dozens of concertos were written by virtuoso pianists and violinists to show off their fabulous techniques, but the number which virtuoso composers wrote for them is small. Only the most intimate friendship or closest admiration would induce a master composer to risk writing a concerto which the soloist might scorn for its lack of display and the critics for its lack of musical depth.

Beethoven, whom no one could scorn, asserted the importance of the orchestra and put it on almost equal terms with the soloist. His piano concertos are symphonies in which the solo instrument gives him an especially bright spotlight to shine, but he never dims the rest to the point of invisibility and they always have something interesting to say. They keep the three-movement form of the eighteenth century, but the keys are already widening in the third piano concerto (C minor: 1800). The fourth (G major: 1805) gives the piano a solo introduction before the orchestra begins the work proper. The fifth (The 'Emperor': 1809) abolishes the first movement cadenza by letting the piano start the coda alone, and the second movement leads without a break into the final rondo (through a beautifully simple en-harmonic change from five sharps to three flats) which again the soloist leads. The piano concertos were written for himself; the Violin Concerto (1806) was written for the best violinist in Vienna and is a near-perfect example of the classical pattern enhanced by the beauty of romantic melody, harmony and (above all) orchestration. It keeps the balance between orchestra and soloist (with places left for cadenzas), and relates the keys of its three movements in the same design as an eighteenth-century concerto, but no one could mistake the changes of thirty years if it is compared with, say, Mozart's finest violin concerto (A major; K. 219).

Mendelssohn wrote the only other Violin Concerto (1844) to keep its place in the repertory of this period. The search for continuity is strengthened by playing all three movements without a break; the composer writes the first-movement cadenza in full, at the end of the development; and no amount of repetition seems to dim the glow of the lyrical slow movement or bring disenchantment to the airy finale. His two piano concertos, and the brilliant *Capriccio* and *Rondo* follow the continuous pattern set by Weber in his *Concert Piece* for piano and orchestra.

The two most fabulous pianists were Chopin and Liszt, each of whom wrote two concertos. Chopin's F minor Concerto (1829) consciously uses the classical forms but juxtaposes unexpected keys and uses all the arabesques of a wizard's handiwork at the keyboard to weave a spell over the orchestra, which succumbs after its first tutti, to comment only occasionally as it accompanies the rest of the work. Liszt was the son of a servant to the Esterhazy family in Hungary and had experimented with a popular Fantasia on Hungarian Tunes (1852) for piano and orchestra before he attempted his first concerto (E flat major: 1855). This concerto is in one movement but has four sections connected by themes which, though they change form, appear in each section.

When Chopin first played his Variations for Piano and Orchestra (on a tune from *Don Giovanni*), Schumann hailed him as a genius. Twenty years later another genius, Clara Schumann, was to play her husband's A minor Concerto (1846) for the first time and put Chopin's concertos in the shade. This work, Grieg's Piano Concerto (in the same key: 1869) and the 'Emperor' are today the most over-played in the concert hall. Beethoven and Grieg can still (in their own ways) manage to survive unsympathetic handling, but Schumann needs a highly-sensitive romantic if his concerto is to touch the heart. Beethoven's grandeur and Grieg's lusciousness are always affecting; Schumann's freshness, poignance and subtlety too easily become jaded, mournful and banal.

Brahms, Schumann's most loyal friend, completed his first work using a full orchestra in 1858: the D minor Piano Concerto. Its first movement was planned as part of a symphony and its immensity in the concerto—it lasted well over twenty minutes—overwhelmed its audience. The piano part had none of the brittle brilliance people expected in the Leipzig of the eighteen-fifties, and was sometimes almost lost in the orchestral sound. The slow movement seemed to continue the eternity of the first (with the same keynote and time signature) and the gypsy-rondo finale was an impertinent contrast. Unbalanced though this concerto may be, it was the omen for an extraordinarily reactionary period in Romantic music. Brahms thought on Beethoven's lines in the symphonic framework of the classical age, with towering passions which needed no stimulus from any other art (or politics); his first symphony was completed in 1876.

CHAPTER FOURTEEN

OPERA HOUSE AND CHURCH

THE merger of symphony with opera in Berlioz and Wagner did
not mean that all opera in the nineteenth century was willing to
be taken over. Italian composers would have been horrified at
the thought of subordinating the voice to the violins; French
balletomanes would never have given up their dancers and
pageantry for all the colours in the orchestra; the German passion
for form and order would not part with an aria unless there was
some other unifying thing in its place.

Opera: Beethoven

Beethoven's only opera *Fidelio* was performed in Vienna in
1805, almost fifteen years after Mozart's last, *The Magic Flute*,
before an audience mostly made up of officers in the invading
French army. Mozart's overtures had almost always been in
strict symphonic form, usually the long two-subject pattern, and
in this last he uses momentarily a passage (for trombones), which
is to appear in the opera. Beethoven tried four times to produce
a satisfactory overture to *Fidelio*; three of them now bear the real
name of the heroine, *Leonora*, and not her masculine disguise as
'Fidelio'. Each has some allusions to tunes to come in the opera
and each is developed symphonically. The Overture 'Leonora
No. 3' began to be played on its own at a symphony concert and
the opera overture was thus re-living its own history, for the

earlier overtures had, in fact, been 'sinfonias'. Now they had appropriated the singer's tunes as well.

The libretto of *Fidelio* was in German though it had been translated from a plot in French, written a year or two before for an Italian composer! It is only interesting as an example of the 'rescue-operas' which pleased French revolutionary audiences so much and which appear whenever politics are uppermost in composers' minds. There is occasionally, as in *The Magic Flute*, spoken dialogue, and a passage of melodrama where conversation is punctuated and accompanied by arresting 'diminished-seventh' chords or questioning chords of the 'augmented sixth' (see example 32). The arias, duets, trios, ensembles and choruses follow the contemporary Italian type for which Cherubini was famous and keep fairly strictly to Gluck's principles. There is a soldiers' chorus, therefore there has to be a march to get them on convincingly; the chorus of prisoners is imaginatively brought on as the convicts are released from their cells with imitative phrases to sing at the sight of daylight (for the first act finale); and a typical Italian 'crowd' tune heralds the entry of the people outside the prison and covers the final release of the prisoners for the last chorus of rejoicing. Elsewhere the theatricality of the plot is too banal for the care which Beethoven gave it; over 300 pages of Beethoven's sketches for the opera have been found, sixteen of them for *one* of the hero's songs. If you listen to *Fidelio* as a symphony, leaving out the dialogue and keeping only the formal 'vocal gems', the dramatic tension of the prisoners' rescue and the heroine's feelings as she plans the escape are far more powerful in the imagination than on any stage.

Opera: The Italians and Verdi

The libretto of *Fidelio* was originally written in Paris for an Italian composer. The Italians held their grip on opera in nineteenth-century France, England and—after the first decade —the U.S.A., through a succession of prolific composers headed by Rossini and Verdi. Opera buffa reigned equally in Vienna, Venice and Milan. *The Marriage of Figaro* in 1786 followed by

Cosi fan tutte four years later had established Mozart as the great master of the Italian style, and no Italian could ever reach into the heart of music as he did through the 'stock' characters of opera; but several, wearing their hearts lightly, could write bubbling, lively streams of melody which almost burst with good humour and the joy of singing. Among Mozart's contemporaries, two lived on to become favourites at the grandest courts of all, Cimarosa in St. Petersburg with Catherine of Russia and Paisiello in Paris with Napoleon. Both were Neapolitans and both excelled in comic opera. Cimarosa's *Secret Marriage* and Paisiello's *Barber of Seville* (another Figaro story) were played in almost every opera house in Europe, but their serious work contributed little to the growth of opera other than establishing the choral finale in all types of opera.

From the old academic city of Bologna came the first of the nineteenth-century successors to Mozart: Rossini. His first triumphs were in Venice, but after being appointed director of two theatres in Naples (including the San Carlo opera house) he swiftly became famous throughout the Western World. His *Barber of Seville* re-set Paisiello's opera and had reached New York in an English translation by 1819. Its two showpieces— Figaro's 'Largo al factotum' and Rosina's 'Una voce poco fà'— are still in many a singer's music case, and the role of Rosina has been filled by all the prima donnas in the hall of operatic fame from the original Giorgi-Rhigeti (who was actually a contralto) through Patti, Grisi, Melba, and Galli-Curci to Victoria de los Angeles and Teresa Berganza. Glyndebourne opera has revived *Cinderella* and *Count Ory* since 1945, the overtures to *The Silken Ladder*, *The Thieving Magpie*, *The Italian in Algiers* and *William Tell* are ideal openings to many a concert, and military bands (adding the overture to *Semiramide* to the list) fill seaside bandstands many times over with Rossini's tunes.

Rossini's contemporaries, Bellini and Donizetti, accepted the conventions of their age completely but within those limits they produced excellent displays for their virtuoso singers. Their orchestral accompaniments are often dull 'vamping' figures and they showed none of Rossini's happy touches of instrumentation, but their gifts for simple, direct and appealing melodies and choice of dramatic plots kept audiences happy. In particular, the shop windows which they provided in scenes for one character alone attracted a public which loved stars, and the operas which contain these great parts are revived today to display prima donnas like Maria Callas ('Casta diva' in Bellini's *Norma*), Joan Sutherland (the Mad scene in Donizetti's *Lucia di Lammermoor*), and not so long ago Caruso and Gigli in the tenor role of Donizetti's *Elixir of Love*. The geography of their opera plots shows how fashionable the small romantic country of Switzerland was becoming. No less than three of the favourites take place there: Donizetti's *Daughter of the Regiment*, Bellini's *La Sonnambula* and, of course, Rossini's *William Tell*.

Italian composers also discovered the romance in British history and the novels of Sir Walter Scott. Bellini was content with one English setting (*I Puritani* in Plymouth) but no less than eight of Donizetti's operas take place in England or Scotland, including *The Castle of Kenilworth* and *Emily of Liverpool*.

Verdi began in the same vein as his predecessors. A year before Donizetti's last comic opera *Don Pasquale* was produced, the first of the three operas which were to spread the name of Verdi all over Europe reached the stage of La Scala, Milan: *Nabucco*, the story of Nebuchadnezzar (1842). The chorus plays a much bigger part as they sing the prayers and lamentations, and in the unrest which then disturbed Italian hearts the great third-act chorus tune (in unison, not parts) struck home with tremendous force. The excitement was whipped up even more by climax upon climax on brass and big drum, but otherwise the orchestra is left to provide very simple accompaniments. Victor Hugo's tragedy *Ernani* had, at its first performance in Paris (1830), pioneered the Romantic movement in French literature. But Verdi's setting was not to do the same for Italian opera; he chose it more for its story of the wronged outlaw and his successful fight against tyranny than because it cried out for music. He had high hopes of being able to retire after a few more successful operas—as Rossini had done before he was forty—but not until he 'discovered' Shakespeare did the true genius of Verdi emerge.

Macbeth, in 1847, was something quite alien to Italian opera tradition, for Verdi insisted that his singers studied the dramatic part first, then the words and finally the music. His sleep-walking scene, compared with Bellini's, has a terrifying ghostly effect. Lady Macbeth was meant to be devilish and to sing nastily, and everything had to be atmospheric and in character. This was true romanticism in opera, which set out to give pleasure by revealing what the composer felt were the real, life-like, reactions of his characters to the situations of the tragedy in the music, requiring the actors to 'live' their parts (not unlike the so-called 'Method' school of today) to complete the illusion.

Verdi was to return to Shakespeare in his last years but he was now ready to begin again on the Romantic French novelists. Hugo's *Le Roi s'amuse* and Dumas' *La Dame aux camélias* inspired him to far greater intensity than *Ernani* and the operas he made of them—*Rigoletto* and *La Traviata*—are both dependent on the right actors for complete success, in spite of the flow of melodies which anyone who has ever opened his ears must still know by heart today. The jester Rigoletto is lost if he plays the part as strong melodrama, and the audience will come away remembering Gilda's 'Caro nome' and the Duke's 'La donna e mobile'; but if the singer can really interpret the character as Verdi's music suggests, the jester will stay the tragic but dignified central figure. Sarah Bernhardt and Eleanora Duse played Dumas' heroine in the theatre, and for his Violetta Verdi wanted a Bernhardt who could also sing. It is no wonder that opera has been ruined for many young listeners who, on their first visit to an opera house, have heard a *Rigoletto* or *Traviata* sung by singers for whom acting is an unnecessary evil or an excuse for exhibitionism.

Il Trovatore, the third inevitable choice for a touring opera company, can stand up to any sort of acting, for the plot is so complicated that no actor could convey any dramatic truths in it, and its music glorifies the voice throughout. The Anvil Chorus for the gypsies, the 'Miserere', and the Troubadour's Serenade have become hackneyed but there is still enough excitement in them to carry the opera through. Historically its characters are wildly romantic but its music harks back to the 'um-cha-um-cha' accompaniments of Bellini under soaring tunes complete with tenor high 'C', the worst and the best in Italian grand opera.

The quest for credible characterization led Verdi to choose duets for many of his crucial scenes, because two people—lovers, husband-and-wife, or father-and-daughter—in dialogue will each bring out the other's character. Soliloquy is limited to moments when the character is really isolated—whether in tears or in mounting rage, the person is always under great stress—and so becomes even more poignant or terrifying. *Don Carlos* shows both duets and solo at their finest in portraying the personalities that Schiller had created on paper.

For the rest, Verdi wrote what was needed until his last two masterpieces again showed his personal genius. He wrote operas on the grand scale where pageantry and chorus-work were all-important for the Great Exhibition in Paris (*Sicilian Vespers*: 1855), and for the opera house in Cairo (*Aïda*: 1871). As the unification of Italy drew nearer he turned back to more political operas, including *The Masked Ball* (1859). The last and best were to come only after his allotted span of life was well-nigh exhausted . . . and they must wait for Chapter XVIII.

Opera: Weber and Wagner

On the 18th of June, 1821, the sixth anniversary of the Battle of Waterloo, Weber's *Der Freischütz* won a memorable battle against Italian domination at the Berlin Opera. The feeling of nationalism in Germany at the time was as much responsible as Weber's music, but there were also features in the score which were to become, through Wagner, the distinctions between later German and Italian operas. The plot was 'a legend of the people', according to its publication in an eighteenth-century storybook, and is a story of true love amongst magic bullets, devils incarnate, monsters, and spooks in a wild country setting. Nothing could have been more tailor-made for the Romantic composer: the situations cried out for dramatic music; nature had to be 'painted' in music to make the settings convincing; and the love affair was heroic and intense enough to bring out the most emotional sounds as the composer transferred his own feelings to the characters. All this needed a highly-sensitive musician, an experienced theatrical mind, a delicate ear for instrumentation, and a gift for expressive melody: it needed Weber.

The overture is in the long symphonic form and is often detached from the opera for concert performance. It is, in fact, a symphonic sketch of the opera's plot, using only themes that appear in the opera. The slow introduction is a melody scored for four horns, heralding the Romantic era with their rich 'middle' sounds and also, of course, creating the magic atmosphere. The tonic group of first subjects is made up of the hero's despairing phrase and a leaping tune which is used for the storm in the grotesque glen (both in a minor key), and the bridge passage, using more horn calls and a slow clarinet passage, leads to the heroine's serene theme (in the relative major) as a second subject. When you listen to the development of these ideas and their re-statement at the end, you may imagine the whole story of the opera but there is no particular sequence which takes you from one situation to another: symphonic form prevents it and the overture needs no knowledge of its 'programme' to be enjoyed. The chances of hearing a professional performance of the opera in England nowadays are slim, but the overture is played frequently. If you listen to the overture to *Freischütz* compared with, say, the overture to *The Magic Flute*, then *Fidelio*, you will hear clearly what a big difference Weber made to the course of operatic history.

Once the themes in the overture are known to the audience, the unity of the whole opera is ensured by using them to pin-point situations and reveal the emotions of the characters they represent. The movement of the drama means that new musical ideas crop up continually but (just as ideas in real life) they seldom develop logically, for something else happens which brings in a completely new thought. So the opera is not, like a true symphony, based entirely on a limited number of subjects which are discussed and then summed up. It is more like a Berlioz 'symphony', but the series of subjects is linked by more than one *idée fixe* (called, in German, *Leitmotiv*). Each leitmotiv in Weber's opera represents a character or a scene.

In *Freischütz* and in the third of Weber's successes, *Oberon* (yet another version of Shakespeare's *Midsummer Night's Dream*, written for Covent Garden in 1826) spoken dialogue connects the arias, scenas and ensembles, and this is bound to break the train of musical thought. But the German singspiel (or musical play) was well established and so near to English ballad opera that English audiences were not taken by surprise. The musical danger in writing Weber's type of opera is that you put all your best tunes in the overture and they may not last the night out without boring your listener. Weber knew this very well and was disturbed if the audience, by applauding and demanding encores of the overture and the first appearance of these tunes in the opera 'fired off their powder too soon'. His second masterpiece, *Euryanthe*, written for Vienna in 1823, has no spoken dialogue and uses all the set dramatic forms of grand opera. The libretto is absolutely incredible and Weber could do nothing to make it possible even to follow the plot. Like *Il Trovatore*, much of the story has happened before the curtain goes up, and the game of who-told-who-what has to be played to put the audience in the picture before the first incredible incident of the story proper happens; unlike *Trovatore*, this has proved too much for the public to bear and so we have lost some of Weber's finest music.

Wagner tackled the vast musical design of an opera in the same way as Weber and finally created the largest of all in his cycle of operas, *The Ring of the Nibelungs*. The change from Weber's type of overture which he used for *The Flying Dutchman*, *Tannhäuser* and *The Mastersingers of Nuremberg* to overtures and preludes which led directly into the acts (as in *Tristan and Isolde*) shows how Wagner's musical thought became more and more continuous. Similarly, the join between recitative and aria is gradually made invisible and inaudible so that, in a sense, we are back at the stage of a complete work in arioso. In the last operas (*The Ring of the Nibelungs*), you can never tell where the composer stopped work for the night, and the music could easily have become force of habit, but with Wagner there remains always the sound of the orchestra, the fascination of hearing a mind develop and enlarge upon striking ideas, and the spectacle on the stage.

Lohengrin, first conducted by Liszt at Weimar in 1850, was the first of Wagner's operas to be completely continuous, without any distinction between recitative and aria. Wagner was returning to the age-old ambition of opera composers, that the singer should 'sing . . . giving each note its value' and so 'have the spoken word completely in his control'. As yet his harmony and instrumentation were not enough to keep his melody interesting for a whole opera and the joins between the set numbers are still obvious, but the libretto shows how clearly Wagner could tell a folk tale and make it all the more vivid by adding to it historical fact (in the person of Henry I of Germany, not in the original story) and concentrating the attention on a wicked kind of career woman (Ortrud) who is recognizable in any age. This skill at re-telling old legend so that it seemed real is seen at its best in *Tristan and Isolde*, written fifteen years later, in 1865, after his return from exile as a political refugee. At this time he had as his patron in Munich the King of Bavaria, Ludwig II, but by the end of the year his strong views on a united Germany and his open association with Cosima Liszt (who was then married to von Bülow, the eminent conductor) led to a second exile.

Wagner's second exile was spent with Cosima in Switzerland. There he wrote his life story, books of criticism, and a guide to conducting, besides finishing *The Mastersingers* and most of *The Ring*. In 1866 he returned to Munich, as an honoured guest of the King, for the first performance of *The Mastersingers* (a story about real Germans, in history). The Prelude to this opera is the most ingenious 'summary' overture of all time. Beginning with the Mastersingers' own theme, Wagner goes on to a tune made up of snatches from his hero Walther's love-songs, then the solemn march of the Gild brings the introduction to its close. The development of these and other phrases suggests the struggle of a Gild competition brilliantly: the song which finally brings Walther the prize alternates with his failures; the apprentices mock the dignity of the march, and the efforts of the comic villain Beckmesser; and half the tunes in the opera combine to herald the processional majesty of the Gild once more. Here as in the prelude to *Tristan and Isolde*, Wagner guides his audience in advance to the central subject of his opera. The *Tristan* prelude uses the figures representing the tragic love of Tristan and Isolde one by one and then all together; there is nothing apart from their love. The *Mastersingers* prelude hardly comments on the love story of Walther and Eva but dwells on the love-songs in their relationship to the Master's contest; the overwhelming triumph of the Gild march shows that the opera is really about its title and not just a simple love story. In glorifying these early composers, Wagner wrote a 'political' opera. Here was the all-powerful bourgeoisie united and democratic, which German unity aimed at. But by sitting in the Royal Box at its première the composer infuriated the bourgeoisie far more than his music might have inspired them. Wagner did not make a very practical politician.

The *Ring* has made Wagner as an idealist almost god-like to his admirers. As Bismarck approached his goal of a united Germany, so Wagner was more and more identified as its representative composer. An appeal was launched in 1871 to build a shrine where the great 'music-dramas' (never called 'operas') could be performed, and in 1876 the first cycle of *The Ring* was heard in this shrine, at Bayreuth. Two of the four works which make up the cycle had been performed in Munich several years earlier, *The Rhinegold* (1869) and *The Valkyrie* (1870). The first became the prologue, one act in four scenes, in which the gold (which in mythology lay at the bottom of the Rhine) is stolen and made into a ring. This ring serves as a link to the other three dramas in which over a score of legendary figures appear (dwarfs and giants, mermaids and warrior-maidens, gods and goddesses, dragons and serpents). The hero, after whom Wagner named his son, gives the third drama its title, *Siegfried*; and the end of the saga, in which the ring returns to its rightful home in the Rhine, is also the end of the old gods of Valhalla, *The Dusk of the Gods*. The symbolism of the legend is endless; the Rhineland is all-powerful, the old order is struck down; small wonder that the music of Wagner played such a part in the Reich of the Nazis.

Wagner was bitterly disappointed at the results of Bayreuth. Instead of becoming the home of idealism for all German people, it became a fashionable meeting-place of princes and high society. It remains the rendezvous of those who love Wagner's music, not (necessarily) his ideals. In his last opera, *Parsifal*, perhaps the composer admitted to himself that his ideals were born of seeking comfort for his own soul; the medieval legends which he took for his libretto tell the story of the salvation which Parsifal brought to the keepers of the Holy Grail by his innocence and by love for his fellow men. But narrowly Christian ideals like these were forgotten in the wide world of Nietszche, and *Parsifal*, produced in 1882, was already out of its period. *The Ring* of 1876 marked the height of Romantic opera, where it had become the unity of 'music-drama'.

Opera: Berlioz and the French

The Ring turns an epic into a philosophical tract as well as a music-drama; its 'grand' manner is very personal to its composer and, by extension, the German people. *The Trojans*, Berlioz's 'Latin Ring', does not turn Virgil's epic into anything except a truly heroic music-drama. The classical subject may seem a strange choice by a Romantic composer whose first opera librettos were planned to break away from the Baroque love of Rome, but Berlioz had loved Virgil since he was a boy and everything which was intense to the ancient poet he felt equally passionately. The historic scenes provided room for spectacle on the stage (the famous March of the Trojans, the description of the Royal Hunt, and the Storm) and listeners could re-live the tragic love of Dido and Aeneas for themselves if they wished. Berlioz succeeded in capturing, for the only time in his life, the other-worldly quality of someone else's poem and setting it to music without intruding his own personality. The opera is not an account of Virgil's effect on Berlioz, but a sincere attempt to think what music Virgil might have demanded if he had been alive in the nineteenth century. Such restraint makes admirable listening, for Berlioz endowed Virgil with a wonderful ear for instrumentation and a delicacy in melody-writing unsurpassed in that opulent age.

Not counting *The Damnation of Faust* (which you have read about as a symphony) Berlioz wrote two other operas which followed his predecessors' examples: *Benvenuto Cellini* (1838) was a grand opera which, with its general vigour and big crowd scenes, looked back to Meyerbeer's *Robert the Devil* and *The Huguenots*; *Beatrice and Benedict* (1862) was a pure comic opera of the sort which Auber, Boieldieu and Halévy had turned out by the dozen. Each set a new example in its genre which culminated in Bizet's *Carmen* in 1875 (which the Paris press thought 'too Wagnerian', without looking back to Berlioz's *Cellini*) and Offenbach's *La Belle Hélène* (1864).

A third kind of opera, somewhere in between 'comic' and 'grand', was 'lyric opera', peculiar to the French. Somewhat sentimental, with attractive melodies and the inevitable ballets, it had recitative (not the spoken dialogue of comic opera) but none of the pomposity of grand opera. The most able composer of lyric opera was Gounod, whose *Faust* (1859) and *Romeo and Juliet* (1867) both concentrate on love affairs with no deep regard for any philosophical or symbolical twists in the plots, nor strong characterization. Saint-Saëns even contrived to do the same with a Biblical plot in his *Samson and Delilah* (1877). French opera was back where it began in this period, slight but charming.

Ballets were indispensable to all French opera and the prima ballerina Taglioni had composed for her in 1841 the first full-length ballet which we may still see and hear: *Giselle*. In 1870 Paris provided another two-act ballet which has remained a favourite, Délibes' *Coppélia*, and the same composer wrote *Sylvia* six years later (1876).

Light Opera

Opera buffa had been raised to such heights by Mozart (in *Cosi fan tutte*) and Rossini that no one knew what to do next. In Germany, the comic bass reigned in operas by Lortzing and Nicolai (whose *Merry Wives of Windsor*, yet another Shakespearean libretto, was first heard in Berlin in 1849), but the mantle of the older Singspiel or ballad opera fell upon the Viennese waltz kings, especially Johann Strauss the Younger with his operetta *Die Fledermaus* (1874). French comic opera was given a brief leg-pull by Offenbach in his *Orpheus in the Underworld* (a romp about the private life of Orpheus and Euridice) at the theatre called 'Les Bouffes Parisiens'. In England, by 1876, Sullivan was sharpening his pencils to write the first of the operettas which were to charm all London.

Opera in Eastern Europe

Western Russia and Czechoslovakia (or Bohemia as it was then) were both much closer to Europe after the peace of 1815 than ever before. St. Petersburg and Prague, musically, were both held by Italians but native composers arose to challenge them. Russian music in western style may be said to have begun with Glinka's opera *A Life for the Tsar* in 1836, but neither this nor Rimsky-Korsakov's first grand opera, *Ivan the Terrible* (1873), could compare for originality with Moussorgsky's *Boris Godounov* (1874, first version). All three are historical operas on Meyerbeer lines, with pageantry in the processions for the Tsars; all have big crowd scenes; and all have a big part for a bass. The singers Chaliapin, at the turn of this century, and Boris Christoff in the post-war era have made *Boris Godounov* known all over the world, but in 1876 the Russians were still not ready to compete in the world's opera houses.

Nor were the Czechs, though Smetana had written one of the most popular of all operas for Prague in 1866, *The Bartered*

Bride. The libretto and music of this opera were to have many successors. It was a story of contemporary village life told quite as a matter of fact and the music used genuine and spurious folk tunes in the dances and choruses even down to the polka and furiant. The circus scene, complete with band, had to be staged with as many real 'turns' as the producer could devise. Smetana took no heed of leitmotiv, idée fixe or summary overture. His opera is a quick-moving series of songs, choruses, duets, and a quintet, with plenty of dances, and its rousing overture (which has no tune from the opera in it) breathes the very air of a village *en fête*. Romance it has, but much of its success depends upon a comic tenor (who stammers) and a blustering bass; at a time when the Czechs were just beginning to recover from harsh Austrian rule, Smetana taught them to laugh again. Next came a tragic legend, *Dalibor*, and finally, in 1876, *The Kiss*, a mixture of grave and gay. Smetana had laid the foundations of a national school of Czech opera.

Oratorio and Choral Church Music

The influence of the Christian church on music in the nineteenth century is very slight, yet each of the supreme masters of symphonic music was inspired by some religious text to produce one memorable work. Wagner's *Parsifal* was his statement of faith, and his contemporaries also chose dramatic ways to show their belief in God. The Mass was set only once with originality and power, in the *Missa Solennis* of Beethoven (1818), whose vehemence answers for all mankind. Fugue forms the climax for the composer whose mind is turned to the future 'et vitam venturi' ('and the life of the world to come'). Time after time he repeats the words and the hereafter is emphasized wherever it it appears in the text. There are no solos (save for a violin in the 'Benedictus') but a solo quartet alternates with the chorus and occasionally sings against it in operatic style; the words, not the solo singer, are given prominence. If Beethoven looked back with the fugal climax to the work, he was the true Romantic (and symphonist) in his view of the movements. 'Kyrie', 'Gloria' and 'Credo' are all long continuous structures, the first calm, the second fiery with only a brief moment of peace at 'who takes away the sins of the world' and the third an astonishing range of moods. 'Dona Nobis Pacem' (the final prayer for peace) is continually interrupted with reminders of the menace of war. The intensity, breadth and drama of the whole construction are unparalleled in the history of church music.

Berlioz and Verdi turned to the more obviously dramatic liturgy of the Requiem Mass. Berlioz wrote his for a huge ceremony at Les Invalides, the memorial chapel of Paris, according to the expectation of his time: four brass bands heralded the Day of Judgment, hundreds of voices and a colossal orchestra (whose strings alone numbered over one hundred) thundered, roared and as suddenly whispered, overwhelming the hearers with what the composer called 'horrifying grandeur'. It may be that the present generation thinks this excessive, though no one who heard Sir Thomas Beecham's performances in the fifties will forget the impact of the music; Berlioz himself wished that, above all his work, his Requiem should be preserved.

Verdi's Requiem was written in equal sincerity and with passionate tribute to an Italian patriot, Manzoni, who died in 1873. He had found his true means of musical expression only in opera and the Requiem was bound to be dramatic; so there is no criticism implied in calling his most emotional religious work his finest opera. It is also a fine example of symphonic development. From the initial phrase of the cellos (a minor triad followed by a four-note descent to the dominant) Verdi derives his first two long movements. New themes come in at will but the rhythm or the melodic material of these first four bars is never far away. The second movement, a spacious rondo on the 'Dies Irae', has eight sections of immensely contrasting moods connected all the while by the chorus theme of the opening words. This 'opening act' is so powerful that the five short 'scenes' which follow always seem a little weak, until the final prayer 'Libera me' brings back the awesome vision of the Day of Judgment and the return of the initial 'Requiem' phrase shows us the Heaven

beyond. Beethoven's music was a testament of his faith in the
world to come; Verdi's is the music of a Christian newly returned
to his faith, to whom the Day of Judgment is still terrifying.

Brahms's German Requiem from Luther's translation of the
Bible is a much smaller work, tender and almost introspective,
which he wrote soon after the deaths of his friend, Schumann,
and of his mother. Three sections are extended and there are four
shorter pieces. Two soloists sing the more personal lines, the
baritone pleading for comfort on behalf of mankind and the
soprano promising the comfort of the Lord. For Brahms, too, the
Resurrection is all-important: at the great cry 'Grave, where is thy
victory?' the chorus repeatedly demands 'where? where?' and goes
on to sing joyfully (in fugue) to the Lord of all Creation; there
lies the climax of the music. Brahms is the least dramatic of the
Romantic composers and fittingly his Requiem has this one outburst only before returning to the usual serenity of its composer.

There remains that curious phenomenon, the 'London-type'
oratorio. Handel had evolved it. London had taught it to Haydn
who took it back to Vienna with his *Creation* and *The Seasons*.
In the 1830s Mendelssohn, from Berlin, returned it to England:
not, by now, only to London but also to the provinces—Liverpool
and Birmingham—where choral societies and orchestras
flourished. The work of Mendelssohn which is loved above all
by English choruses is *Elijah*, completed for the Birmingham
Musical Festival in 1846. Thoroughly Handelian in its layout,
Elijah has forty-two airs, recitatives, duets, quartets, and choruses
with an opening prophecy by Elijah and an orchestral overture.
Its popularity amongst singers is still widespread and Oratorio
Classes in musical festivals today seldom go by without someone
choosing one of the songs as a test piece.

CHAPTER FIFTEEN

SALON AND DRAWING ROOM: BALLROOM AND MUSIC HALL

SLOWLY in Vienna, abruptly in Paris, the court handed over the patronage of music first to the nobility and then to the middle class citizens. For the first quarter of the nineteenth century gatherings in Viennese houses adored Schubert's songs; after Liszt and Chopin arrived in the 1830s the salons of Paris resounded almost continuously with piano music. In Vienna educated people still remembered how to play stringed instruments, and commissioned trios and quartets while Beethoven and Schubert were alive. Prussian aristocrats accepted dedications of string quartets from Mendelssohn, and Schubert wrote quartets for his fellow-musicians to play, but this was no age for the amateur string player. The middle class sang and played the piano; so they loved listening to their 'own' virtuosos, singers at the opera, pianists at the large recital rooms or in their salons. Virtuoso string players (except the phenomenal Paganini) taught in the new Conservatoires until their pupils began to storm the concert halls as concerto soloists and even (like Joachim) in recital quartets.

A touring pianist does not need a large repertoire of big works, nor will his audience take long pieces. He needs a number of attractive contrasts in short numbers, some to establish his virtuosity, some to tempt his audience into feeling that they might attempt them. A romantic composer still needed money and publishing houses were sometimes hard-headed. So there are fewer sonatas and more suites, fewer song-cycles and more collections of songs; it was the beginning of 'music for the million'.

The million took to the ballrooms, too, and no composer after Schubert could keep up with their thirst for waltzes and still write concert music. Specialists like the Lanner and Strauss families in Vienna and Waldteufel in Paris attempted nothing but dance music, and others specialized in music-hall ballads: the gap between 'classical' and 'pop' music was widening.

Chamber Music: Beethoven

Among the thirty-two piano sonatas and twenty-five string quartets, Beethoven left enough music to make his name immortal even if he had written no symphonies, concertos or the Missa Solennis. The very first sonatas published in the collected edition show his individuality grafted on to the style of Haydn and C. P. E. Bach. He had written three—'my first works'—before these three which form op. 2 (dedicated to Haydn: 1795) and he was ready to branch out on his own. Four movements (not three) began to include a scherzo in place of a minuet; bold modulations put his second subject into a strange key before he ended the exposition in the dominant; the piano writing revelled in octaves and handfuls of notes; and the dynamics changed so abruptly over so large a range that the pianist needs to re-tune his ears to feel the infinite grades of intensity.

Few pianists play Mozart and Beethoven equally well: eloquence too easily replaces elegance instead of being added to it, and mere weight often passes for strength. It is easier to train on Haydn's sonatas, particularly those in op. 54, op. 66 and op. 79, though one big Mozart work (the C minor sonata of 1784) served Beethoven as an obvious model for his 'Pathétique' sonata (1798) and these two pieces might well be learnt side by side. The 'Pathétique' shows the new concern for continuity in its first movement through the repetition of the 'Grave' opening at two later places (almost like an idée fixe), and the key of the well-loved slow movement (like so many when Beethoven begins his sonata in a minor key) is the sixth on the flat side (see page 178).

After 1800 Beethoven turned the old sonata patterns inside out, re-arranging all the time. First movements may be theme-and-variation and the order of quick and slow movements reversed (as in op. 26); the whole sonata may be planned to be played without a break 'like a Fantasia' (op. 27, nicknamed the 'Moonlight'); opera recitative may be transferred to the piano in midmovement (op. 31); or a slow movement may be made by contemplating pieces of its adjacent quick movements (op. 53, the 'Waldstein'). At times he could be the complete Romantic, inspired by reading Shakespeare to write a work with a hidden programme (op. 57, the 'Appassionata'), or (op. 81A, the 'Farewell') moved by a friend's departure to write an annotated programme sonata about his feelings. The last five sonatas (1816–1822) exploit the piano in every possible way and one of them has attracted a title grand in its simplicity—'Piano' or 'Hammerklavier' (op. 106). Like Bach, Beethoven spent his last years exploring the fugue but in his case the aim was to discover how to use it in sonata form.

The last piano sonata (op. 111) came in 1822 in Beethoven's favourite key for a fight, C minor. The first subject is torn to pieces by a fugue in the first movement, to be countered hesitantly by a second subject built entirely on the harmony of a perfect cadence (on the flat sixth again), and put together with increasing force to end the first half. After such an opening (with its even more powerful development), the Arietta (= little song) which follows as the last movement is the most serene of romantic tunes. Beethoven decorates it with three contrasting variations full of contrapuntal ideas without once disturbing its serenity, and introduces its last appearance with a magical enharmonic passage through C minor to the light of C major, the 'natural' key.

The early quartets also owe a little to Haydn but show the same extension of form and tonality. These extensions characterize the first three of the mature quartets written for the Russian Ambassador in Vienna (the 'Rasumovsky' Quartets op. 59: 1806), which astonished the first-rate players (of whom Count Rasumovsky was one) and the audience who suspected that Beethoven was mocking them. Codas became second development sections, and there were so many themes that no one could follow their metamorphoses. The three 'ABC' Quartets of his last two years (A minor, B flat major and C sharp minor) and the final quartet of 1826 (F major, op. 135) reiterate the pre-occupation with fugue announced in his last piano sonatas, but here there is a mystical quality comparable only with Bach's *Art of Fugue*. All three 'ABC' quartets grow from a single subject of seven notes centred on the leap of a sixth. The first has five movements, the second six and the last seven; whatever the symbolism of numbers, these quartets (with 'Et vitam venturi' in the Mass and the 'Ode to Joy' in the Ninth Symphony) are visions of another world. The final quartet was to be Beethoven's last utterance in this life and he seems (like Mozart in the Requiem) to have known that he would complete nothing else: his sketch for the slow movement in his beloved 'flat sixth' key of D flat major has by it the words 'Sweet song of rest or peace'; and over the last he wrote a phrase, 'The hardest decision of all', meaning the acceptance of death. 'Must it be? It must be! It must be!' Beethoven faced the question and answered it in this last movement.

We have over 600 compositions by Beethoven and you have read of a mere dozen in any detail. If you are a pianist look and listen for the Variations (twenty-three sets), waltzes, polonaises, écossaises, and bagatelles (how many childish fingers have picked out *Für Elise?*); for string players there are violin sonatas, cello sonatas, variations and trios with piano. Singers have solos ranging from arrangements of folk songs (with piano, violin and cello accompaniment) to canons on the words 'Ars longa, vita brevis' and 'Happy New Year', and the wistful song cycle *To the Distant Beloved*; wind players can join in the Septet for clarinet, horn, bassoon and four strings and have their own Sextet and Octet. Even collectors of antiques have tunes that Beethoven wrote for mechanical clocks and music-boxes.

Chamber Music: Schubert (1797 – 1828)

Beethoven's single song-cycle set the pattern for Schubert's two great contributions to the German songbooks, *The Beautiful*

Maid of the Mill (1813) and *The Winter Journey* (1827), but, though the pattern is sharper in Beethoven's design, individual songs in Schubert's stand out in their striking beauty or perfect shape. The song writer's problem was not one of length but of fitness. Even the long Romantic ballads were short compared with the movement of a symphony, and the words (usually narrative and dialogue alternatively) provided their own form, but it was still hard to find music which would fit all the sections without constantly needing new phrases. If you try to write a tune which will hold the ear for more than sixteen bars without repeating, you will find it impossible: long ballad tunes depended for their unity on figures in the accompaniment or dramatic sections in a sort of recitative breaking up the melody. Short songs with three verses or so in the same metre were less obviously dramatic, but they allowed for more spontaneous and lyrical melody which could be repeated for each verse and they were simpler for most people to sing.

Schubert wrote over six hundred Lieder (= songs) in his pathetically short life, nearly 150 in 1815 alone. The next year 120 more filled his manuscript books; between the two song cycles the harvest included the Shakespeare settings 'Hark, hark the Lark' and 'Who is Sylvia' (1826). After his death at the age of thirty-one his publisher issued a third song-cycle which included the 'Serenade' and was labelled (no doubt to catch the sentimental if not the romantic) *Swansong*. Scarcely a poet escaped, from the late court poet of Vienna, Metastasio, to Heine, the Laureate of the German romantics by the time Schubert died. Obviously some of his songs were 'pot-boilers', but among the 600, Schubert fashioned some of the most delicate (and some of the most awe-inspiring) in musical history.

The first masterpiece 'Gretchen at the Spinning Wheel' (1814) has one of those piano parts which Schubert could seemingly conjure up as he pleased, to suggest here the whirring wheel or elsewhere the bubbling stream ('The Trout' 1816) or a galloping horse ('The Erlking' 1815). They are the unifying factor and they must not only help to set the scene but create the right mood; or the words. Gretchen is agitated, the trout is carefree (until he is in danger: minor change!), and the father in 'The Erlking' is frantic with worry. How easy it is to see how apt Schubert's figures are, but how difficult now to make similar figures even suggest a horse let alone a frantic parent; 'The Erlking' is a once-for-all treatment.

When there was no need for characterization, Schubert always had his store of lovely melodic phrases. 'To music' (1818) has survived years of being a signature tune in B.B.C's *Music Magazine* (even as a piano solo), and 'Hedgerose' (1815) a million school singing lessons without a blemish. Such music is now almost folksong to generations.

In his chamber music his song-tunes served for two of the four great string works, the 'Death and the Maiden' quartet and the 'Trout' (1819) quintet for four strings and piano. England's 'Schubert' of 200 years before, John Dowland (see page 145), had used his most famous song 'Flow my tears' in the same way for his 'Lachrimae' pavans for strings. In Schubert's Octet (1824) for clarinet, horn, bassoon and five strings it is clear that no composer contemporary with Beethoven could remain uninfluenced by him. The idea of a song-cycle had come from him and his Septet must have spurred Schubert to write the Octet, using the same wind instruments and adding only the second violin; both are survivals of the eighteenth-century divertimento. In the 'Trout' he even leaves out the second violin in favour of a double bass, just as Beethoven had done in his Septet. The String Quintet (1828) is exceptional in having two cellos rather than Beethoven's two violas, and the rich sounds it contains—particularly in the lyrical second subjects—are unsurpassed in music before 1830. As in the Octet, Schubert makes small numbers of instruments sound almost as resonant as full orchestras without straining at all. The 'Trout' has perhaps remained in the repertory because so many people know the song on which Schubert based the fourth movement. It is pretty, but not to be set beside the String Quintet.

Schubert completed his life's quartets strangely like Beethoven.

Last but one came a reflection on death which has its savage side as Schubert struggled with the 'hardest decision'. The chorale-like tune of his own song 'Death and the Maiden' provides its slow movement, and the finale has the turbulence of a Beethoven. The final quartet (G Major: 1826) begins with a large question mark made by the major-minor alternation so dear to Schubert. This seems to be *his* question, 'must it be?' and the answer is not in any sense resigned, but an abrupt, sweeping reply in one of his most lyrical veins (as much as to say, 'Yes, but death has its own beauty'). The end of the movement begins with a pianissimo reversal of the major and minor of his opening question (whispering to the imagination, 'it must be') and all seems resolved; but the slow movement has two raging interruptions and the finale is a ferocious rondo. Schubert, on this musical evidence alone, was not anxious for the early death which his already wretched health was beckoning.

The B flat major Sonata (1828), the thirteenth and last, is Schubert's most monumental work for piano, but there are many smaller treasures in the catalogue among the Impromptus and *Moments musicaux* (which are really 'songs without words') and the friendly duets for four hands (which include overtures, marches, waltzes and polonaises, much neglected by piano teachers). His piano writing needs no virtuoso (except in the 'Wanderer' Fantasia) and amply repays a little practice.

Piano Teachers' Music

Schubert's last piano sonata was dedicated to Hummel, a virtuoso who had been a favourite pupil of Mozart and Director of Music to the Esterhazy family at Eisenstadt. This musical businessman, living in the same Vienna as Beethoven and Schubert, had far more influence than his music would nowadays suggest. His *Pianoforte School* (1828) was the first comprehensive book on keyboard technique since C. P. E. Bach's seventy years before, and his transcriptions of Beethoven's symphonies for piano duet set the fashion for the countless transcriptions which swamped the music shops later in the century. His brightest pupil,

Czerny, carried on his work to make an industry of writing studies and making transcriptions for piano teachers and family parties (where you could play two, four or eight hands on one piano and up to thirty-two on eight pianos). Clementi and Cramer built up a similar trade in London between 1786 and 1830 on the foundation of the former's hundred studies (*Gradus ad Parnassum*: 1817) and sonatas, which even Beethoven kept in large numbers on his shelves.

Piano music: Liszt, Field and Chopin

Czerny taught Liszt to play; Clementi's pupil, Field, was touring Europe at the same time as Liszt; Chopin knew both Field and Liszt in Paris. Of the three, Chopin is undoubtedly the most original. In 1832 he gave his first Paris concert in the salon of Pleyel (the great firm of instrument makers whose 'Salle Pleyel' is the 'Wigmore Hall' of Paris today). Liszt and Mendelssohn were there to applaud, and the eminent Belgian critic, Fétis, immediately recognized something new in piano music. When Field gave a concert later the same year, he was thought old-fashioned and Chopin himself was very disappointed. Field, however, had provided Chopin as a composer with useful models in his piano concertos and the impromptus which he called *Nocturnes*.

Chopin, like Mozart and Purcell, could assimilate any style he heard amazingly well and could usually turn out something which was better than his model. Italian opera recitative and bel canto at the piano, Hummel's and Field's virtuosity, and his native folk music are clearly separate but totally absorbed in the early rondos, nocturnes, polonaises and mazurkas. His last years in Poland, the upheaval, and his friendship for Liszt whom he met as soon as he arrived in Paris coincided with the writing of his twelve Grand Studies (dedicated to Liszt in 1833). Here, for the first time, was 'teachers' music' with real romantic insight worthy of performance in its own right: the technical exercises are there but so is the poetic feeling which, brightly labelled, was to appear in later piano cycles. No study had its name given to it by Chopin, though some have acquired nicknames (The 'Revolutionary' and 'The Black Keys'). They were so popular that he wrote a further set of twelve (published in 1837) and contributed three to a famous tutor of the nineteenth century, Moscheles's *Piano Method* for the Leipzig Conservatoire.

The first six Studies were connected by key in pairs of major-relative minor but the effort was too great to last; in the twenty-four Preludes (published in 1839) Chopin completes a cycle of keys which does for the romantics what Bach did for the baroque in his '48'. The number is halved by a romantic way of looking at keys: starting with C major and its relative A minor there is an 'outward' series of increasing sharps up to F sharp major (six sharps); the next key (C sharp) has seven sharps but if you re-christen it enharmonically ('D flat' for 'C sharp', the same black note on the piano) it has five flats; the 'inward' series of preludes has, successively, a flat less until you arrive at the last pair, F major and its relative D minor, with only one flat and your next would be C major again, the 'natural' key. It may be that Chopin called these pieces 'preludes' with the old Bach idea of the name in mind, for he was a great student of Bach. Some are short and some long; like Bach's, some are made entirely out of chordal progressions (both composers do this in arpeggio for their first prelude in C major) while some improvise on one keyboard figure; some are just beautiful tunes, others sound like dances. But no fugues follow Chopin's poetic prologues.

Devotees of the salons, on the whole, preferred their music short and would certainly never have sat through a complete performance of the Preludes as many do in recital rooms today. Their favourites were the big E flat Waltz (op. 18) and the E flat Nocturne (op. 9) which are still the pillars through which most music-lovers pass to the rest of Chopin's music. The Waltzes which Chopin wrote from time to time throughout his life were far removed from the ballroom and music hall (or beer-garden). Weber had written his *Invitation to the Dance* in 1819 but Chopin did not know it when he arrived in Paris; Hummel was his model for a series of short contrasting waltzes which work up to an exciting coda. Chopin's waltzes have no programme (whereas Weber's is a description of a love affair); they are unique and stand as a perfect example of his gift for enhancing unremarkable prototypes. The same gift applies to the Nocturnes. Chopin's harmony and melody are far beyond Field's (though the piano writing of the prototype remains), and the tracery of his ornamentation, the delicately balanced proportions in the later pieces were things which Field could never have created in his comparatively heavy-handed way. Most of Chopin's Nocturnes are light salon music, but the C sharp minor and, even more, the D flat major of op. 27 demand more than a passing ear. Two other 'nocturnal' pieces worth hearing are the Barcarolle and the Berceuse.

The Polonaises and Mazurkas run the whole gamut of Chopin's patriotic emotions. As he grew older the pieces became longer and more complicated until they have the heart of the old dances but the body is almost unrecognizable. Listen to the difference between the two most popular polonaises (in A major, op. 40: 1838, and A flat major, op. 53, composed four years later) and, more striking still, between the little B flat Mazurka (op. 7: 1830) and that in C sharp minor (op. 41: 1839). Other countries' dances could also bring out this skill in conveying the spirit without the letter, as in the Bolero and Tarantella. Seven major works which have no Polish connexions at all are the two Sonatas, the four Scherzi and the F minor Fantasy. In all of them Chopin laid down his own rules of form and their unity is sought in many different ways. The Sonatas (B flat minor and B minor) defy analysis other than by picking out their themes, but the listener is aware of the single mind which created them and there is an inevitability about the movements that is as secure as classical sonata form: the spirit, not the letter. Chopin's Scherzi startle his audience with sudden, unexpected happenings but there is nothing childish about them: complete in themselves, the contrast between teeming notes and a simple Christmas carol in the B minor Scherzo, and the struggle of the broad tune to be heard against all the other dramatic ideas in the B flat minor Scherzo are exciting but exhausting 'jokes' for the pianist to play and the audience to follow.

Long pieces for piano which had no particular classical forms, but which re-arranged and adapted them to suit the expression of a composer's ideas as they occurred to him, needed a new name other than 'Sonata'. Chopin found his in the title 'Ballade', for in the poetic ballad the story-teller repeated himself as the drama demanded it but continually introduced new incident, occasionally saying 'but remember when . . .?' The first Ballade (G minor) is an outstanding example on two main characters (or subjects) with a frighteningly difficult *dénouement* in the story at the end; the second (F major) has one idea (or, rather, day-dream) which is thrust out of the way by a furious torrent of thoughts but returns to haunt the ear, a sort of nightmare aria form; the third (A flat major: 1841) is built on its first two lilting bars (a true fantasia); and the last (F minor) has a prelude and two main subjects which are transfigured into one outburst of ardent melody. Chopin was an ardent figure in life, in his loyalty to the memory of Poland, in his passion for the notorious George Sand and in his love for the piano which still lives for us in his music.

Patriotism played a great part in Liszt's later life and he, too, loved the piano. As a virtuoso, he was to pianists as Paganini was to violinists; this kind of flamboyant virtuosity brings fame and fortune, but not many friends. In Paris his friends were Berlioz and Chopin in the 1830s, but the friendship was uneasy. Both admired Liszt as a pianist but neither as a composer nor as a man, yet both had much to thank their friend for. Born in Hungary and trained in Vienna, Liszt came of age in Paris, went into social 'Coventry' at Geneva, toured the continent from Scotland to St. Petersburg, was resident conductor at the fashion-able court of Weimar, sometime a semi-recluse in a monastery at Rome and always a showman in his crowded seventy-five years of life.

His name could have been seen on a music-copy in any house where music was made, for he arranged for piano or organ with prodigious industry almost everything that could be judged popular from an excerpt of someone's 'Ave Maria' to the latest operatic overture. He orchestrated some of Schubert's song accompaniments and transcribed many of the songs for piano solo; and besides all this he left over 220 original works for salon, drawing-room and practice studio.

Liszt's imagination was fired only by poetry or beauty seen from afar. No love affair moved him half so much and his best piano music is contained in the 'tone pictures' left in his mind by a view of a Swiss lake, a spectacular storm, the sound of distant bells, a Petrarch sonnet he read in Italy or the fountains in his garden at the Villa d'Este (the same garden in Tivoli where Palestrina had once worked); all these and many others are collected in his three volumes, *Years of Pilgrimage*; but pictures fade and few of these pieces attract pianists any longer. His years of turning to religion inspired a book of *Music of Poetry and Religion* (1853), two impressive *Legends* (1863) one of which pictures St. Francis of Assisi feeding the Birds, and (by reversion) the devilish *Mephisto Waltzes* (1860, 1883 and 1885).

Even genuine admiration for a human being only produced virtuoso studies to tax his friends' technique in the twelve Studies (1834) for Czerny and the 'Paganini' Studies (1852) for Clara Schumann; his only Sonata (1854), written for Robert Schumann, has been held to be a self-portrait, humble and grandiloquent by turns, leading nowhere but always seeking the path to Paradise. Certainly the pianist can get no better picture of the sentimental exhibitionist than by playing this sonata, with its transformation of the subject in each movement.

Chamber Music: Mendelssohn, Schumann and Brahms

Despite Liszt's friendship for Schumann (and, though neither understood the other's way of life, Mendelssohn) German composers followed Beethoven and Schubert in their songs, chamber music and piano scores.

Mendelssohn went even further back—to Haydn, Mozart, Domenico Scarlatti and J. S. Bach—for his keyboard models.

His six Preludes and fugues for piano (1832–1837) brought Bach in new dress into the nineteenth-century drawing-room, wearing more highly-coloured chromatic harmony and more deliberately ear-catching: the first, beginning in E minor and ending with a booming chorale over bass octaves in E major is a winner for any musical evening. The Serious Variations (1841) are again remarkable for the rise and fall of the dramatic temperature, and he could translate his celestial 'fairy' music with complete success to the piano as in the Andante and Rondo Capriccioso (1824). Scarlatti and Bach are both echoed in the contrapuntal *Seven Characteristic Pieces* (1825) and Beethoven nods in more than one place in the three sonatas, especially at the opening of the B flat major Sonata if you know the Homeric 'Hammerklavier'. Mendelssohn's reputation as a composer of piano music is made by the eight books of *Songs without Words* which are dignified (without the ardour of Chopin or the showmanship of Liszt) but very easy on the ear. Some are too hackneyed ever to sound fresh again (*Spring Song*, 1842 and *The Bees' Wedding*, 1845) but many are worth a moment or two if you are feeling at peace with the world and just a little sentimental.

Organists still admire Mendelssohn's three Preludes and Fugues (1833–1839) and his six Sonatas. For their Mozartian freshness and occasional reminders of Beethoven, the two String Quintets (1832 and 1845), some of the quartets and the fine String Octet (1825) are high on string players' lists. But few singers would now give anything for the complete songs, vocal duets and part-songs in any sale; 'On Wings of Song' is enough to show how lovely some of these can be and perhaps, one day, someone will discover Mendelssohn for the world as Mendelssohn discovered Bach for us.

Schumann was the first notable composer of Lieder after Schubert's pitiful *Swansong*, and the first of the Germans to recognize the value of Chopin's piano music, adding something of Chopin's youthful poetry to the revolutionary inheritance of Beethoven and the wisdom of Bach, his musical ancestor by adoption. The three sides of Schumann's nature which reflected these composers had each its own human form in the composer's imagination. He often named the three figures in his writings and portrayed them in his music as Florestan (the Beethoven side) or Eusebius (the Chopin side), or as a group of Davids fighting the Philistines in the *Davidsbündlertänze* (1837) and in *Carnival* (1834–1835). Trained in Leipzig, Schumann was in the traditional centre of German music; in 1834 he founded a magazine which helped to establish the reputation of Schubert and Mendelssohn by its criticism and introduced among others Berlioz, Brahms, Chopin and even an Englishman (Sterndale Bennett) to a wider public. The first of the piano cycles was *Papillons* (= Butterflies) in 1832: eleven contrasting pieces ranging in length from twelve bars to 102, almost all in four-bar phrases and all but one in waltz-time (at many different speeds) follow each other apparently in haphazard order with an introduction and a finale in D major providing a sort of 'home' key. The Finale begins with Schumann's March for the supporters of David (which he was to use in later works), then refers back to the opening waltz. As the sounds of the march fade the waltz peters out, the clock strikes six, and (in Schumann's words) 'the noise of the carnival dies away'. Already he was creating his dream world.

Fantasy ruled Schumann's life. His Intermezzi (1832) and *Kreisleriana* (1838) are sub-titled 'fantastic pieces'; there are four Fantasy pieces for piano trio (1842) and eight more for piano solo (1837); *Novellette, Humoresque, Arabesque, Nocturne* (called *Nachtstück* in German), *Romance, Dream Picture* and *Woodland Sketch* are his titles for single pieces; and he looks back to the fantasy world of children in *Scenes of Childhood* (1838) and *Album for the Young* (1848). He tried to come to terms with the hard facts of life as a conductor (Düsseldorf 1851–1854) but, like Bach, he was no choir-trainer. As a teacher his career began and ended with his transcriptions for piano of some Caprices for violin by Paganini which Czerny included in his *Modern Fingering Method* (1840). He had married in Clara Wieck a virtuoso pianist far better than himself and he had to live as a virtuoso composer. This the dreamer found hard. After two attempts at suicide he entered a lunatic asylum (1854) and lingered there, not permitted to see his beloved wife yet still able to write to her the most poignant letters, for two years more.

The songs were nearly all written in the happiest year of his life, when he married Clara (1840). The cycles *Dichterliebe* (= The Poet's Love) and *Frauenliebe undleben* (= Women's Love and Life) contain the best of the 128 songs, together with the two popular 'flower' songs ('Die Lotosblume' and 'Du bist wie eine Blume') and 'The Two Grenadiers'. All of these except *Frauenliebe* were settings of Heine. The piano accompaniment assumes great importance and sometimes the songs are virtually piano solos with a vocal obbligato, yet Schumann was probably more sensitive to words than any of his predecessors and each syllable finds its due place, so that it is unusual to find strict repetition of a vocal line even in strophic verse. These are the songs of his courtship; later he works with greater care but less inspiration in the Goethe songs from *Wilhelm Meister* (1844) and he seems already tired of struggling with life in setting poems by Mary Stuart, Queen of Scots (1852).

A similar explosion of energy brought, within the one year 1842, his three string quartets (dedicated to Mendelssohn), two works in E flat major (a Piano Quartet and Piano Quintet) and the four Fantasy pieces for violin, cello and piano. Odd beauties flit across most of this chamber music—a golden tune here, a silvery harmonic sequence there—but none really grip the attention throughout. He was no Beethoven.

But Brahms is a true disciple of Beethoven in his two string sextets (1862 and 1867), the Piano Quintet (1864), the Horn Trio (with violin and piano: 1865), and in 1876 (the first year of the final great period of chamber music in the old Germany) the B flat String Quartet. Here counterpoint and formal design come absolutely naturally, themes develop as if their evolution is inexorable; still the storms and sunshine of the impulsive and the reflective Romantic are somehow there. Some of his early piano works have titles in keeping with the age (four 'Ballads' 1854) but only after 1876 does he start to use 'Capriccio', 'Intermezzo' and 'Rhapsody' for his title-pages. The rest show his sympathy with older forms. The first three published works are sonatas, then followed experiments in eighteenth-century dance-forms and five sets of variations. There are echoes of Liszt in the grandiose sonatas, and the best of the three is also the most difficult, in F minor (1853). The variations reflect Brahms's increasing interest in counterpoint, with their canons, inversions, and fugue (in the Variations and Fugue on a Theme by Handel: 1861) and his up-to-date outlook on virtuosity (in the Variations on a Theme by Paganini: 1863). His final bars in variation form before the remarkable examples in his symphonies and major chamber works were written in the well-loved Variations on a Theme by Haydn (1873) for two pianos (*or* orchestra), also called 'St. Antony Chorale' variations.

Preludes and Fugues for organ—above all, the late Chorale Preludes—show once more the conservative view of music which made Brahms so old-fashioned in the eyes of his critics. These critics naturally trotted at the heels of Wagner but before long Brahms had a champion at his side: Hanslick, the powerful critic of a Vienna newspaper. Brahms, a kindly man, did not relish the fight, but Wagner struck a glancing blow by his parody of Hanslick as 'Beckmesser' in *The Mastersingers*. The career of neither man was in jeopardy, for the public was large enough to divide between those who were always searching for new music and those who found themselves fascinated by the products of the recent arrivals on the musical scene—the musicologists. The first faction eagerly followed Liszt and Wagner; the second, marvelling at the treasures dug up by men like Chrysander (sometime editor of Schumann's *Musical Gazette*) from the age of Bach and Handel, hailed the man who gave them the best of both Romantic and Classical worlds, Brahms.

In his songs, duets, partsongs and choral works with orchestra, Brahms is thoroughly Romantic, although he relies on counterpoint in the larger choral works. There was still one very classical trait in the solo songs; to him music was more important than words. In this he followed Schubert rather than Schumann, sacrificing correct accentuation occasionally for a beautiful melodic line (as in the first line of 'Wie bist du meine Königin': 1864). He finds other Schubertian touches in his love for the repeating folk-song type of setting such as the familiar 'Cradle Song' (1868) and in his catholic taste in poets (which ranges from the traditional Old German through Shakespeare and Goethe to Heine and Eichendorff.) After 1876 the line of lyricism is peculiarly his own, almost introspective and at times as dreamy as Schumann; the heroic line breaks out in the opposite direction in the Ballads (1877) but the folk-song type becomes scarce; the best, as in other fields, was yet to be heard. Meanwhile, duets, choruses for female voices, and mixed vocal quartets of genteelly-arranged popular dances kept his publisher (Simrock of Bonn) happy and contributed to his private fortune. Among these the *Liebeslieder* (= Love Songs: 1868 and 1874) have outstripped in popularity the *Zigeunerlieder* (= Gypsy Songs: 1887) and the Songs for Female Voices, Two Horns and Harp (1862).

Chamber Music: Russia, Norway and back to France

Moussorgsky may well have had Brahms in mind when he wrote his cycle of *Children's Songs* (1872), for his education had been in the hands of a German-trained musician, Balakirev. The other two Moussorgsky song cycles, *Sunless* and *Songs and Dances of Death* (1874), point to the Oriental influence of the future but his well-known 'Song of the Flea' looks straight back to Goethe's Mephistopheles and the Romantic image. Borodin, too, has two sides to his nature, looking ahead and Eastwards towards the nationalists in his songs but turning to western convention in the two string quartets and towards Italy in his early choral music. Tchaikovsky absorbed Russian, French, Italian and Schumann-esque features into his early songs such as 'None but the weary heart' (1869) and, curiously enough, he too reached his most original after he had composed a set of *Children's Songs* (including the famous carol 'Legend'). But this was well after 1876: in that year, Russia's first 'international' composer—his B flat minor Piano Concerto had its première in Boston, U.S.A., in 1875—

was too busy with his third string quartet (op. 30), his third symphony and the ballet *Swan Lake*.

Norway's comparable figure, Grieg, was equally occupied with the music for Ibsen's *Peer Gynt*, but he had already shown where his strength lay in his short piano pieces (*Lyric Pieces*: 1867 onwards, till there were ten books over thirty years later) and in his songs to German, Danish and Norwegian words of which a simple but effective piece of sentiment, 'I love thee' (words by Hans Andersen: 1864) still warms many a 'Winter-Garden' heart in an English summer.

In France, two miniaturists of great delicacy had declared themselves by 1876, to counteract the snake-like fascination which Wagner held for the 'big' composers in their twenties (like d'Indy): Duparc and Fauré. Duparc's reputation has been built up by singers on surely the smallest number of works by which any composer entered the dictionaries of music, for there are but fourteen songs, six little piano pieces and a symphonic poem (which hardly anyone knows); the one song 'Invitation au voyage' (words by Baudelaire: 1870) justifies singers' confidence. Fauré's early *mélodies* were all written by the age of twenty-one and they include two gems in 'Lydia' and 'Après un rêve'; they were the fruits of meeting Saint-Saëns, then newly appointed music master at the boys' school, but in their sudden turns of harmony the pupil's songs held far more interest than the sweetly charming tunes of his master, and the younger man was to reach middle age in a new era for French music.

The year 1876 is an artificial dividing point in musical history, but I have chosen it for several reasons, and the number of stirring musical events within this one year is unique. It is, in fact, the clearest year in which to show that 'music' was no longer—as it had been in 1786—one art. The year included first performances of Wagner's *Ring* in the opera house; in the concert hall, Brahms's First Symphony; in one home, Fauré's 'Lydia'; in another, Sullivan's 'Little maid of Arcadee'. Only in the ballroom could you prophesy what sort of music you would hear: the ubiquitous Waltz, the odd Polka and the 'old' Lancers. The way was open for the 'isms'. Dégas and Manet had almost reached middle age as 'Impressionists' summing up all in a glance; Cézanne and Van Gogh were well on the way to establishing two different traditions, the first examining form with the closest analysis, the second pushing emotion to the fore at the expense of everything else in art. Composers, striding ahead of their public, were not far behind the painters; and the ingenious Mr. Edison was already tinkering with the gadgets that led to the telephone, the gramophone and television.

CHAPTER SIXTEEN

TRADITION AND
EXPERIMENT

FEW composers in history have been so deliberately regardless of
their interpreters as those of the past forty years. The signs were
apparent in 1876: vocal line in Wagner and even in late Brahms
makes tremendous demands on the singer's ear to sing in tune;
string players had to develop their harmonic sense very highly
to hear some of the chords which they had to take part in; wind
players were expected to be almost as agile as the strings; and
conductors had to have phenomenally panoramic eyesight or
highly-cultivated memories to read or remember the orchestral
scores of Wagner and his followers. This gulf between the
composer and his performance has widened.

Many will combine together to overthrow a tradition, but few
will agree on what is to replace it. The 'Ars Nova' of our century
has as many different and separate movements as that of the
fourteenth century, and many of its composers are experimenting
with the same materials. Synthetic rhythms and fixed series of
notes are on the workbench of present-day serial composers
much as they were, in colors and taleas, on Machaut's table.
Not all have experimented with the 'Nova' materials. Some have
tried to extend the materials of traditional rhythm and harmony
still further along nineteenth-century lines; some have re-
analysed old forms to find new; and some have followed the
emotional side of Romanticism to the exclusion of all else. So we
can divide the sounds of the past eighty years or so, roughly, into
'traditional' and 'experimental'.

Range: Traditional

Voices have tended to settle into smaller compasses. Baritones are far commoner than basses and they keep to a middle range, leaving notes above 'F' to the tenors for preference and not too happy below the bass stave. Tenors no longer consider a fortissimo high 'B flat' sufficient excuse for an operatic career but concentrate on an effortless flow of tone. Contraltos have taken over the lower mezzo-soprano range in the name of richer quality, and sopranos are left to be *either* 'coloratura' *or* 'mezzo'. In the search back to the past there have been some attempts to revive the male alto as a soloist, and the parlando bass (who speaks rather than sings his notes) has re-invaded comic opera bass parts. Dynamic ranges have had to be completely revised with the invention of recording and broadcasting equipment (which Edison was testing successfully for the first time in 1877), so that many a reputation made on disc or radio might not now survive in opera house or concert hall.

Choirs have again taken up madrigal singing, though the basic range is still SATB. Looking backwards, composers have used massed voices and double choruses with and without orchestra, and the amateur singer in the more progressive choral societies has had to increase his understanding of tonality to sing even the harmony based upon tradition.

Orchestral instruments have not increased their compasses but some departments have acquired new members, and others replicas of old favourites. Bass flutes and baritone oboes have re-appeared in modern works, while harpsichord, clavichord, lute, chamber organ and recorders have been adopted by the purists in performances of old music, and used by contemporary composers for new music. Brass players have had to learn some of the 'tricks' of jazz such as the 'flare', and their instruments have been muted more often than before; the saxophone and flugelhorn have still not established themselves in the concert orchestra though they have been with us for over a hundred years. Percussion players now have a vast array of possible instruments: since 1876, the Celeste, Xylophone, Wind machine,

Whip and various South American instruments (Maraccas, Claves, Bongos) have added to the 'effects' of the orchestra following the traditional use of percussion to add rhythmic excitement.

The range of traditional tonality based on major and minor keys could hardly be said to have extended since Wagner's *Tristan and Isolde* (1865), though composers working with the old key systems have continued to find new relationships by thinking out possible orders for themselves—a cycle of keys a minor third apart, say, instead of the earlier tonic-to-flat-sixth device—or by deliberately keeping the tonic-subdominant-dominant relationship exact but increasing the chromatic harmony about it. There are still many young composers who do not believe that the nineteenth-century system is dodo-dead: one evolution they may claim is that the ear can now move happily through any key-cycle, without needing the 'signposted' enharmonic change of example 30, and this has opened up new sounds in the old box of magic. The other important traditional approach to tonality has been in carrying further the research into old modal systems started by early Romantics like Berlioz and the relatively un-skilled but highly-gifted Russians of the 1870s.

Range: Experimental

Composers, having subdued the singer in the opera house of the nineteenth century have experimented by first making him or her *speak* half the music (*Sprechgesang* = speech-song) and then by turning the voice into an instrument, singing without words (*vocalise*). Both these experiments are, musically, the equivalent of Gauguin's primitivism in painting (see folksong, page 14). For both of them, the compass of the voice has been ignored and exploited in the extremes, by turns.

Choirs have also had to take up choral speech and been told to 'hum with closed lips' (how else?), snarl and shout, often with striking effect.

Electricity has affected the range of instruments which composers have to experiment with. Melodies have been written for the Ondes Martenot (= Waves, after the name of the inventor), electric organ, amplified pianos and electric guitars and the combination of these is still a fascinating field for study. The popular amplified instrument on the old principle of a glockenspiel is the electric Vibraphone, played with hammers like any other instrument of the bell family but on which the player can regulate the length and intensity of the notes. In Germany and the U.S.A. electrophonic instruments have been built since the 1940s which make no attempt to imitate normal instruments but aim to extend the range of expression with totally new sonorities. The invention of the tape recorder helps these last experiments and has also led to tests using recordings of 'live' music (or *Musique Concrète* according to its French musico-scientists) which have been superimposed one on the other, played at different speeds, backwards or upside down. Ballet or film has so far been the most successful medium for *musique concrète*. Abstract music like this has developed alongside abstract art.

As you have read, there was no room for experimental tonality in the old keys after 1876, so composers explored polytonality—mixing up the old keys simultaneously—and turned their attention to the construction of scales to produce, first, 'whole-tone', then 'twelve-note' series. Polytonality guaranteed new orders of chords but you have a feeling of schizophrenia in listening to polytonal music: if your right hand plays in C major and your left accompanies in A flat major—to use a traditional earlier pair of keys—the example tune of this book needs one ear while the accompaniment demands another and the two come together only at the beginning and the end in a single chord of A flat. Whole-tone harmony may be mixed with diatonic melody to make new progressions (the scale had six notes separated by whole tones, and only those six notes are used in the harmony), or a whole-tone melody may be harmonized in the old system. Here are extracts to play which will give you an idea of the sounds (see example 33).

Twelve-note music (or dodecaphonic, or simply 'serial' as it is now known) denies the old system of keys with cadences

Polytonality: Right Hand in C; left, A flat

Diatonic melody,
harmonized to whole-tone scale

Melody in whole-tone scale:
harmonized diatonically

Example 33

altogether, ignores the physical laws of music, and insists that there is no home note; there is only home ground. The twelve semitones which exist between one note 'C' and its octave are placed in any order you like in a row, and this is then your ground: it may be used at any pitch but you must use *all* the twelve notes before you may repeat any of them. The order of the notes must be kept, though the rhythm may change as in a medieval color (see page 61), and the series may be transposed. But this is not the counterpoint of set numbers of voices and you may use as many notes of the color as you like at any time as a sort of chord. Finally, the actual order of the notes may vary (as it used to do in canon) so that the series may be back to front ('crab'), upside down ('inverted'), or both. Obviously it would be impossible to use the example tune to illustrate serial technique as each note is repeated (and would therefore have to have all the other eleven notes used in between), but you could use its first six notes as the first of a twelve-note series and set off to cover the first ground like this:

Example 34

This can be done mathematically and, until some musical laws are agreed on, the serial technique is open to charlatans; but as an experimental basis it is the only development in musical theory comparable to the theories of atomic physics and it may be that someone will succeed in making the theories intelligible (and musically stimulating) to the ordinary listener if not in the street at least in the concert hall. The most successful serial music at present attracts by the sonorities of its instrumentation and the motion of its rhythmic pattern rather than by its melody or harmony.

Rhythm and accent: Traditional

The interchanging 3/4 and 4/4 of Romantic music was carried further by music which changed time between 2, 3, 4, 5, 7, and 11 beats in a bar but kept a steady crotchet pulse (see also folk music, page 13); increasing numbers of pieces in the 'odd' times characterized the late nineteenth and early twentieth century. The rhythms of the two-step, ragtime and jazz became an unsatisfactory mixture of primitivism and sophistication in the concert hall. (For more about Jazz rhythms, see *Teach Yourself Jazz* in this series.) Syncopation became so regular as to be ineffective in a single 'time' and the traditional two-against-three of earlier days was reinforced by frequent combinations of simple and compound times: 6/8 and 3/4 together, 12/8 and 4/4 and so on.

Some composers preferred not to use any time signatures but to indicate the pulse and define the accent by phrasemarks; others (learning from folk-music) added up the accents in their time signatures as in 2+2+3/8 or 3+2+3/8; but in fact these were only different from plainsong and the free phrasing of the Romantics if the music was fast and the accents emphasized.

The division of beats which the Romantics had used since Beethoven to build up or relax tension by varying the number of quavers, semiquavers and demi-semiquavers was altered even more by the use of rests followed perhaps by a scurry of notes and then a long-held pause. Rests of this kind occasionally served to destroy the beat entirely, and continuously changing accent with sudden rests and isolated figures has led in part to the technique of—in the presently fashionable word—'pointillism'. This term is borrowed from painting where it means a picture built up from separate dots of colour instead of mixed pigments: so far, it has proved most enticing in chamber music for curious combinations of instruments.

Rhythm and Accent: Experimental

The pointillist technique, although a logical development of traditional rhythm and accent, finally destroyed the tradition of accents in twos or threes and rhythms dependent one upon the other. In the last few years some composers have begun to experiment with new series of rhythmic numbers (not unlike the proportions of the Renaissance, see page 89) to vary the old series which was always the same (semibreve = two minims = four crotchets = eight quavers = 16, 32, 64 of the shorter values). These are mathematically arranged in alarming proportions such as 11:10 and 7:5; musically, the pieces in which new series of pitch *and* rhythm are employed (total serialization) remain, for now, theorists' exercises and not practical music. Critics, like ordinary men, are left to concentrate on instrumentation and dynamic contrasts; performers, faced with proportionate notation and as many different dynamics as there are notes in a bar, are left to reflect on the powerful eccentricity of the modern composer; musicologists scratch their heads and recall the similar rhythmic devices found in Morley's *Plain and Easy Introduction* (1597).

Melody: Traditional

Melody in the diatonic system depended more and more upon harmony and appoggiaturas in the late nineteenth and early twentieth century, but two or three effects of the new outlook on old tonality made tunes differ. In song, those who wished to return to the inflections of speech wrote melodies of very narrow compass. Those who were studying folk-song elements found themselves using modal and primitive scales. All composers expected singers to pitch any intervals, often without any help in the accompaniment.

Melody: Experimental

Large intervals gave way to small as the big problems (for string players especially) in music using the whole-tone scale—it is surprising how much further than a semitone it seems from E to F sharp if your ear, accustomed to the old scales, expects F natural—*and* in experiments with quarter-tones. Since the total break with the immediate past in serial music, melody has ceased to exist for old ears, and new ears which can follow the patterns melodically must have the gift of 'absolute pitch' as a basis. No performer stands much chance with this music unless he can hear any note of music accurately 'out of the blue'—or unless he has, like the pianist, an instrument that will make the notes in tune for itself.

Cadences

Cadences were vaguer about the turn of the century and imperfect endings, on indeterminate chords, became common. Interrupted cadences such as had helped Wagner to maintain the flow of his music became too vulgar and often a keynote sounded alone was sufficient to form a satisfactory ending, however it was approached. Mixtures, as you may expect, of plagal and perfect cadence together lived alongside polytonality. Really, once the feeling of home and away keys has gone, any repeated note or held chord will rest in the ear as a suitable end, as long as you repeat it often enough or let it die away as 'infinitely' as possible. In serial music, the question of cadence (being a musical convention, not mathematical) does not arise.

Harmony

Chromatic and modal harmony are still explored by the traditionalists. The thickness of harmony has fluctuated considerably. In the late 1800s and up to the 1920s chords had more and more appoggiaturas piled on them; some, particularly the augmented sixths (see example 32) on different degrees of the scale and the derivatives of the dominant seventh (ninths, elevenths and thirteenths, see example 35) became 'common' even as chromatic chords and were left unresolved. Meanwhile chords associated with the Impressionists, built on successive fourths or triads with augmented fifths, sounded 'thinner' and encouraged others to leave out many of the components of post-Romantic harmony to provide a more piquant style of harmony.

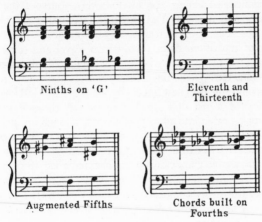

Ninths on 'G'   Eleventh and
                        Thirteenth

Augmented Fifths   Chords built on
                        Fourths

Example 35

Others—again in France—emphasized this piquancy with deliberately intrusive discordant notes, called by many 'Wrong-note harmony'.

Harmony is concerned with the relationship of chords formed in a similar way and serial music does not form its chords similarly, nor consider discord and concord. Experiments with harmony must be traditional and it is pointless to analyse new views with old prejudices.

Forms

Two new words have hung on the lips of those who have written books on form in this century: cyclic and organic. Neither means anything new in the history of musical forms but both are useful. The first involves an extension of the motto-theme (leitmotiv or idée fixe) of Weber, Wagner and Berlioz, mostly by Franck and his companions; the second which means 'variation' or 'fantasia' in the sense of experimenting with one compound (an interval, perhaps, or a rhythm) is suited to the atomic age and is associated particularly with Sibelius. The Impressionists—Debussy and his followers—pursued the emotional aspect of music as Van Gogh did, excluding any niceties of form but bound by laws which still came naturally, particularly the law of repetition. After them—with Ravel and some early Stravinsky—came those who re-analysed old dance-forms, contrapuntal techniques, and older composers' melodies, dressing them incongruously in new finery. By the 1920s musical form was something of a rag doll which had passed through thirteen generations, beaten into all sorts of shapes, crushed up, stretched to breaking point, re-painted so many times that its face was now unrecognizable. Serialists have finally locked the old doll away in an untouchable glass case and proclaimed a law to strip away the only rag that remained: 'There shall be no repetition of patterns'. But many composers still look through the glass and try to copy her in fresh colours, for not everyone welcomes the atomic age of music.

CHAPTER SEVENTEEN

THE LINE OF TRADITION

The World Scene

Musical life has been changed beyond all recognition during the past eighty-five years by the astounding development of communications. Virtuosos and composers meet and their music is heard across continents in hardly any time at all in concert hall and opera house; the mass communication of radio and gramophone has even done away with the need for concert hall and opera house, though there are still some who miss the 'live' atmosphere of a concert in a loudspeaker or two. Music has become international; even Eastern music is becoming a commonplace in Western radio broadcasts. The results so far show that similar musical experiments are being made nowadays in New York, Paris, Athens, Rome, London and Cologne, to take only a random selection. The old traditions die hard, but everywhere young composers are searching to replace them.

This need for some 'new music' has grown stronger as the old political régimes have been swept away. After the French Revolution musicians had left their traditions in the dustbin, there grew up in Paris the more novel Romantic music; after the October Revolution in Russia (1917) the most promising Russian composer—Stravinsky—broke new ground for the first time from his refuge in Switzerland; after the First World War, the

Austrian Schoenberg's serial ideas first gained currency in Berlin (until the rise of Nazi ideas about the old grandeur of the German Reich brought back primitivism in 1933 and the music of Carl Orff); and once Mussolini had marched on Rome (1922) no Italian composer found any inspiration in the Romantic vein of Puccini, even in the land of melody.

England, Finland and Denmark, separated from the musical mainland of Europe in the first half of this century, can all claim greater gifts in their composers than they had known for two hundred years, quoting Vaughan Williams, Sibelius and Nielsen. Indeed, the British have had a revival of gifted composers only comparable with the 'Golden Age' of the late sixteenth and early seventeenth centuries, including their first international opera composer, Britten.

The United States of America was already attracting European composers and virtuosos by 1876 and this century has sent many eminent refugees to their hospitable shores. Most of these have earned their living by teaching, and there should before long (if history has laws) be an international American composer. The even newer countries, like Australia or Africa, seem still to be finding a culture in which they can grow their own music.

This picture of the world is one of evolution and revolution; the tapestry of musical tradition is not yet quite threadbare, though only faint traces remain in the centres where that tradition began—Vienna and Paris. It is stronger in Rome, London and New York but weakening with successive generations of composers. Meanwhile, the taste of vast audiences is far behind, varying from thirty to sixty years (according, roughly, to the age group).

The Symphonic Tradition: Brahms, Dvorak, Tchaikovsky and the Russians

Vienna, Prague and Moscow were, between 1876 and 1914, among the grandest cities in Europe and there these three Romantic composers produced their best symphonies: all four of Brahms' date from 1876 to 1886, the last three of Tchaikovsky's six from 1878 to 1893, and Dvorak's D minor (no. 2), G major (no. 4) and 'From the New World' (no. 5) between 1883 and 1893.

Brahms had the finest symphonic brain of the three. Nowhere does the form of the symphony seem to restrict him, whereas in both lesser symphonists the seams show as they join together sections which, conventionally, should 'join'. Tchaikovsky is, to most new listeners, easiest to follow and the most immediately appealing. Dvorak's style is the most difficult in its harmonies for the student.

In his first symphony, in C minor (finished in 1876), Brahms is at once at his most Romantic and his most Beethovenian. There is an immediate severity about the music after, say, a Mendelssohn or Schumann symphony, and a feeling that here is a man who has considered every note carefully. The slow introduction gives way to the controlled passion of the first movement proper, which has the remarkable balance of subjects (both of which use the same material from the introduction), and even the rhythm of Beethoven's C minor symphony in a subsidiary tune. Canon, augmentation, inversion—all the old polyphonic devices are there; but with them is Brahms's wonderful sense of Romantic key relationships and harmony . . . and his gift of melody. The slow movement displays his equal command of orchestration with its solos for the 'romantic' oboe and clarinet contrasting with the 'classical' violin coda. The third movement is not the usual scherzo but a delightful pair of pieces in duple time, the first simple (2/4) the second compound (6/8) lasting only five minutes and using only part of his large orchestra. His finale has one of *the* horn calls of the nineteenth century and a solid chorale-like tune worthy of the Gild of Mastersingers in its introduction, a first subject that could serve for another Schiller 'Ode to Joy' and a fairy-like second subject worthy of Mendelssohn: the best of all possible nineteenth-century worlds.

The D Major Symphony (no. 2, 1877) is a similar summing-up of the pastoral side of the Romantic age. It is absolute music and needs no programme but in it Brahms has recalled all the pleasure

which a holiday in the Austrian Tyrol gave him. The first movement opens with another horn call (dreamy this time) after a three-
note introduction on the cellos and basses; where in the first
symphony he made the whole movement out of his introduction
here Brahms finds room for one of the most haunting tunes ever
written in a symphony as his second subject (played by cellos,
singing a third higher than the violas). The slow movement is the
first symphonic example of Brahms's art of phrasing immensely
long tunes across the bar-lines so that the accent continually
shifts without changing the time signature; this one is contrasted with a lilting and graceful melody which seems to have
floated in from the ballet. Again Brahms scorns the normal
Scherzo for his third movement, preferring an impish set of
variations on a pretty *ländler* tune which he may well have
refined from a country-dance song which he heard on holiday.
The finale brings back his initial three notes as if by coincidence
to lead off a string of happy figures which recall a Haydn rondo,
then to form a 'tranquillo' episode (which usually, in Brahms,
sounds 'misterioso'.) The crowning gaiety of the coda has all the
spirit of carnival, ending with a tingling fortissimo triad on
trombones which can only fall flat in performance if the conductor has his hands behind his back. (Dvorak uses the same
effect to close his concert overture *Carnival*.)

The last two symphonies, in F major (1884) and E minor
(1886) bear out the theory that the greatest composers all became
fascinated by counterpoint in their last works written in the 'big'
form of the day. In the F major, Brahms blinds you with a 'bi-
lingual' subject which is in F major and F minor alternately,
using all the conjuring tricks of counterpoint: the finale has more
rhythmic variants of his tune than any polyphonic motet, still
passing the two tonalities before your eyes until you are mes-
merized. The last movement of the E minor is a Passacaglia (see
page 115) to make all such exercises in counterpoint and harmony
pointless in future: only Brahms could make thirty variations on
five steps of a scale and a perfect cadence climb so unrelentingly
from peak to peak.

Variations ended Brahms's symphonic life. Dvorak's Symphonic Variations for orchestra (1877) heralded his musical maturity. In them he quotes Slavonic dance-themes of the sort that keep on turning up in his major works: where Brahms (except in the deliberately 'gypsified' Hungarian Dances: 1874) will evoke a folk-dance type of tune, Dvorak openly builds his subject on them. Indeed, his two series of Slavonic Dances (1878 and 1886) which, like Brahms, he transcribed for orchestra from piano duets, still require re-printing more frequently than anything else. Outside influences also led him to concentrate in later life on concert overtures, symphonic poems and suites rather than on Brahms's symphonic model, yet he left one masterpiece in his 'New World' Symphony and two other welcome additions to the repertory of real symphonies. The D minor (1883), although it has suggestions of Brahms *and* Wagner in it, has that quality of humble yearning mixed with an unfortunate streak of pomposity which was to appear in almost all his works. The G major (1887) is sometimes called 'The English' because of all his symphonies this is the only one published, not by Simrock of Bonn, but Novello of London. It is the most 'Bohemian' of all his symphonies in sound, from the finger-snapping flute tune in the first movement through the pleading Slav notes of the Adagio and the Waltz (in G minor) to the final set of variations on the flute tune in new guise.

Dvorak's fifth symphony 'From the New World' (1893) is too well-known to need description, but it may be well to recall the composer's words in an interview with the *New York Herald** about Negro songs which were, to him, 'pathetic, tender, passionate, melancholy, bold, merry, gay or what you will'. Here is a detailed vocabulary to his last symphony, composed when he was director of the newly-opened National Conservatory in New York. The words are true equally of the Slav temperament; both races knew the meaning of slavery, and Dvorak's symphony belongs neither to the Americans nor the Czechs but to all who have known poverty and oppression.

*Quoted by Alec Robertson in *Dvorak* (Master Musicians, Dent 1945).

Tchaikovsky's three principal symphonies were all written after the composer had been working on programme music, and each had a personal programme. The F minor (no. 4) was the first orchestral work to follow the Symphonic Fantasy *Francesca da Rimini* (1876) 'after Dante'; the E minor (no. 5) followed the so-called symphony *Manfred* (1885) after Byron; and the last, the 'Pathétique' in B minor, was composed after he had made the orchestral suite from his ballet *The Nutcracker* (1892). Their programmes (apart from no. 4) remain an enigma, but many commentators have wasted pen and ink in speculation, starting from Tchaikovsky's letter in which he told his patroness that the opening of the Fourth represented Fate. There is no evidence for labelling the opening theme of no. 5, 'Fate'—but there is no harm in guessing. The symphonies last because their tunes are so good, the orchestration is sumptuous, and the emotions are so easily transferred to the listener who is not afraid to admit them. Few composers can claim that their slow tunes are so immediately recognizable as these played by the oboe in no. 4, the horn in no. 5, and the 'lamentoso' strings in the Finale of the 'Pathétique.'

All three composers used the title and shape of an earlier symphonic form in Romantic style in their serenades, of which Tchaikovsky's is the most well-known (1880). Dvorak and Tchaikovsky turned also to the suite. Russian composers have since used the symphonic suite to great advantage from Rimsky-Korsakov's tedious *Schéhérezade* (1888) to the exhilarating suite from Stravinsky's ballet *The Firebird* (1910). 'Capriccio' is another old term revised in Rimsky-Korsakov's 'Spanish' and Tchaikovsky's 'Italian' works for orchestra. Tchaikovsky's symphonic poems or fantasies set a pattern which Tsarist Russians loved to use under every circumstance, from the geographic (Borodin's *In the Steppes of Central Asia*: 1880) to the erotic (Scriabin's *Poem of Ecstasy*: 1908, using chords built up of fourths as in example 35 almost exclusively) and the necrophiliac (Rachmaninov's *Isle of the Dead*: 1907). Real symphony has been universally acclaimed in Prokofiev's first, the 'Classical' Symphony

(1917, which uses an Esterhazy-size orchestra), and in two by Shostakovich, in F minor (no. 1: 1925) and E minor (no. 10: 1950).

The Symphonic Tradition: Bruckner, Mahler and Strauss

Bruckner lived in Brahms's Vienna and suffered by comparison. A devout Roman Catholic and an admirer of Wagner, his symphonies were a serious and rather stodgy mixture of religious ecstasy and secular pride. They are immensely long and the composer rarely smiles in his music: the Scherzos sometimes have the rustic humour of Austrian dances, but elsewhere the organist keeps a solemn face to impress his choirboys. On the other hand, there is a majesty about his solid walls of sound (which build up in the orchestra as if an unseen organist is pulling out more stops at convenient intervals) and about the chorales which end three of the slow movements in his nine symphonies. He was always revising his work, and six symphonies exist in two or three versions; two of them have nicknames, the third (from his dedication) the 'Wagner' and the fourth the 'Romantic'. The publication of the original versions of many of his symphonies shows that many alterations were later made to suit conductors who knew what the public wanted; in their original form Bruckner's symphonies show him to be a man of singular concentration with a true sense of symphonic form who should be studied closely. In one development of tradition he looks understandingly back at those who first evolved the 'long' sonata form as an extended two-fold pattern (see page 123): when he has three subjects (not two) there is no repeat of the exposition but they develop *as they recapitulate* to make a balancing second half. He uses leitmotiv only in pairs of movements, never throughout; but in three finales he brings back all the main themes of his earlier movements. A composer more for the student than the ordinary listener, opportunities of hearing his symphonies are few; the fourth, seventh and ninth are the most likely to appear in radio or concert programmes.

Mahler also wrote nine symphonies and four song-cycles with

orchestra which would have been called 'symphonies' half a
century earlier. Like Bruckner's, they are very long and their
form is complicated. The resources swelled as Mahler, by
profession primarily a conductor, needed new sonorities. They
reached their peak in the eighth symphony (1907), called exagger-
atedly the 'Symphony of a Thousand', for eight solo voices,
double chorus, boys' chorus, organ and abnormal numbers of the
usual orchestral instruments; at the other end of the scale is the
Fourth Symphony (1900) for soprano and small orchestra.
Altogether four of his symphonies needed voices and we are at the
logical end of the line started by the Choral Symphony of
Beethoven, continued by way of the orchestral niceties of Berlioz,
and over-stretched by the prolixity of Bruckner.

Romantic music is perhaps at its most personal in Mahler. As a
first-rate opera conductor, he had more than his fair share of the
sense of drama in life, but he chose the symphony rather than the
opera to put it down on paper. The first few symphonies show him
becoming more and more subjective. The D major (no 1: 1888)
begins with one of his own song melodies, uses a favourite canon
('Frère Jacques') in the third movement, and yet another of
his earlier songs later. They are not sung but treated symphonically, as if the composer was remembering incidents in his life
and re-living them for the pure pleasure of composing during a
holiday from conducting. Bruckner had revived the idea of a
two-section 'long' form: in the C minor symphony (no. 2: 1894)
Mahler goes one further and conceives the whole symphony in
two large parts with a very long first movement and, after a
pause, a series of four shorter movements (five in all) which are
to be played as a balancing group. Here, too, he builds his four
short movements regardless of practical resources and as the
whim takes him. The Andante is a slow waltz, the next another
fantasy on one of his own songs, the third a short new setting of an
old text he was fond of (for contralto solo) and the last a vivid
setting of an ode on the Resurrection for soprano, contralto,
chorus and orchestra. The D minor (no. 3: 1895) is in the same
pattern, with women's and boys' choirs and an extra section

added to make a five-movement 'second-half', and a record time-
length for a symphony of two hours.

In 1900, Mahler seems to discipline himself, allowing himself
only four movements, one soprano and no trumpets or trombones
for the G major symphony (no. 4) For the last time in his symphonies he uses one of his own songs, and (for the first time)
he provides no detailed programme except to say that the queer
violin solo in the Scherzo is 'Death' fiddling away. He was
converted from the Jewish religion to Catholicism in 1895 (just
after writing the 'Resurrection' symphony) and a new feeling
for simplicity had to fight with a natural tendency for the man's
mind to dramatize and heighten every emotion. The next three
symphonies for orchestra only, which made up his middle period
(1902–1905), have something of the plain statements of faith
and fun which Haydn used, and much of the older composer's
skill in counterpoint. With the Eighth (1907) Mahler burst out
again, this time with mature confidence, on the subject of life
after death: from the Catholic point of view in the forty-minute
'Hymn' based on the old Latin *Veni Creator Spiritus*, which
opens the work; and from the Humanist attitude in the hour-
long setting of the closing scene in Goethe's *Faust* (where Faust
is redeemed and his soul enters Heaven) which forms the second
half. This gargantuan symphony was to the Romantic period
what Bach's B minor Mass was to the Polyphonic period: it
also united the two periods by insisting on the compatibility of
old church dogma and the romantics' humanist outlook through
the mediation of music.

Richard Strauss was another eminent conductor in opera
houses from Weimar to Vienna and in concert halls all over the
world. He began to compose for orchestra with a couple of early
symphonies, but he found his true *métier* in 1888 when he wrote
the first of his symphonic poems on the character of *Don Juan*.
From then on all his symphonic works have programmes
and Strauss's success, like Beethoven and Mahler, lay in his
ability to absorb sounds with an 'outside' meaning into pure
music. Three poems have legendary heroes (*Don Juan, Don*

Quixote: 1897, and *Till Eulenspiegel*: 1895) and one glorifies himself as hero (*Ein Heldenleben*, or *A Hero's Life*: 1898). These are the most readily understood and so most often played: Don Juan's love-song with its wink at the beginning, the tuba which plays Sancho Panza to the cello's Don Quixote, and Till's mocking horn call immediately conjure up their own images. *Heldenleben* in which Strauss is angry at his critics was followed by a much more peaceful piece of autobiography about his family life, *Domestic Symphony* (first performed in New York: 1904). The last of his programme pieces was *Alpine Symphony* (1915) which is a simple descriptive piece waiting to be used as background for a travelogue.

Strauss's two most serious symphonic poems need a separate paragraph since both are concerned with philosophy and both are musically the most advanced in the old tradition. *Death and Transfiguration* was written five years before Mahler's 'Resurrection' symphony, in 1889, but Strauss was not only putting down his own views in music; he firmly believed that his music could express those views so clearly as to make people believe in them. He tried further, in *Thus Spoke Zarathustra* (1896) to convey a whole philosophical doctrine in terms of music which would put hearers in the state of mind where they could understand Nietzsche's argument in favour of the superman. Strauss himself was evidently attracted to Nietzsche's doctrine and was one of the few musicians of the older generation not to condemn Hitler for his doctrine of the German superman. He was even moved by the dictator so much (like Beethoven before him, by Napoleon) that he quoted from the 'Eroica' funeral march at the end of his last symphonic work, the strangely beautiful *Metamorphosen* for twenty-three solo strings, finished in the year of Hitler's death.

It is now (1960) only just over a decade since Strauss died and yet he is usually thought of as a nineteenth-century composer, for he never departed from the traditional Romantic warmth of emotion. His harmony, with its triple and quadruple appoggiaturas making chromaticism even more chromatic, has been imitated until it has become old-fashioned and the orchestral effects have been transferred to the luscious light orchestras of the television screen, but there are still prophetic passages (such as the dual tonality of *Zarathustra*) for disciples to fulfil, and many experimentalists written about in Chapter XIX had reason to thank Strauss for showing the way.

The Symphonic Tradition: Franck and the French

Seldom has one symphony had such an influence on a composer's countrymen as Franck's D minor (1888). It is a cosmopolitan symphony, not unlike Liszt in its germinal growth, full of academic procedure but with a Wagnerian disrespect for correct modulation. Nowadays it has a fascination for those who like to play at 'functional anaylsis' which proves how everything derives from everything . . . and there is always the broad F major tune to wait for expectantly. Chausson's Symphony in B flat (*c.* 1890) was the first offspring to grow up, while d'Indy's *Summer's day on the Mountain* (1905) and Dukas's *The Sorcerer's Apprentice* (1897) were short-lived symphonic poems brought up on Franck's teaching. One of d'Indy's pupils, Roussel, returned to the true form after a first which had a 'programme' poem, and his remaining three symphonies (written between 1919 and 1934) look back to the French tradition.

The Symphonic Tradition: Sibelius and Scandinavia

Sibelius has become very well-known in Great Britain and the United States but few other countries of Western Europe have shown any interest. Perhaps the climate has something to do with it. There is a northern wind blowing through all his symphonies whose cold we catch easily but which does not seem to affect the Latin temperament nor yet, apparently, the German constitution. Sibelius was, as it were, on his own iceberg drifting apart from the flow of European music, showing little above the surface which can be called original, yet having so much depth below that there is always plenty to listen for. The E minor (no. 1: 1899) begins with a long clarinet solo over a low, soft and grumbling drum-roll pedal which has the morning cold in its bones. The first theme shows the typical Sibelius technique of letting a long note disappear finally in a flurry of much shorter ones. Next comes a fingerprint of Sibelius orchestration using woodwind in the lowest registers and preferring not to mix 'families'; and within a matter of fifty bars a composer has announced his style to the world. The rest of the symphony may remind you of Tchaikovsky, Grieg or Brahms from time to time but the iceberg is already adrift.

In the remaining six symphonies the iceberg gradually sinks until there is so little left on the surface in the seventh that the listener must know something of the music which has 'gone below' in previous symphonies to understand what significance the remaining shapes have. The finales of the D major (no. 2), the C major (no. 3) and the E flat (no. 5) all have warm, broad tunes which pile up from earlier elements, rising through the orchestra from the lowest to the highest registers; these are perhaps the most popular movements in Sibelius and carry a dignity entirely their own. Elsewhere the music often seems fragmentary and when, as in the finale of the A minor (no. 4) the fragments seem on the verge of coming together to make another great tune, only to dissolve again, the Romantic listener is often frustrated. The D minor (no. 6) is from this viewpoint the most frustrating and aloof of all. It sounds as if Sibelius had his broad tune at heart and writes all the fragments down in a jig-saw but is then only interested in the pieces as pieces. The picture of the whole jig-saw is never completed, but remains under the surface—the hidden four-fifths of the iceberg. The Seventh (also in C major) is the ultimate example of his process of leaving out anything which he can claim is clearly implied. Here all the movements are concentrated in one. It begins with a few fragments which do not seem to have any connection as an opening Allegro, then goes on to a short 'slow movement' with a new group of jigsaw pieces; these two sections develop *together* to a climax which proves to be the Scherzo, and a whole row of pieces seem to fall into shape as a Trio tune; but before you can sit back for this to grow, Sibelius starts the 'last movement' which looks at all the fragments again (recapitulation). The subjects are implied but never stated: as the Fantasy mass in the sixteenth century had become a set of 'variations on an unknown theme' at the end of the period of unaccompanied polyphony, so Sibelius's Seventh Symphony (1924) brought to an end the period of symphonic form based on the diatonic system.

Sibelius has also rightly earned a place in history books by his remarkable symphonic poems such as *The Swan of Tuonela* (listen to its magical string fluttering of wings against the cor anglais 'swansong'), *Pohjola's Daughter*, *A Saga* and *Tapiola*. Even in his over-familiar pieces, such as *Finlandia* and *Valse Triste* there is still the strength and sureness of a master.

Norway's master Grieg was no symphonist; his friend and compatriot Svendsen, who had learnt his craft in Leipzig and Paris, might have become the Sibelius of Norway had he not also had to earn his living as a conductor. His memorial in modern concerts is a cheerful symphonic poem, *Carnival in Paris* (1870). Sweden's finest symphonist, Berwald (who died in 1868) left no school to follow up his undoubtedly original ideas, but the Danish Gade (himself thoroughly 'Leipzig' in outlook) left a pupil of some account in Nielsen, composer of six controversial symphonies which extend the normal resources of harmony and tonality to their limits. Three of Nielsen's symphonies have titles, though the composer published no programmes for them. Two are occasionally heard in England, the 'Four Temperaments' (no. 2: 1902) and the 'Inextinguishable' (no. 4: 1914–16), notorious for its drum parts.

The Symphonic Tradition: Elgar and the English

The first 'German' symphony written by an Englishman was Stanford's Symphony in B flat, in 1876, one of seven. Elgar, then only nineteen, was working in a solicitor's office and keeping music his hobby. Nearly a quarter of a century later, a thoroughly professional composer, Elgar still remembered his amateur musical friends who are—many of them—pictured within the

first 'international' symphonic work by an Englishman, his
Enigma Variations (1899). This set of fourteen pieces, all of them
headed by the initials or the nickname of their subject, started
Elgar's fame as a symphonist as surely as the Symphonic Variations had done for Dvorak. His concert overture, *Cockaigne*
(In London Town)—complete with Salvation Army Band coming
down the street—and the *Introduction and Allegro* for strings
further confirmed his gifts as an orchestrator and as a man who
could work in long forms.

Elgar's two symphonies (and tantalizing sketches for a third)
and the big symphonic study *Falstaff* are all monuments to the
Edwardian age in England. The A flat symphony (no. 1: 1908)
has for its first theme a simple tune to be played *nobilmente*
(Elgar's favourite adverb); these first few bars characterize their
composer's music as succinctly as Sibelius's had in his E minor
Symphony and the two should be played side by side to point the
immense contrast. Both are simple, but Elgar's tune has the
comfortable warmth of an English fireside where the brandy is
taken for pleasure and not to unfreeze the limbs. Elgar, like
Sibelius, makes use of fragments but he plays the complete tune
first. It is one of the last memorable tunes in the history of the
symphony and its composer was the last serious symphonic
writer that the public at large could understand. Here was the
man who had written their favourite *Pomp and Circumstance*
marches, including 'Land of Hope and Glory'; his symphony
had over one hundred performances during its first year of life.

The E flat Symphony (no. 2: 1911), dedicated to the memory
of Edward VII, announces a haunting motto-theme in its third
bar which returns to point to the end of each movement. Finally
lingered on by the flutes, it ends the whole symphony in a deep
contentment, a mood which Elgar must have felt as he wrote an
extract of Shelley on the fly-leaf, 'Rarely, rarely comest thou,
Spirit of delight.' Already nostalgia had begun to settle in. In
Falstaff (1913) the composer uses his years of study in Shakespeare to provide a detailed programme of the events involving the
old rogue Sir John in *Henry IV* and *Henry V* which he was

portraying, but there is an almost unbearable Edwardian nostalgia in the farewell to his hero which was also Elgar's farewell to the symphony. Although he was to live for another twenty-one years he felt himself to be a relic of a bygone age and the sketches for a third symphony defeated the seventy-five year old composer as he tried to make them grow in an attempt to fulfil a B.B.C. commission.

In the year following Elgar's death in 1934, Vaughan Williams produced his most dissonant symphony, the F minor (no. 4: 1935) and dedicated it to another Englishman who was as great a craftsman but no genius: Arnold Bax. Vaughan Williams' first orchestral masterpiece, the Fantasia on a Theme by Tallis, had been performed at Elgar's beloved Three Choirs' Festival (see page 279) in 1910, the very year of Edward VII's death, and a new era—perhaps the last in the old tradition—had begun. The same year his first symphony was given at the Leeds Festival, called, despite the fact that it used a choir and soloists (shades of Mahler) the 'Sea' Symphony. The second and third symphonies also had programmes but the composer had learnt remarkably quickly how to orchestrate (with a few lessons from Ravel) and he now needed no words to stimulate his imagination. The second portrayed the capital in music again—the 'London' Symphony (no. 2: 1914)—and the third was his 'Pastoral' Symphony (no. 3: 1922) which has a wordless cadenza for soprano at the beginning and end. This last is the first symphony in which Vaughan Williams can 'have his fingerprints taken' (as Elgar and Sibelius had in their opening symphonic bars): after the *vocalise* which mixes folk-song and plainsong in equal parts, the lower strings have rows of parallel close triads while the violins play a broad tune in octaves, both unmistakably by Vaughan Williams.

The F minor (no. 4) was first performed by the B.B.C. Symphony Orchestra and begins with a howling clash between C and D flat, a fight about which is to be the dominant of 'F' which reflects the first parting of the ways between the eighteenth and nineteenth centuries, for D flat is, of course, the sixth on the flat side of 'F'. By the end of the first movement D flat is uneasily supreme, unsure now whether to be 'minor' or 'major' (a hovering which was to become another fingerprint of Vaughan Williams's hand). A powerful, restless Scherzo leads without a break to the Finale where, for the first time, the 'relative' D minor enters the lists to be followed by the least attractive 'V-W' fingerprint— a galumphing 'um-cha, um-cha' rhythm for brass with the tuba as a bass—and a lively epilogue. The Epilogue is a tightly-packed fugato on a subject made up of two repeated notes, the first pushed out by the semitone below, the second weighed upon by the semitone above (thus, F-E-G flat-F). The last four bars are a final vehement utterance of the driving thoughts behind the symphony: six *ff* repetitions of an F minor chord with both major and minor third in it and a note 'G flat' howling defiance again on top; and *fff* chord of F with *no* third, major or minor, in it. If the Sibelius Seventh marks the end of the road for classical form in its balance of movements and thematic development, Vaughan Williams's Fourth is surely the cul-de-sac of diatonic harmony.

The D major (no. 5: 1943) reverts to the more usual peaceful temperament of Vaughan Williams, using many of the tunes which occur also in his morality, *The Pilgrim's Progress*. The opening of the E minor (no. 6: 1948) again raises the argument between major and minor tonality, but the Epilogue there, in one of the strangest passages in all music, seems resigned and immune from the quarrel. The last symphonies are 'entertaining' by comparison: the 'Antarctic' (no. 7: 1953) was extended from a film score and pays tribute to the polar explorers, especially Captain Scott, and the Eighth (1958) is an orchestral showpiece in which the brass and strings have movements to themselves and 'all manner of bells and 'phones' play a Toccata.

The other English symphony established in the repertory is Walton's first, completed in 1935, which in a curious way ties together the three ends of Elgar (in the majesty of its finale), Sibelius (in its tunes which scurry away at the end) and Vaughan Williams (in its indeterminate tonality). Walton calls it his Symphony in B flat minor, but the tonal argument is never settled any more than in Vaughan Williams's Fourth. Its fury is almost without parallel. The Second Symphony (1960) resolved much of the struggle and is a mellower work, though it has Walton's unmistakable idioms in it. One other work of this century in England, Holst's symphonic suite *The Planets* (1916), also fought for a compromise between traditional dignity, exotic oriental ideas, and the fast-failing grip of tonality, and has at least reached a fairly wide public. For the lover of English music, there are also the six well-designed and richly-coloured symphonies of Holst's pupil, Rubbra; the grim intensity of Fricker's two symphonies; and the open-hearted gaiety of Arnold's symphonies and symphonic poems (of which *Tam O'Shanter* is currently very popular).

The Concerto Tradition

Virtuosos have kept many a composer's name alive by adopting one of his concertos and most of the popular pieces written since 1876 are not music to assess or quarrel about; we talk about the performance, not the work. A few have become war-horses for every aspiring interpreter and those may be worth a little study to the historian.

Among piano concertos, Brahms's B flat major (no. 2: 1881) deserves most attention for it has real symphonic thought in its first three movements and an infectiously joyful finale. The piano part needs a master who has no technical worries whatever but who can think in terms of long developments and distant climaxes. Once the piano is 'introduced' to the orchestra by a most courteous French Horn, Brahms makes the two discuss his tunes with equal vehemence and persuasion, never leaving the pianist empty-handed unless the orchestra has something highly important to say. The second movement, surprisingly in a concerto, is a scherzo which sometimes blusters, sometimes wheedles, surrounding a trio based on one of the proudest themes in the repertory. The slow movement begins and gradually unfolds one of Brahms's almost endless tunes which a solo cello sings in uneven phrases as if he was improvising from line to line. Finally, in a wicked test for a virtuoso, Brahms strings together four very typical tunes—perky, wallowing, restless and jaunty again—to make an ending almost too lightweight for the rest of the work.

There is no cadenza to write about in the Brahms' Second, but no one can escape the cadenza Grieg wrote in his celebrated A minor Piano Concerto (revised in 1907): the measure of the two composers' sense of evolution and development could not be taken more exactly than by noting this. Brahms lets his piano develop themes constantly in full partnership with the orchestra where Grieg keeps to the well-worn path in which a clearing has to be made for the soloist to impress the whole assembly by his discourse on the chosen themes. There is no lack of poetry, though, in Grieg's slow movement (in the foreign but rich key of D flat major) and the Norwegian gets the maximum excitement and enchantment from a contrasting pair of tunes (pitched a flat-sixth apart) in his finale. The last stage in the journey of this type of concerto was made by Rachmaninov, in the second and third of his four piano concertos and the Rhapsody on a Theme by Paganini (1934): their unashamed virtuosity and their full-blooded romantic spirit have provided many a background score for the film industry and have become almost an inescapable model for arrangers of light music working with large orchestras; the composer died, appropriately enough, in Beverly Hills, California (1943).

Violin concertos also stem from Brahms, who wrote only one (for Joachim, 1878) but succeeded in making the music live in its own right as well as providing a vehicle for the soloist. The first movement is again the largest and most deeply thought out: its three main tunes (in 3/4 time) are models of contrast—slow arpeggio, jerky repetition and a Viennese waltz-tune with swooning appoggiaturas—and are all enlarged upon and enhanced in the development. Brahms left the cadenza to Joachim and you may still hear what that virtuoso supplied, though in this century Kreisler and Heifetz (among others) have adopted their own and you may hear any one of them nowadays. Whichever cadenza the soloist uses, listen to the intonation when the opening tune returns, high up, accompanied by the orchestra; Brahms sets out the remainder so beautifully that your ear is recaptured from the first note of the orchestra's return and the cadenza immediately takes its place in the proportions of the movement. The slow movement tune is so simple but haunts the ear for days, and the Finale is a rollicking Hungarian dance. Benefiting from Joachim's advice, Brahms has provided a near-perfect piece for the Romantic violinist who is willing to think; technique must be assumed to include octave-playing, treble-stopping, flying fingerwork and immaculate bowing before an artist can begin to use his ears to prepare the work properly. Most of the other violin concertos which you may hear from time to time usually require one of three approaches: considerable technique (Wieniawski and Tchaikovsky), panache with a sentimental touch (Bruch, Goldmark, Lalo's *Symphonie Espagnole*, Svendsen's *Romance* and Chausson's *Poème*), or high-mindedness coupled with devotion (Sibelius, Delius and Elgar). Brahms needs something of all three.

Bruch, Delius and Elgar also provided cellists with showpieces which each have movements of great beauty (as in the heartbreaking Elgar slow movement). Brahms tried to provide for violin and cello together in his Double Concerto, but Dvorak is the only composer to write a masterpiece for cello and orchestra. His Cello Concerto (B minor: 1895) was written for the cellist of a trio with which he had toured Bohemia; Dvorak—unlike many, including Brahms—would brook no interference with his very short cadenza passages by a well-meaning virtuoso, and made only minor alterations at his friend's request. How right he was you may judge for yourself, but incontestably, Dvorak's ear has let the cello 'come through' the orchestra better than any before or since, leaving plenty of room for fireworks, singing melodies (listen for the horn in the first movement) and grandiose climaxes in the highest Romantic tradition. Casals has made a memorable recording to prove that the cellists had no reason to mourn their lost cadenza.

CHAPTER EIGHTEEN

TRADITION IN THE
OPERA HOUSE, CHURCH
AND RECITAL ROOM

Verdi and the Italians

France and Germany had both reached their pinnacles of operatic grandeur by 1876 in *The Trojans* and *The Ring*; Italy's comparable summit was conquered by Verdi in his last two operas—both Shakespearean—*Othello* and *Falstaff*. *Othello* (La Scala: 1887) is a near-perfect opera. Not a word is wasted in the compression of Shakespeare's play into a quarter of its original length and Verdi does not waste a note in setting it. The music helps the tenor to portray the Moor in every mood which Shakespeare had created, as the imperious man of authority, the poetic lover (in perhaps Verdi's finest love duet which ends the first act), wretched with jealousy, relentless in rage, and finally, noble in despair after killing Desdemona and discovering his trust in Iago mistaken. Iago's repulsive power reaches its height in his notorious 'Credo' ('I believe in a cruel God') but Verdi also gives his baritone music to suggest brilliantly the villain's crafty cunning; Desdemona, in all her innocence, has in her Willow Song a most exquisite matching of Shakespeare's intentions, and her final scene is set by an orchestral prelude of heart-searching

270

intensity. *Falstaff* (La Scala: 1893) is a mixture of what Shakespeare showed Sir John to be in *Henry IV* as well as in *The Merry Wives of Windsor*—twice as large as life. The music is full of the kindly wit an old man might well feel for the affable, fat knight whose unceremonious failures in love give the opera its story, and the whole sparkles at a crackling speed; in the words of Verdi's last fugue, 'man is born to be jolly'.

There is nothing jolly about the tragedies of Verdi's most famous successor, Puccini, if you except the short one-act *Gianni Schicchi* (1918) and the party scenes of *La Bohème*. The rest nearly all concern *femmes fatales*. *Manon Lescaut*, the first, was performed in the same year as *Falstaff*, in Turin (1893), and tells the story of a woman too fond of luxury who is banished to New Orleans as a wanton only to die there despite the presence of her faithful lover (who has managed to go into exile with her). *La Bohème* (1896) deals also with a wanton, Mimi, who dies of consumption almost at the moment she has re-found happiness with the lover she had previously deserted. *Tosca* (1900) becomes involved in politics at the time of Napoleon's invasion of Italy, kills a vindictive police chief to save her honour (and at the same time to provide for her lover's escape from prison) only to see the prisoner executed before her eyes and to throw herself over the parapet of the gaol. *Madam Butterfly* (1904) marries an American Navy Lieutenant, who sails away (leaving her with a child) and returns three years later with another wife; he only wants the child and Butterfly commits suicide by the side of the little boy just as the Lieutenant re-enters her house. The young wife of a much older man falls in love with a youth in *Il Tabarro* (1918) but at the end of the opera's single act the curtain comes down on her gazing at the body of the lover her husband has strangled. *Sister Angelica* (1918), an unmarried mother who has become a nun, poisons herself on hearing that the child whom she had to leave is dead. In this last, though, Puccini chose a text which ended with Angelica being forgiven by a vision of the Virgin Mary and his unfinished opera *Turandot* was to have closed on a love duet surpassing any of his earlier passionate romances, as the Princess Turandot discovered the secret of love.

Perhaps it was fitting that only sketches of this last duet were found after Puccini died, though it is tantalizing to imagine what beauty it might have contained. The emphasis on tragic plots is important to operatic history not so much for their tragedy but for the characters who are afflicted. Turandot apart, these are *credible* women—not fairytale—living real lives in real environments; they come from novels and melodrama, not historic literature or legend; they follow *La Traviata* and *Carmen*, not *Othello* or *The Ring*. This realism is admittedly as highly-coloured as a glossy magazine story or a Tennessee Williams drama, but it was significant. Leoncavallo in *I Pagliacci* (1892) invites the audience to believe that the singers are people they might meet in the street in the celebrated Prologue—there were historical precedents but not for well over a century before; Mascagni in *Cavalleria Rusticana* (1890) took a contemporary short story of the sort which everyone was reading. Italians call this period of opera 'verismo', yet opera and real life are incompatible in the lyric vein of Italian melody. People do *not* sing the impassioned phrases of Puccini's lovers nor do they ask for whisky naturally on a melodic interval. All the *verismo* operas which survive do so because of their store of unending melody rather than because they make sense; knowing this, many singers treat them as if they were early nineteenth-century showpieces, helped by conductors who play to the dress circle. A sincere performance of any of them as straightforward drama can still be a revelation and, meanwhile, there is still a spine-tingling moment or two to be had in phrases sung by a good tenor and soprano in octaves. Menotti has kept the form alive in operas such as *The Medium* (1946) and *The Consul* (1950), both also concerning tragic women; and having emigrated to America as a young man, he has helped towards giving Italian *verismo* a new life in the American musical which is acquiring more and more music at the expense of the dialogue.

Italian tradition in Italian opera houses has been in the hands of Malipiero and Pizzetti since Puccini's death, but both composers have gone back to earlier traditions for their operatic philosophies. Malipiero has adopted a Gregorian outlook involving him in modal harmony and continuous melody which never develops a theme but endlessly invents new material, as in *L'allegra brigata* (The Jolly Company) produced in Milan (1950). Pizzetti insists on characterization with Verdi's vehemence but returns to the spontaneous declamation of the medieval lay or canzo as his model with, occasionally, monotonous results as in his setting of *Ifigenia* for the Italian radio in Turin (1950). A third successor to Puccini who also reacted against nineteenth-century lyricism was Respighi. At first he wrote in the cloying style of Richard Strauss at its most sickly and could never find dramatic music to replace his native leaning towards pouring out lyrical melody. His last—*Lucrezia* (Milan: 1935)—sought to cut out dramatic music on stage and to go back to bursts of recitative in the seventeenth-century manner declaimed by a singer in the pit, thereby leaving the stage free for the lyrical outbursts which have, traditionally, become sacred in Italian opera.

Busoni's *Doctor Faust* looks backwards also, but only as far as Verdi, for the composer's chief pre-occupation was with form within a free arioso style and not in set arias. Chances of hearing it are thin, even in Busoni's adopted country, Germany, but many claim greatness for it.

Richard Strauss and the Germans

Richard Strauss chose two quite horrid women for the subjects of his first operas, *Salome* (Dresden: 1905), and *Electra* (1909), and makes of them equally horrid character studies in music. His experience of symphonic poems had taught him how to paint the mood of his characters, but the decadence of Oscar Wilde's version of the Bible story about Herod, Salome and John the Baptist needed a corresponding decadence in the music, which Strauss supplied by means of complex harmony in his orchestra and dissonant melody for his singers. Using the Wagnerian style of arioso with most of the melodic interest in the orchestral polyphony, he extended the leitmotiv systematically even to associating particular keys with some of the characters in *Electra*, and his juxtaposition of common chords contributed much to the decay of tonality.

Viennese operetta had captured the pre-1914 world, led by *The Merry Widow* (1905), Léhar's sensational success. The lilt of their waltzes and the gay life of their plots affected even the neurotic Bavarian Richard Strauss. Whether he wanted to live up to the coincidence of his surname (that of so many Viennese waltz-kings), whether his love of the Viennese masters of the eighteenth century (specially Mozart) led him to want to re-create their elegance and wit, or whether (never lacking in business sense) he thought he could write a grand opera to raise the level of operetta and still keep the same public pouring into the theatre, Strauss wrote the wittiest German opera since *Figaro* and caught the most elegant strains of the operetta waltz in *Der Rosen-kavalier* (Dresden: 1911). At last his gifts of musical character-ization joined with his consummate orchestral skill and feeling for singable lines. The Prelude is a symphonic poem of love and the Waltzes (which you may quite often hear in a separate suite) are sumptuously scored for a huge orchestra needing well over one hundred players. The trio at the moment when the aristo-cratic Marschallin (the 'Field Marshal's wife') forgives the young lover whom she has given up to a younger woman for his earlier part in the plot, touches luxurious heights in writing for female voices which are almost unbelievably beautiful; and the shabby Baron Ochs is given a most infectious waltz tune with which a bass can hardly fail to steal the show and win the audience's sympathy even though he is in fact 'the villain'. As *The Ring* left nothing to be said after it in German Romantic opera, so *Rosenkavalier* was the last word on Viennese comic opera. Even Strauss himself never achieved its poise or warmth in his later operas, though *Ariadne on Naxos* (1912) and *Arabella* (1933) occasionally come close.

Tchaikovsky and the Russians

Before 1877 Tchaikovsky had already composed four operas,

and the glitter of the stage continually attracted him for the remaining sixteen years of his life. Two of the six which he completed during these years are still worth seeing: *Eugen Onegin* (Moscow: 1879) and *The Queen of Spades* (1890). Both owe their stories to Pushkin, whose poem about Onegin was a classic among cultured Russians. Tchaikovsky makes Tatiana rather than the man his main character and seems to feel most deeply for her in music such as her 'Letter Scene', in which she writes a simple but passionate love-letter to Onegin; this song provides most of the material for the rest of the work as her declaration of love first is refused by Onegin, then, in the last scene, taken up when it is too late (for Tatiana is by then married, and loyalty to her husband triumphs over the love she still admits for the subject of her letter in Scene I). *Eugen Onegin* is unique in having *two* ball scenes—one famous for its Waltz in a country house, and the other, equally popular for its Polonaise, in a fashionable town house—and masterly in its form by which Tchaikovsky lovingly shows the development of his heroine from the naïve girl who writes her sweetheart a letter in the first scene to the mature aristocratic beauty who tragically remains true to her code of honour in the last. Next to *Boris Godounov*, *Onegin* is the finest opera yet written by a Russian. *The Queen of Spades* is melodramatic by comparison both in its story—about the downfall of a young officer through gambling and the resulting death of two women—and in its sudden contrasts in the music, but it is most successful on the stage.

The figure of Rimsky-Korsakov towers over all Russian music from his appointment as professor of composition and instrumentation at St. Petersburg in 1871 to his death there in 1908. Apart from an impressive list of pupils—including Glazunov and Stravinsky—he made two editions of Moussorgsky's *Boris Godounov* which helped to win that opera its world renown; completed (with Glazunov) Borodin's *Prince Igor*, which has now reached an even wider audience than *Boris* through concert performances of its overture, the choral dances and its 'musical' version, *Kismet*; and found time to write twelve operas of his own.

The most interesting are *Snow Maiden* (Maryinsky Theatre:
1882), *Sadko* (1896) and *The Golden Cockerel* (1909). In the
world between the two great wars only Prokofiev's *The Love for
Three Oranges* (Chicago: 1921) became popular with Western
audiences, though Stravinsky in a non-Russian vein has much
space to fill in the next chapter, and Shostakovich's *A Lady
Macbeth of Mtsensk* (Moscow: 1934) was also performed in
London and New York. Since 1945, the only first performance
to be heard outside Russia has been of one of Prokofiev's earlier
works, *The Flaming Angel* (finished 1925), hailed by some as a
masterpiece.

The French

After Saint-Saëns' *Samson and Delilah* (Weimar: 1877) the
traditional grand opera (with ballet) was maintained by Délibes
in *Lakme* (1883). Massenet, in his three tragic love stories
Manon (1884), *Werther* (1892) and *Thais* (1894), foreshadowed
something of Puccini's psychological interest in his characters
and was a master of melody comparable even with Fauré; and
Charpentier, in *Louise* (1900), produced a curious mixture of
realism, symbolism and nationalism about a sewing girl's
dilemma in coping with life in Paris at the turn of the century.
It was left for Debussy and Ravel to experiment with opera in
French on completely new bases and for Milhaud in *Christopher
Columbus* (1930) to revive the old large-scale musical tradition—
only to find that his poet Claudel's symbolism and the new devices
such as the use of a cinema screen to extend the scenery have
successfully barred its stage performance ever since its Berlin
première.

Nationalists in small countries

The Czech tradition which was born on the first night of
Smetana's *Bartered Bride* in 1866 deepened in emotion with the
years. In his two operas *Jenufa* (1904) and *Katya Kabanova*
(1921) Janacek reflects the bitterness which grew in Czech hearts
until the country disappeared once more as an independent name

from the atlas (1939). In the first, the vocal lines match the characters exactly and in place of the cardboard figures of Smetana's opera, Janacek conveys the feelings of real people in his music: the warmth of Jenufa, the intense pride of her foster-mother, the harsh young man whose love drives him to attack her and yet ends in devotion; all are worthy of a Zola, and the music intensifies the drama subtly throughout. *Katya Kabanova* recreates the atmosphere of the nineteenth-century struggles between the old Slav régime and those who fought for emancipation, ending (after one of the most convincing and scaring storms in all music) with an immensely sad scene which leads up to Katya's suicide. London has been fortunate to have had both operas in the repertory, the first at Covent Garden and the second—still to be seen occasionally—at Sadlers' Wells. They are probably among the finest examples of traditional opera to be written in this century. Weinberger's *Schwanda the Bagpiper* (1927), which countless schoolchildren in this country know from its Polka, is a riotous, topsy-turvy version of the Faust legend transported to the Czech countryside and it could make a nice change from *The Bartered Bride* for an amateur opera club. The orchestral suite from *Hary Janos* by Kodály might also tempt enterprising schoolmasters into looking at the 'opera' which the Hungarians call the play that goes with the music.

English opera 'tradition' had been that of ballad opera—plays with songs—ever since *The Beggar's Opera* (1728), with a couple of nineteenth-century exceptions in Balfe's *Bohemian Girl* and Wallace's *Maritana*. London's 'Opera Comique' and 'Savoy' theatres were given over to the operettas of Gilbert and Sullivan from 1877 to the end of the century, and Sullivan's one attempt at grand opera (*Ivanhoe*: 1891) in a new opera house (now the Palace Theatre) was only a paper success. Edwardians preferred to be 'Savoyards', to watch *The Yeoman of the Guard* changing, and—eventually—to revel in Edward German's *Merrie England* (1902). Vaughan Williams provided an English counterpart to *The Bartered Bride* in his country opera *Hugh The Drover* (1924), using folksong as his musical ground. The atmosphere is not so

gay as in the Czech opera; the story and the music are true to
small-town life in the Cotswolds during the Napoleonic wars and
have their own comfortable English climate. *The Poisoned Kiss*
(Cambridge: 1936) is a sophisticated fairy-tale ballad opera, and
Sir John in Love (1935) is a very rural comic opera.

The first English grand opera which, like Janacek's *Katya*,
lifts the 'country' plot into intense tragedy, is Britten's grim
version of events in East Anglia towards 1830, *Peter Grimes*
(Sadlers' Wells: 1945). It, too, has a magnificent orchestral storm,
and Britten's characterization is equal to any in the whole field
of opera. *Grimes* is traditional opera, with arias, duets, arioso,
trios and choruses which include a fugue, but in place of an
overture, each act has an Interlude for orchestra which seems to
suggest the prevailing weather at sea—all-important to a
borough which lives by fishing and to Grimes who is himself a
fisherman. These *Sea Interludes* may quite frequently be heard in
the concert hall. None of Britten's later operas may be truly
called traditional, though *Billy Budd* (1951)—another pathetic
story of a man misjudged—and *Gloriana* (1953) use the full
resources of the opera house. Tippett's *Midsummer Marriage*
(1952) has some choral dances which might compare favourably
with the hackneyed 'Prince Igor' dances if they were not so
difficult to perform, and Bliss (though he was more hailed for
ballet music like *Checkmate* in 1937 and *Miracle in the Gorbals*
in 1944) wrote a score with memories of Puccini and Richard
Strauss together in *The Olympians* (1949).

La Vida Breve (1913), Spain's only contribution to traditional
opera on the international stage also calls Janacek to mind, for its
composer, Falla, chooses a powerfully tragic 'peasant' heroine—
this time a Spanish gypsy. He uses folk-dance with Andalusian
song to the full and the opera has become most famous for its
dances; so has Falla himself, through the ballets, *Love the
Magician* (1915) and *The Three-Cornered Hat* (1919).

Tradition in Church

Church traditions, by definition, seldom change. As the

patronage of religious leaders died in the nineteenth century, so most composers of the past hundred years have buried their religious thoughts in allegorical works. Some works have still been commissioned for cathedral or parish church festivals (notably 'The Three Choirs' in England where each September choral societies attached to Worcester, Gloucester and Hereford Cathedrals join forces to sing oratorios and cantatas in one of the three cathedrals); a few have come from the stimulus of bereavement; and there have been attempts to revive dramatic oratorio.

Settings of the Mass for festival performance range from Bruckner's three colossal Roman 'Grand Masses' through Janacek's 'Glagolitic' Mass (1926) for operatic soloists, chorus and vast orchestra, to Vaughan Williams' High Anglican Mass in G minor (1923) for unaccompanied chorus and Britten's Missa Brevis (1960) for children. Among Requiem Masses, that by Fauré (1887) is pre-eminent and the Italian Pizzetti's setting for twelve solo voices (1922) is a most moving work. Oratorio, as you may expect, has survived mainly in England.

English oratorio, begun by Handel and continued by Mendelssohn, has reached three peaks in this century. The first, Elgar's *Dream of Gerontius*, was written for the Birmingham Festival in 1900; Walton's *Belshazzar's Feast* was for the Leeds Festival in 1931; and Vaughan Williams' *Pilgrim's Progress*, called a 'morality' but most nearly a dramatic oratorio, was given in Covent Garden Opera House (1951). Elgar made a fervent setting of a poem by the Roman Catholic Cardinal Newman, Walton went to the Old Testament and Vaughan Williams to the Puritan Bunyan for their texts; and the music betrays the different sources immediately. *Gerontius* is the exotic and ecstatic work (specially in the tenor's cry 'Sanctus fortis'), with even its great hymn 'Praise to the Holiest' set for complex chorus. *Belshazzar* hurls its paeans of praise at the audience with barbaric force and has in its bones the pre-Christian prophet's power of foretelling doom and the crowd's exultation at the fall of Babylon. *Pilgrim* preserves the Protestant strength in simplicity through its rather naïve drama, its foundation on the grand psalm-tune 'York', and the final antiphony between unison voices on earth and the choir in heaven. All three works have that nobility which inspires Englishmen and puzzles foreigners—a reasonable summary of the English oratorio as a whole. For all its apparent 'formula', though, English oratorio does not come easily even to very gifted composers. Fricker's *Vision of Judgment* (Leeds Festival 1958) missed its mark, Britten in his cantatas *St. Nicolas* (1948) and *Noyes Fludde* (1958) turned to the German Passion scheme with hymns interpolated for the congregation, and the only foreigner to try it in the last hundred years, Dvorak, met disaster with his *St. Ludmila* for Leeds in 1886.

Tradition in the Recital Room

The reigning instrument of the recital room has for long past been the pianoforte, on its own or as equal partner in sonata work, as accompaniment for a singer or as part of an ensemble of instruments. The 'chambers' of chamber music have been public rooms for almost every work needing few performers since 1876, yet modern 'traditional' composers of symphonic or operatic stature are seldom heard there; instead, a new category of miniaturist composers working in the traditional line has appeared on the programmes. The major modern composers of chamber music have nearly all been experimentalists. If you write experimental works and you want to hear them performed, write for chamber groups: promoters seldom take risks on financing large-scale 'advanced' works.

Piano Solos

The traditional solo piano forms—Preludes, Variations, Fugue and Dance—have, since 1876, come from Russia and the Spanish-speaking world, with isolationist groups of minor composers providing · pieces for teachers to use in several other countries. In the styles of Mendelssohn and Chopin, touched up with late Romantic harmony, pianists offer us Rachmaninoff and Shostakovich preludes, Franck's Prelude, Chorale and Fugue, and Fauré's nocturnes; after Brahms, Dvorak and

Grieg's concert folk dances, fanciful tone-pictures, or plain rhapsodies, came Medtner's *Fairy Tales* and *Forgotten Melodies*, Reger's more romantic titles, Dohnanyi's rhapsodies and (adding the appropriate 'fire' of their country's folk dance) the numerous pieces of the Russians Kabalevsky and Khachaturian, and the Spaniards Falla, Albeniz, Granados, Nin, and Mompou; a long way after Schumann's *Children's Pieces* came the pieces which fill piano stools in homes where children plod their way towards the next examination grade.

Songs

The interest in collecting and arranging folksongs has made for an international collection assembled and arranged by the 'big' names in small countries: Pedrell and Falla in Spain, Bartok and Kodaly in Hungary, Sharp and Vaughan Williams in England, Villa Lobos in South America. The collection of tunes continues, but the most interesting by-product of this work has been the 'folky' idioms which have entered art-songs almost to the exclusion of genuine lieder style. The jolly songs of Peter Warlock and Vaughan Williams, the blarney or whimsy of Moeran, Bax and Ireland belong to the tweedy sentimentalizing of 'the simple life' in the twenties and thirties, fine examples as some of them are.

Art-songs proper divide into the English ballad, French mélodie, and German lied. Sullivan's gushing Victoriana, such as 'The Lost Chord' (1877), imposed their stamp on many ballads by composers with genteel names, among them Guy d'Hardelot ('Because') and Amy Woodforde-Finden ('Pale hands I loved'), whose fame has rested on a single song. A more lasting type of English song was first written by the Brahmsian Stanford, in pieces like 'The Fairy Lough' and there is a most poetic line of English songwriters which runs through Elgar ('Sea Pictures'), Quilter ('Love's Philosophy'), Warlock ('Fair and True'), Butterworth ('A Shropshire Lad'), Gurney ('Sleep'), Vaughan Williams ('Songs of Travel') and Gerald Finzi ('Dies Natalis'), to poets ranging from the Elizabethans to Housman and Walter de la Mare. The song-cycles and solo cantatas of Britten, though difficult to perform, contain some of the most beautiful phrases of all, among the settings of sonnets to words of Michelangelo and John Donne, 'A Charm of Lullabies', and the Serenade for tenor, horn and strings.

French mélodies were synonymous with the name of Fauré until his last cycle, the mysterious 'L'Horizon chimérique', in 1922. Hahn was left to carry on this tradition and his popularity both as songwriter and conductor of opera led to his appointment as director of the Paris Opera in 1945, at the ripe age of seventy. Even more advanced writers such as Jolivet and Sauguet still write mélodies in the sweetest harmony: the French air de cour maintains its stately charm even in the Fifth Republic.

German lieder had faded into pale imitation of Schumann in the songs of Franz and Cornelius. Brahms had re-found some of Schubert's freshness, but the last great composer of lieder— Wolf—had a hero to worship in Wagner, and the impulse of this affection coupled to the heritage of Schumann (which was inescapable to any German song composer in 1876) inspired a remarkable series of songs. The first to be published were written in 1876 and three of them had words by Heine, Schumann's 'own' poet. This influence lasted in some measure until 1884 when Wolf seemed to find the right poet for a style entirely his own in Mörike. He had already, four years earlier, been moved to set one of Mörike's poems, but by 1889 he was ready to publish fifty-three in the Mörike Collection. Obscure chromaticism beyond Wagner and straightforward, almost naïve harmony after the way of Schumann go hand in hand with a care for word-setting second to neither of his forerunners; and dramatic force gives way to gentle persuasion or wry humour in successive songs, to make the contrasts in the collection absorbing to the ear.

Wolf never quite touched the same heights again. His fame in Vienna rested (far more than on his songs) on his articles maligning Brahms in favour of Wagner and his paper war with the venerable Hanslick, and the Mörike songs were written in his first years of freedom after giving up his job as a critic. Collec-

tions to words by Eichendorff (1889), Goethe (1890) and translations from Spanish and Italian poets ('Spanisches Liederbuch':
1891, 'Italienisches Liederbuch': 1892 and 1896) include some
magnificent music, but no later collection equals his first. Perhaps
most revealing in the later works are the intensely restless love-
songs and the stark, agonizing religious settings in the Spanish
book. There is a strange calm about the Italian songs; in the year
of their publication (1896) Brahms was also writing his last, the
haunting 'Four Serious Songs'. Within a year Wolf's mind gave
way and he suffered four and a half years anguish in an asylum
before his death in 1903. The manner of his dying, as with
Schumann, adds much poignancy to any performance which has
even a portion of the sensitivity that was their composer's
downfall. Some of this sensitivity permeates the work of the
Finnish Kilpinen, writer of over 700 songs; hardly any pene-
trates the lieder of Richard Strauss or Rachmaninov.

Sonatas and Ensembles

In 1876, Brahms published the sunniest of all his chamber
works, the B flat String Quartet . . . and ignored chamber music
for the next four years. When he next composed a small-scale
work, the G major Violin Sonata (1880), he was again in a happy
vein and the mood lasted through two more Violin sonatas, the
two string quintets (1883 and 1887) and the last three piano trios,
completed in 1892. As with Mozart, Brahms wrote his most

intimate chamber music for clarinet, and both composers chanced to meet their clarinettist friends late in life. Brahms's Clarinet Quintet contains the whole of its composer, miniature in ensemble but packed with feeling: the wistful opening which also sums up the work at the end is the only sign of an old man; for the rest there is the impulsive first movement, an aria-form adagio with the middle section a typical Brahms rhapsody, a twinkling third movement 'presto non assai', and lastly an effortless set of variations to divert all the players. For the same friend there are also two sonatas with piano and a trio with cello as well, all treasured by clarinettists today. Even Wagner started a clarinet quintet, but his place in a history of chamber music is safe through the delightful *Siegfried Idyll*, written to be played by thirteen friends on the terrace of his villa in Switzerland, to celebrate his son's birthday.

Dvorak wrote the second of his three piano trios in 1876 and this work proved to be the sign of his maturity as a composer of chamber music. There followed seven string quartets, one of which, in F major (1893) has become very widely known under its nickname 'The Nigger'; two string quintets, the second also written in America (in E flat major, 1893); and a string of concert dances for violin, cello and piano, called the 'Dumky' Trio (1891) which has a charm unique in its field. The melodious Violin Sonatina (1893) is also within the fairly good amateur's reach.

Of those following Brahms in Germany, Reger wrote too much chamber music (including eleven sonatas for unaccompanied violin, harking back to Bach), Mahler wrote none at all, and Richard Strauss turned to wind instruments for preference after the Serenade for thirteen Wind Instruments (1881). The Czech, Janacek, also wrote a lightweight Wind Sextet (1924), but his Violin Sonata, the two string quartets (fiendishly difficult to play) and the Concertino for piano, horn, clarinet and string quartet make him the most interesting composer to work on the traditional harmonic system (enormously extended) in the twentieth century.

César Franck's Violin Sonata (1886) for the virtuoso Ysaÿe has a theme used, as in his symphony, in various forms to link the movements. Its most extensive movement comes second and the final rondo theme is one of the few examples of strict canon in the nineteenth century that sound musical rather than academic. Franck's other brilliant chamber work—overweighted by the piano—is the Piano Quintet (1879) which bears a dedication to Saint-Saëns, as prolific a composer of chamber music as in all other forms, whose works are now almost unknown but for *The Carnival of Animals* (1886), a 'zoological fantasy'. This work, which needs two pianos and only a few other instruments can justifiably be called 'chamber music', as Saint-Saëns wrote it for a romp at a musical evening with his pupils before it was adopted by the concert merchants and educational music advisers. His Piano Quintet (1858) preceded Franck's by twenty years but the form seems to have attracted all the major French composers of the 'Conservatoire' tradition, Fauré's two (1906 and 1921) and that of Vincent d'Indy (1925) taking the form well into the new generation of experimental French music.

English romantics also in the Conservatoire tradition, such as Parry, Stanford, Ireland, Bridge and Bax, have written scores of piano trios, quartets for various combinations of wind and strings and ensembles up to nine for the pleasure or instruction of their student friends, professional colleagues and pupils. The pieces were often useful training for their composers and are still good practice for budding instrumentalists. Judged as music alone not many are completely satisfying to listen to: among the best are Ireland's 'Phantasy' Piano Trio (1906: dedicated to Stanford) and Clarinet Sonata (1945: for the then incomparable Frederick Thurston), Bridge's Piano Sonata (1925) and sets of easy Miniatures for piano trio, and Bax's Piano Quintet (1915). The traditional individualists—Vaughan Williams, Holst, Elgar, Tippett and Walton—have written little chamber music. Among the best pieces are Holst's Terzetto (1924) for flute, oboe and viola, Elgar's Violin Sonata (1918), Tippett's Piano Sonata (1938), Walton's Violin Sonata (1949) and powerful String

Quartet (1947) and *Façade* (1926). *Façade* was originally an entertainment for a reciter (of poems by Edith Sitwell) and an ensemble of wind instruments, cello and percussion, but the revised version (1942) and suite for orchestra have presented it to a far wider public, including balletomanes.

CHAPTER NINETEEN

EXPERIMENT EVERYWHERE

THE crisis over the future of harmony in the key systems which
grew to full flower between 1600 and 1750, became overblown by
1850, and started to decay by 1870, has caused successive *avant-
garde* composers to experiment in concert hall, recital room,
opera house, music hall, dance palaces, film studios and now
laboratories. Some of these composers are isolated and un-
classifiable; others have had pupils or disciples who succeeded
beyond their master's success; and a very few seem secure in
international history of the future. Geographically, Paris has
remained in the height of fashion, producing one lost cause
(Impressionism between the wars), an inconclusive iconoclasm
and, since the Second World War, a group of new designers in
music as difficult to evaluate as their counterparts in the world
of costume.

Paris

Three Frenchmen still under forty in 1900 were experimenting
in an anti-Wagnerian spirit: Debussy and Ravel especially
explored the chordal relationships of harmony; Satie, who worked
on medieval, classical and (later) jazz forms, used every musical
antidote that came along to prevent the Wagnerian disease from
spreading, including whole-tone and polytonal harmony, coinci-
dental counterpoint, and pointillist registers. The first two have
no 'school' of followers, the last influenced everyone in the
second period of modern French music, in the 1920s.

Debussy was the chief Impressionist composer (as Manet was

the chief Impressionist painter), breaking sharply with the
German Romantic tradition. His first successful orchestral piece
was, true to the earlier Romantics, a musical account of a poem,
Mallarmé's *L'Aprés-midi d'un faune* (1894). It was, in this sense,
an impression of the same sort as Liszt's or Berlioz's Byronic
works; but, as with Impressionist painting, the orchestral and
harmonic colours were diffused and there was no clear line
between one group of instruments, one chord and another—
everything was slightly blurred at the edges to merge into the
whole. As an Impressionist painting is made up of multi-coloured
dots and dashes melting into each other, so a symphonic sketch
by Debussy takes shape through an immensely complicated
arrangement of instruments. Occasionally an instrument may
throw out a line of melody against a background—dots on top
of dashes in all directions—but Debussy's tunes are usually
short, narrow in range, and indeterminate in their beginning and
end. Many chords are built up from modal or whole-note scales,
each a sound in its own right, mingling with more familiar
Romantic chords not in any agreed progression involving discord and resolution but constantly on the move and related only
by their 'colour': if a 5/3 chord is one colour, a 6/5/3 or 7/5/3
are others, so Debussy may have a stream of sevenths (the same
colour) which will not necessarily belong to the same tonality.
Add to this the diffusion of such chord colours by appoggiaturas
which make them vaguer and you will appreciate that the sound
of *L'Aprés-midi* caused orchestral players (and conductors) to
alter their listening habits considerably, concentrating much
more minutely on the balance of the orchestral parts.

Pianists too, need new ears if they try to play Debussy on the
lines of Brahms, Schumann or early Liszt. Here the vagueness
may be increased by using the sustaining pedal almost constantly,
and in many of his twenty-four preludes (1910–1913) the form,
too, is entirely rhapsodic with nothing to hold on to except a
series of ravishing sounds which meander rather than develop
because you cannot remember them in enough detail to follow
any logical variation. In the most supposedly logical country in

the West, Debussy himself realized that this was a denial of what civilization had meant to music, but not before he had scored a succession of pieces whose appeal was wholly sensuous: *Nocturnes* (1893–99), *La Mer* (1903–5) and *Images* (1906–9) for orchestra; *Estampès* (1903), *L'Isle joyeuse* (1904) and *Images* (1905–7) for piano.

Debussy's only opera, *Pelléas and Melisande* (1902), also meanders and there is very little action in either drama or music. The orchestra murmurs unbroken impressionist language under a succession of highly symbolical conversation-pieces for the medieval mystic characters in supple recitative; interludes for orchestra connect the scenes and have an inner meaning, too. *Pelléas*—not surprisingly—is unique in the opera house. Nationalism attracted Debussy to countries other than his own. Spain had attracted Glinka and Rimsky-Korsakov before him, Chabrier and Ravel among his contemporaries; the Paris Exhibition of 1889 had an Indonesian *gamelan* orchestra (almost all exotic percussion instruments: dulcimers, drums and gongs of all sizes). So the rhythms of Spanish dance and the clanging gamelan gongs both found their way into his piano music. Classical dance-forms from minuet to saraband and passepied served him in his early piano suites *Pour le Piano* (1901) and *Suite Bergamasque* (1905), which includes the very popular 'Clair de Lune', but waltzes were represented only by an early romantic piece and the wan *La plus que lente* (1910). In his last works Debussy returned more often to the forms of his French musical ancestry (Couperin, Rameau) and of the adopted French Chopin in the two books of Etudes for piano (1915). But the String Quartet (1893), classical in form, César Franck-like in its cyclic themes, and strangely exotic in sound, is of all his works the most 'impressive'.

Ravel had similarly wide interests in music which led him to try modernizing old forms and techniques in early works (*Menuet antique*: 1895) and his widely-known suite for piano, *Le Tombeau de Couperin* (1917). Spain, too, attracted him and the only two published works originally for orchestra have Spanish dance-rhythms, *Rhapsodie Espagnole* (1907) and *Boléro* (1927);

like Debussy, he commented wryly on the waltz in his *Valses Nobles et Sentimentales* (1911) for piano, and wrote some charming pieces for children in his five little duets *Mother Goose* (1908), which match the older composer's *Children's Corner* (also 1908). While Debussy was alive Ravel had less of the limelight, though his first opera *L'Heure Espagnole* (1907), a farce about the love affairs of a watchmaker's wife which markedly resembles English Restoration Drama at its most immoral, met with a great deal more approval than the mystical *Pelléas*. Ravel solved the problem of convincing people by recitative in prophetic advice to his singers: 'speak rather than sing'. *Sprechgesang* (= Speech-song) has been a plank on many a modern composer's platform down to Loewe's songs for Professor Higgins in *My Fair Lady* (1954). Ravel's modishness was assured when Diaghilev commissioned him to write for his company (then the rage of Paris) the ballet *Daphnis and Chloe* (1909–1912), from which two suites are now established in the concert hall.

When Debussy died in 1918, Ravel was his obvious successor, but his style of writing (less vague than Debussy's and so more easily copied) was in danger of becoming stale to the post-war generation. As an orchestrator of his own and other composer's piano pieces (such as Moussorgsky's *Pictures from an Exhibition*) he was incomparable; his very early String Quartet (1903), the Introduction and Allegro for harp, flute, clarinet and string quartet (1906), *Miroirs* (1905) and *Gaspard de la nuit* (1908) for the piano, were still exquisitely original; yet Ravel himself was growing tired of his facile dialect. The first musical signs of his dissatisfaction can be heard in the frenzied last pages of *La Valse* (1919–1920) which seem to snarl at the slick orchestral player and the sensual listener alike.

In his second opera, *L'Enfant et les Sortilèges* (1925) Ravel looked back to his own most youthful work in the lyrical passages, looked down on the youth of the twenties in his use of jazz tricks in the notorious foxtrot, and looked sideways at Satie in the mewing duet for two cats; it is truly an original *tour de force*, and Colette's fantasy about a bad boy cured of ill-treating and breaking everything by the animals and other objects of his temper is hard to resist, particularly in the magical performance which the gramophone can now give. The orchestral Bolero (1927), although it may now seem hackneyed, was a savagely original treatment of a harmless Spanish rhythm. His visit to the United States of America in 1928 gave him a little more insight into the world of jazz and his last work, the G major Piano Concerto (1931) uses the idiom completely absorbed in his own dialect— with some polytonality in the first movement, a nostalgic glimpse of his own past in the second, and a clattering finale showing off the pianist's technique in the grand manner. After that, a film contract came to nothing and a motor-car accident hastened a nervous breakdown leading to permanent brain trouble: two of the amenities of modern life were the end of Ravel as a composer and as a man—an ironical commentary on one who had always, above all, been up-to-date.

The third founder-member of twentieth-century French music before 1939, Satie, is perhaps too famous as an eccentric to be justified as a serious composer here, but his *Parade* (1916)—music for a ballet by Cocteau, Picasso and Massine—is a landmark which should at least justify the same attention as the names of his collaborators do now. The names of many professed disciples of Cocteau's dogmas and Satie's musical asides are widely known: Milhaud, Poulenc, Sauguet, and Honegger in France and America, Lord Berners and Constant Lambert in England. Their mixtures of polytonality, imitation jazz, primitivism and neo-classical formulae does not always do justice to their leader's fastidious example, particularly when it becomes involved with the traditional symphonic seriousness which Roussel and their early teachers at the Paris Conservatoire had tried to teach them. Poulenc's opera *The Carmelites* (1946), Honegger's dramatic oratorio *Joan of Arc at the Stake* (Basle: 1938) and some of his symphonies have probably more stature than any other works by this group.

The works of this last group of composers—all born in the 1890s—have a competence comparable to the minor composers of the eighteenth century and their style is almost as formal: they mock elegance, which is so often used as a synonym for 'France', as they point their music very sensitively for a time and then, suddenly dropping the mask, write something crude or downright vulgar; their humour is that of Tony Hancock, not Noël Coward. Of the younger French composers, Jean Françaix is the most refined pupil of this style, which his teacher, Nadia Boulanger, has taught highly successfully to decades of young Americans and a few British, notably Copland and Berkeley. Copland's *El Salón México* and Berkeley's *Divertimento* are perfect specimens of this art.

In 1936 Jolivet and Messiaen formed a dissenting group called 'La Jeune France'. Their manifesto was a strange mixture of Catholic theology, Romantic impulse, interest in Oriental instruments and medieval methods of composing. Most of Messiaen's pieces have religious titles: *Visions de l'amen* (1943) for two pianos and *Vingt Regards sur L'Enfant Jésus* (1944)— a piano solo lasting two and a half hours—have baffled audiences the world over. He has had some success in America with his 'Turangalila' Symphony commissioned for Boston in 1948, and Jolivet's teacher, Varèse, has also a following among advanced New Yorkers who applaud his music for electrophonic instruments. Jolivet himself slips back into the style of Boulanger and Ravel too easily to give his music consistency.

Messiaen's *Trois Petites Liturgies de la Présence Divine* began a new era for French music in 1945. It is scored for unison women's voices, celeste, vibraphone, Chinese gong and cymbals, maraccas, piano, strings and an electronic instrument (the Ondes Martenot); this pre-occupation with curious timbres and strange instruments characterizes the new party led by Boulez who give concerts under the banner of 'La Domaine Musicale'. Messiaen's insistence on the importance of exploring new proportions of rhythm has become allied in his pupil Boulez not to the Frenchman's equal emphasis on modal foundations for harmony and counterpoint but to the serial pitch techniques originating in Vienna. Now everything in this Paris circle is 'organized'—intervals, rhythm, tone colour and dynamics—but in Boulez the group has a leader who has written down firmly that no one can equate organizing with composition; in some odd way, there *is* a certainty when you listen many times to the timbres of a work like *Le Marteau sans Maître* (1954) that he has been able to hear music beyond the methodical organization.

Paris has also welcomed many distinguished foreign composers in this century as in the last. The Russian Scnabin was a sensation in the 1890s as a pianist playing his own works: studies, preludes, impromptus, mazurkas, and—unique in the pre-war period—ten sonatas. They were full of new sounds, sometimes as vague as Debussy's, usually characterized in their harmony by chords built up of fourths, and clothed in an aura of magical, mystical ideas by the composer's philosophical utterances about his mission in life. The English Delius settled in Paris about 1890 with a strangely-mixed background: English folk-song heard in his youth (uppermost in his rhapsody for orchestra *Brigg Fair*, 1907); American Negro songs remembered from days as an orange grower in Florida (most obvious in the variations on a slave song for chorus and orchestra, *Appalachia*, 1902); a short and un-appreciated course in German romanticism at Leipzig Conservatoire; a fond affection remaining from a visit to Grieg in Norway (manifest in the twelve Norwegian songs: 1886–90, and to some extent in the Piano Concerto: 1906); and an ear for the orchestra as intent as Debussy's. Impressionism using all these early colours made beautiful pictures in Delius's later music such as *Summer Night on the River* and *On hearing the first Cuckoo in Spring* (1912) for small orchestra. Only a reader of 'The Times' would be expected to take the last subject seriously, but there is a cosmopolitanism about all Delius's music that typifies the foreigner resident in Paris, nowhere better shown than in his nocturne for orchestra, *Paris: the Song of a Great City* (1899).

A year after Ravel's ballet for Diaghilev, the Russian impresario introduced to Paris a remarkable young pupil of Rimsky-Korsakov as composer of his ballet *The Firebird* (1910): Stravinsky. For the next twenty-five years, Paris heard the first nights of all but two of Stravinsky's operas and ballets. *Petrushka* (1911) was original enough with its polytonality and frequent changes of time, but *The Rite of Spring* (1913) caused something of a riot with its primitive rhythmic drive. *Les Noces* (1923), a ballet with songs and choruses, was the first of the three most splendid choral works which should be safe in the archives of the future. In it, Stravinsky did away with the huge orchestras of his earlier ballets, accompanying the singers with four pianos and percussion. He had practised with smaller forces in war-time pieces written in Switzerland (*Ragtime* for small orchestra and *The Soldier's Tale*, a narration with mime and a few assorted musicians on the stage, 1918), and after *Les Noces* he picked his orchestra and voices to suit each situation: the dramatic oratorio *Oedipus Rex* (1927) has only male voices in its large chorus part and an eighteenth-century orchestra; the *Symphony of Psalms* (1930), written while he was settled in Nice but performed for the first time in Boston, uses a large wind band with cellos and basses to contrast with a mixed chorus.

Stravinsky has written a great deal about his attitude to music in the Chronicle of his life up to the moment when he became a naturalized Frenchman—and a Parisian—in 1934. From the book, he emerges as a thoroughly professional composer in the way that the classical and medieval masters were professional, working to order and under the rule of a self-imposed discipline. This was not simply a reaction against the Romantic composer's imagined lack of discipline, but a way of life which Stravinsky found inescapable. The resulting music is sometimes dubbed 'Neo-classical' but Stravinsky has always denied that he looked back in the same way as Debussy and Ravel, in any sense imitating his musical ancestors. Everything he wrote is pure Stravinsky: when Diaghilev gave him a collection of tunes by Pergolesi to make into a ballet the professional composer immediately imposed on himself some of the restrictions which Pergolesi might himself have imposed. The orchestra is small, the form dictated by the tunes, but the sound is twentieth century.

History is made to serve the present in this ballet, *Pulcinella* (1920), in *The Fairy's Kiss* (1928) on music by Tchaikovsky, and in the Greek melodrama *Persephone* for reciter, tenor, chorus, children's choir and orchestra, the last work to be staged in Paris (1934), with a libretto by Gide.

In 1939, Stravinsky left Paris for the United States of America. Paris still attracts young composers, but 'La Domaine Musicale' needs no foreign leader. After Stravinsky's re-creation in modern terms of old melodies and forms, the new generation of scientist-musicians have taken the next logical step, re-creating even modern music in their studies and laboratories by feeding it into tape recorders—making music from music which has already been written and is, on the label, 'concrete' music. This is the small world of the French Radio Group under Schaeffer: so far England has heard *Symphonie pour un homme seul* (1950), the ballet *Orpheus* (1953), background music for experimental films on television and (particularly by Marius Constant) radio programmes. Whatever its ultimate musical value *musique concrète*, its 'bleeps' and its 'whooshes', are part of the space age experiments which no one should ignore. It is an odd piece of French logic that the music of the fifties should be as much addressed to the nerves as the Impressionism of Debussy was at the dawn of the century: understanding does not yet enter into either sort of music, and the effect of both is primitive in our ultra-civilized world.

Vienna—Berlin—Munich—Darmstadt

Vienna, the second capital of European music since the eighteenth century, heard the first attempts at a theoretically new system of tonality after, roughly, a quarter of this century had passed. Schoenberg in his Five Piano Pieces (1923), Berg in the 'Lyric' Suite (1925) and Webern in Three Songs for Voice, Clarinet and Guitar (1925) form a starting point for the student of serial music. Schoenberg was the propagandist for the system in his literary writings and as a dedicated teacher, working from 1924 to 1933 as a professor at the Prussian Academy of Fine Arts in Berlin; Berg and Webern, who had both been his pupils before the First World War, taught in Vienna from 1918 onwards.

Theory apart, the chief difficulties in listening to Schoenberg's music lie in connecting the notes of his tremendously angular melodies which choose deliberately to explore dissonant leaps, and in following any formal plan. The vocal music has two further obstacles for beginners in the Sprechgesang (half-sung and half-spoken lines) and in the seemingly inevitable morbid subjects. These characteristics apply to almost all Schoenberg after the *Gurrelieder* of 1900, even before he renounced all previous tonal systems in 1923 for serialism (which he preferred to call 'pantonal' and not 'atonal'). Experiments like this seldom court or receive popularity and though, currently, some of Schoenberg's works—especially the Five Pieces for Orchestra (1908)—are valued as masterpieces by knowledgeable critics, performances of fifty-year old pieces (the monodrama *Erwartung*: 1909, the fifteen settings of Stefan George in 'Das Buch der Hängenden Garten': 1908) are still 'experimental'. The most widely-played chamber music is *Pierrot Lunaire* (1912), twenty-one poems for singing-speaking voice and five instruments, each set for a different combination of sounds.

Many of Schoenberg's pupils in Vienna and Berlin have enjoyed greater success by a more flexible use of theories than the master usually allowed himself. Berg's opera *Wozzeck* (Berlin: 1925), his Violin Concerto (1935) and his 'Lyric' Suite for string quartet (1925) have almost certainly now established themselves in the three homes of opera house, concert hall and recital room. *Wozzeck*, although its story of a private soldier's degradation and ultimate compulsion to murder is so sordid, carries the most powerful impact of any opera in current fashion—if you are in the theatre. As concert music on radio or gramophone it is more difficult but not impossible, for its orchestration is continually fascinating and the underlying classical formulae of march, lullaby, passacaglia, fugue and variation (even though you should not consciously try to trace them) give the opera a unity which much of Schoenberg's music seems to lack. Berg's Violin

Concerto, too, is comparatively easy on the ear because the choice of note-series on which it is based allows him to use two major and two minor triads *and* almost a complete whole-tone scale, so that many of the sounds come within the old harmonic tradition of Romantics and Impressionists. In later works Berg always made the theory fit the 'fact' of any sound which, as a musician, he wanted: there is never any danger of theory freezing the bones of his music.

Webern is the supreme pointilliste in music. His pieces are concentrated and the pill—though sometimes sweet—is often hard to swallow: the permutations of three or four notes (which are never truly fixed in the ear as even the tiniest melody) have to be taken so quickly that the mind cannot digest them. The Five Orchestral Pieces fill no more than ten minutes between them: when the movement of parts is slow, even old-fashioned ears can sort out the sounds, but when rhythm disappears altogether and the lines of counterpoint are shared at long range by a different instrument for each note, you need new ears. Otherwise, the music of Webern must be regarded as the end of Debussy's trail of impressionism and you must let your nerves tell you whether the music bores or delights you, without any interventions from the mind. The early songs for voice, clarinet and guitar (1925) and his last orchestral work, the Variations (1940), reflect the charm of a composer who was adored by his pupils and at all times an idealist.

In 1927 the Berlin Music School appointed as one of its professors Hindemith. He was best known as an outstanding viola-player whose compositions were played where the 'cranks' met— at the Festivals of the International Society for Contemporary Music in Salzburg, Venice and Prague and at the Donaueschingen Festivals of so many *succés de scandale*. His early compositions were not revolutionary in the manner of his elders Stravinsky and Schoenberg. The forms he chose repaid his debt to traditional teaching: sonatas for unaccompanied strings, string quartets, a clarinet quintet and a piano quintet. But he was working in the shattered country of Germany after the First World War:

classical though his musical forms may have been, Hindemith had to mock everything or shock someone to avoid being accused of the then awful crime of taking himself too seriously. The young man was in any case very obviously an extrovert, dashing notes on to paper at an alarming rate, inventive and full of humour (particularly, as in the United States of America in the fifties, grotesque humour): jazz, neo-classicism, and an obsession with counterpoint at the expense of harmony make his earlier works impossible to take seriously, except perhaps the song-cycle to Rilke poems 'Das Marienleben' (1924) for soprano.

As a professor, Hindemith had to stop being an *enfant terrible*, although it was a few years before he settled down. These first years as a teacher were marked by a number of pieces meant for domestic performance and for schools; evidently the new professor thought that the gap between a modern composer and his audience should be sealed by educating the amateur performer to play technically simple but up-to-date, dissonant pieces. This thoroughly professional attitude developed side by side with a more thoughtful style of writing as, like many teachers, he learnt to tackle his own problems through those of his students. When the Nazis came to power in 1933, he set to work on his own artistic protest, an opera *Mathias the Painter* which was performed in concert version as a symphony in 1934. The question of the composer's place in a totalitarian system, surrounded by temptations to conform and appeals to his compassion, has never been more eloquently debated in music than in this historical allegory based on the painter Mathias Grünewald's ill-fated entry into politics during the Peasants' War in about 1525. The painter came from Mainz, Hindemith's birthplace, and the operatic hero who defied the State in the name of God was too thinly disguised for the Nazi Reich: no works of Hindemith were performed in Germany between 1934 and 1945.

The professor held his job until 1937 but was more absent than not, as a practising musician once more, playing, conducting and preparing his monumental textbook by which people might understand and learn to write his kind of music: *The Craft of*

Musical Composition (1937). In 1939 he emigrated to America. Schoenberg had been there since 1933; some of his pupils, notably Krenek, and others trained in Berlin by Busoni such as Weill had already followed him; Webern was living in obscurity near Vienna and Berg was dead. The musical art of Germany was in the hands of men like Orff.

Orff lives and works in Munich. He, too, had been pre-occupied as a composer with problems of teaching. Between 1930 and 1933 he published his *Schoolwork*, three volumes of elementary training for children using a wide range of xylophones, glockenspiels, drums and other percussion with recorders rather like a European *gamelan*. His theories were most ingenious, highly successful and have now (1960) reached England. So, too, has Orff's *Carmina Burana* (1937), a cantata on medieval poems from Benedictbeuern Monastery, set as robustly or as sweetly as the text requires. A second attempt at this formula, *Catulli carmina* (1943), uses four pianos for accompaniment like Stravinsky's *Les Noces* but there the resemblance ends. Orff's style relies on a childlike faith in repetition, motor rhythms and an ever-lasting background of colourful noise. His more adult 'fairytale' operas *The Moon* (1939) and *The Wise Woman* (1943) have been followed by the classical stories of *Antigone* (1949) and *The Triumph of Aphrodite* (1953) and have been performed at European Festivals of Music since the war as 'primitive' attractions.

Since the war serial composers have come to light in Germany following the re-introduction of the music of Webern. The most advanced men like Stockhausen employ serial rhythm as well as pitch and dynamics (*Kontrapunkte* for four pairs of instruments: 1953), and team up with the scientists of the German radio in Cologne to explore electrophonic music. The pre-war avant-garde Festival at Donaueschingen now has a serious rival in the Summer School for New Music at Darmstadt where the most devoted of all advocates in contemporary music, Scherchen, conducts the works of Schoenberg's successors as faithfully as he once gave the first performances of Schoenberg himself.

Budapest—Prague—Athens—Venice—Florence

Hungary and Czechoslovakia continued to nourish nationalist composers, but their late Romantic style of writing was enlivened by new experiment between the wars. Janacek had shown the way with his operas and the Sinfonietta (1926) in Prague, and he was followed in a more neo-classical fashion by Martinu whose four symphonies (1942–1945) and comic opera *Comedy on·the Bridge* (1950) are the high mark of his restless style. Haba, schooled in Schoenberg technique, evolved his own atonal system which included the quarter-and micro-tones which he heard in collecting Czech folk music, but the musical world's initial interest in it has waned until very recently. In Hungary, Kodaly learned a personal language from his study of folk music that had the inflections of sixteenth- and eighteenth-century counterpoint on a basic vocabulary of late Romantic harmony: this language is most powerful in his choral masterpiece *Psalmus Hungaricus* (1923) and in the *Missa Brevis* (1942–45); his prodigious work as a teacher has also made it a native tongue for the thousands of Hungarian children who use his songbooks in school.

Bartok was the laureate of all the Central European nationalists when it came to experiment. He collected and analysed thousands of folk tunes from Hungary and Rumania to Turkey and North Africa, and absorbed their atmosphere until it became part of his own breathing; as a piano-teacher at the Budapest Academy he wrote six books of graded teaching pieces (*Mikrokosmos*: 1926–37) which open the door not only to his own works but also to much modern piano music far removed from Hungary. As a composer Bartok nibbled at all the experiments of twentieth-century music except the twelve-note series, but fed mostly on Magyar folk melody. The different '-isms' may be followed something like this: French impressionism in the opera *Duke ·Bluebeard's Castle* (1911), in which like *Pelléas*, absolutely nothing happens on stage (except in this case the opening of seven symbolical doors); erotic primitivism in *The Miraculous Mandarin*, a ballet (1919) and the Allegro Barbaro for piano (1911); neo-classicism in the first two piano concertos (1926 and 1933);

polytonality and the 'modern impressionism' of curious sonorities in the Music for Strings, Celeste and Percussion (1936) and the Sonata for Two Pianos and Percussion (1937). The remarkable series of six string quartets written at different times between 1908 and 1939 summarizes all the influences within the always distinctive Hungarian flavour of Bartok. No man has explored deeper into every corner of music in one form than Bartok in these quartets. For most amateur players, such asymmetrical rhythms as 9/8 equalling 4+2+3/8, and the need for a consummate technique with fingers, bow (and back of the bow) and a near-perfect ear put the quartets into the category best played on the gramophone.

A last stage in this journey through Eastern Europe takes us south to Athens, where the Greek Skalkottas developed his very personal style in respect for his master Schoenberg but not in strict obedience to his teaching. Four Greek Dances (1933–36) are the only orchestral pieces to have reached England; they are ample evidence of his skill in orchestration and individual solution of twelve-note problems. Florence and Venice complete the tour of experimental workshops: Dallapiccola has transplanted serial music to Italy, his oratorio *Job* (1950) has attracted much attention, and he himself has attracted many younger composers by his ability as a teacher at the Florence Conservatory; the latest group of young Italians, centred on Venice, are post-Webern impressionists led by Maderna and Nono, whose appeal has so far been mainly confined to the Darmstadt Summer School, though the latter's *Incontri* for twenty-four instruments is intriguing. The Venice Festival has also claimed Stravinsky's post-war opera *The Rake's Progress* (1951), his latest essays in serial technique, and Nono's first opera, *Intolleranza*, 1960.

Zurich—London—Moscow—New York

The Swiss conductor of the Zurich Music School, Paul Sacher, shares with Scherchen in Germany a remarkable reputation for interpreting experimental music of this century, and is in some part responsible for the success and popularity of Switzerland's most interesting composer, Martin. Martin is a composer who, understanding Schoenberg, links the idea of a twelve-note series with old notions of tonality—a compromise which many audiences find easy to accept. The technique is probably clearest in the opening of his best-known work, the Petite Symphonie Concertante (1945) for harp, harpsichord, piano and double string orchestra: the twelve semitones of the octave are arranged in a singable tune of sequences; as they repeat, first a bass then an alto is added (not unlike a thirteenth-century motet, see page 42); and on the entry of the soloists the theme is varied to suit the composer's idea of beauty whenever he wishes. The piquant sounds of the curious combination of instruments entice the ear in this work immediately, but in the eight Preludes for piano (1948) the test is sterner and few pianists can communicate them clearly enough. His oratorios have had some performances in England and choral conductors might tax their societies to good purpose in preparing In terra pax (1944) or Golgotha (1948).

The conservative tradition of many English choral societies brings us back to considering what experiments have been made in this country. You will realize, from the number of English composers who were mentioned in the last two chapters, that the Englishman prefers to digest new continental delicacies slowly and to take his time over choosing his musical menu. Many criticize this attitude, but it has advantages and allows English composers to strike a balance between many divergent styles to make an unmistakably 'English' sound even with the modernities of Europe . . . about twenty years later. Britten and, to some extent, Rawsthorne have a personal style compounded from Strauss and Stravinsky, Berg and Bartok; Vaughan Williams learnt some of Ravel's manners; Berkeley takes after the French of Boulanger and Françaix most elegantly; Cooke anglicizes the counterpoint of Hindemith, and Tippett adopts the rhythmic extensions of Bartok almost to Messiaen's lengths; but each of these composers retains his English accent even in the most dramatic foreign phrases, as the Tommies of the First World War who stayed on in France speak today. Britten's accent shows in his vocal lines despite the cosmopolitan (and internationally successful) language of his chamber operas, *The Rape of Lucretia* (1946) and *Albert Herring* (1947) for Glyndebourne, and *The Turn of the Screw* (1954) and *A Midsummer Night's Dream* (1960) for his own Festival at Aldeburgh. Rawsthorne speaks most fluently in instrumental music but the brevity of his points in the Violin Concerto (1947), the Clarinet Quartet (1948) and the Symphony (1950) is unmistakably English.

The followers of serial masters must speak a common language and there is far more exchange between Britain and the Continent amongst the works of the twelve-note composers Searle and Lutyens. Searle, who was taught by Webern yet admires Liszt, has found the more convincing utterances so far in his three Symphonies.

Cheltenham has become the British Donaueschingen and Dartington the summer Darmstadt: there the enthusiastic may hear the youngest generation of post-Webern persuasion; Bennett and Hamilton at present emerge at the front of the guard, with electrophonic experiment in the names of Bradshaw, Wilkinson and Cary travelling cerebrally alongside. Gerhard, Spanish by birth, Viennese by training and British by adoption, is still a reminder of the tragic upheavals which scattered Schoenberg and his contemporaries about Europe and the U.S.A. in the 1930s, and musical authority, if not yet the English public, has begun to recognize his remarkable gifts in performing his Violin Concerto, Nonet for an unusual combination of instruments which includes a piano accordion, and Symphony which has a fascinating movement of counterpoint for percussion. Seiber from Hungary enlivened concerts with his mixture of jazz and twelve-note technique and, as a teacher at Morley College, London, played a prominent role in musical education.

As the U.S.S.R. is, up to now, adamantly against experiment with any musical technique which has been born in the decadent West of the twentieth century, and the U.S. has sheltered and welcomed every new advance in music, the contrast between Moscow and New York as modern musical cities is too sharp for comfort. New music in Moscow, as far as the radio reveals, is still predominantly Romantic, diatonic and in the grand manner. Shostakovich is announced as having written a musical and there may be a big future for Russian ballad-opera, starting—as the Singspiel in Germany and the *Beggar's Opera* in England began over two hundred years ago—a national style which will be inescapably Russian. Ballet music in concert excerpts from Shostakovich's *Golden Age* and Khachaturian's ubiquitous *Masquerade* explores folk-rhythms and could lead to a new type of 'people's opera', if its composers could turn a deaf ear to the music of Tchaikovsky. Moscow's modern composer, meanwhile, still searches for ideologically acceptable sounds with which his brilliant performers can impress the West.

The presence in America of so many musical refugees from Europe has given their adopted country a formidable list of premières which includes Schoenberg's Violin Concerto (1940) in Los Angeles, Stravinsky's Symphony in C (1940) and Three-movement Symphony (1945) in New York, Bartok's Concerto for Orchestra (1943) in Boston, and Hindemith's American Requiem (1946), many wind sonatas and the set of piano fugues in all twelve keys linked by interludes, *Ludus Tonalis* (1942 = 'Musical Game'). As teachers, many of these refugees have given the young musicians of the U.S.A. an unrivalled opportunity, from the beginners whom Hindemith had in mind at Yale Music School when he wrote his two most useful textbooks *Elementary Music for Musicians* and *Traditional Harmony*, to the advanced students who could have individual lessons from the most eminent American and European composers at Summer Schools like Tanglewood (the American 'Dartington').

What America will eventually gain from the presence of these foreign masters it is too early to tell. In the concert hall the '-isms' have all had their champions. Virgil Thomson has transported Boulanger's fastidiousness and Satie's eclecticism to the new Continent in his two suites of Portraits for orchestra, the opera *Four Saints in Three Acts* and four piano sonatas; his background scores for films (especially *The River* and *Louisiana*

Story) have become classic examples of this difficult craft. Another pupil of Nadia Boulanger, Piston, has written four symphonies, a violin concerto, and a good deal of chamber music which reflect very personally the common re-discovery of counterpoint in the last fifty years. This neo-classicism is now passing and composers in their forties are finding new heart in well-learned techniques, writing music for a wide public. Among these Gillis, Ward and Barber are the most accomplished; Barber's opera *Vanessa* had the distinction of a European première at Salzburg Festival in 1958, and his Adagio for strings, cantata *Dover Beach* and suite from the ballet *Souvenirs* have crossed the Atlantic many times.

The man who mostly strikes Europeans as an all-American composer is Copland. The fusion of angular and precise thinking (which he, too, absorbed from Boulanger in the twenties) with an open-hearted wish to please has led him into the highly productive and popular style of his Third Symphony and the gentle *Quiet City* for trumpet, cor anglais and strings. Before this maturity Copland, like Stravinsky and Hindemith, had his de-bunking period when the jazz tricks of the Piano Concerto and *El Salón México* amused or horrified his audiences; but like his European contemporaries, a mellowness came into his music about twenty years ago and ballets like *Billy the Kid* and *Appalachian Spring* have a wide appeal. The Piano Quartet of 1950 shows new signs of restlessness and maybe Copland, like Stravinsky, will turn to serial music. So far, no young master of serial technique has emerged in America and it seems that the practical if not the sentimental side of the Americans may prevent it; in such a highly-industrialized society, if a man wants to organize a number of notes in a very complex series he can build a machine to do it for him. The invention of just such a music computer in 1959 may be a sinister sign for the future American composer.

Ironically, the path of American music may well lie in the same direction as that of Russia, towards a new folk-opera. Apart from the high-powered musical like *Oklahoma*, jazz and the folksongs

of Cowboy and Negro alike are at the core of such works as
Copland's ballet *Rodeo* and Gershwin's opera *Porgy and Bess*.
Already Bernstein, concocting his music with the lyrical skill of a
Menotti and the orchestral ear of a budding Stravinsky, has built
a uniquely American product on jazz in *West Side Story*. Since
1918, this American path has been almost overgrown by jazz.
Now that modern jazz has begun to compete seriously with
traditional and mainstream styles, the gap between the techniques
of classical and jazz composers is narrowing rapidly, the jazz suite
is on its way to being a symphony, and concert chamber music
contains the most original work in jazz. Jazz awaits its Beethoven;
he will surely, one day, be born in America.

LIST OF ILLUSTRATIONS

(With notes on musical instruments)

Page 9: Poet-singer, playing the cithara or lyre. In his right hand is a large plectrum. Based on a drawing of Apollo on a Greek jar in the British Museum.

Page 21: An Egyptian feast. The audience watches a dancer, who is accompanied by (from left to right) oboe, drum, rattle, harp, castanets and flute. The three percussion instruments are roughly equivalent to the bongo, maracca and claves of a South American dance band today (see page 242). From Egyptian paintings.

Page 22: A Roman dance band, playing tambourine, cymbals and a tibia (= Roman form of the Greek aulos, a double pipe with a reed). From a mosaic at Pompeii.

Page 23: Musicians in a Roman amphitheatre. On the top row, an organist is flanked by two players of the cornu (= horn); below, two trumpeters frame a tibia player.

Page 26: The minnesinger, Walther von der Vogelweide, surrounded by his minstrels who play (left to right): shawm, psaltery, bagpipe, rebec, and a small drum (hung round the neck). Based on various pictures in the Manessisch Manuscript.

Page 31: Choir singing plainsong from one large leaf of music.

Page 44: Musicians in a church gallery as they might have looked in the fourteenth century. The instruments, from left to right (top row), are: long trumpet, harp, rebec, and bent trumpet. In front, a portable organ and a psaltery.

Page 60: Fifteenth-century composer.

Page 80: A fifteenth-century organ, played on a table, with two pairs of bellows (for which you needed an assistant). Based on an engraving in the Bibliothèque Nationale, Paris.

Page 92: A band playing for a procession *c.* 1600. The instruments are, from left to right: small shawm, cornett (a small

INDEX OF MUSICAL INSTRUMENTS

(A number in *italic* type indicates that the instrument is shown in the illustration on that page)

309

INDEX OF COMPOSERS

GENERAL INDEX